SHOPPING IN EXOTIC SINGAPORE AND MALAYSIA

Ronald L. Krannich
Caryl Rae Krannich

IMPACT PUBLICATIONS
Manassas, VA

SHOPPING IN EXOTIC SINGAPORE AND
MALAYSIA: Your Passport to Traditional
and Modern Cultures

Copyright © 1989 by Ronald L. Krannich and Caryl Rae
Krannich

Library of Congress Cataloging-in-Publication Data

Krannich, Ronald L.
    Shopping in exotic Singapore and Malaysia: your
    passport to traditional and modern cultures / Ronald L.
    Krannich and Caryl Rae Krannich
        p. cm.
    Includes index.
    1. Shopping--Singapore--Guide-books. 2. Shopping--
    Malaysia--Guide-books.   3. Singapore--Description--
    Guide-books. I. Krannich, Caryl Rae. II. Title.
TX337.S55K73 1989   380.1'45'0025957--dc20   89-7477
ISBN 0-942710-15-0

Cover designed by Orion Studios, 1608 20th St., NW,
Washington, DC 20009

For information on distribution or quantity discount
rates, call 703/361-7300 or write to: Sales Department,
IMPACT PUBLICATIONS, 10655 Big Oak Circle,
Manassas, VA 22111-3040. Distributed to the trade by
National Book Network, 4720 Boston Way, Suite A,
Lanham, MD 20706, 301/459-8696.

TABLE OF CONTENTS

PART III
SECRETS OF EXOTIC MALAYSIA

PREFACE

Exotic Singapore and Malaysia offer some of the world's most exciting shopping opportunities for those who know what to look for, where to go, and how to shop these two Southeast Asian countries properly. For more than 20 years we have repeatedly discovered the pleasures of these two unique countries as we have returned again and again to shop their many centers, arcades, department stores, shophouses, factories, and markets.

Singapore and Malaysia offer many shopping opportunities for clothes, jewelry, arts, antiques, handicrafts, tribal artifacts, and home decorative items. From each trip we return home with unique and quality items to enhance our home and wardrobes. If approached properly, we believe Singapore and Malaysia may well become two of your favorite travel and shopping destinations.

While Singapore and Malaysia are still exotic places to us, they no longer present the mystery and confusion that often confront first-time visitors to many parts of Asia. For they are very modern, convenient, comfortable, clean, and orderly countries to visit. The people speak English, the transportation and health systems are excellent, the food and hotels are outstanding, service is exceptional, prices are still reasonable, and the people are interesting and delightful to meet.

The chapters that follow present a particular perspective on traveling in Singapore and Malaysia. Like other volumes in our *Shopping in Exotic Places* series, we purposefully decided to write more than just another descriptive travel guide primarily focusing on hotels, restaurants, and sightseeing and with only a few pages on shopping. While our primary focus is on shopping, the book had to go beyond other shopping guides that only concentrate on the "whats" and "wheres" of shopping.

Our experience convinces us that there is a need for a book that outlines the "how-tos" of shopping in Singapore and Malaysia along with the "whats" and "wheres". Such a book should both educate and guide you through the shopping maze in these two countries. Consequently, this book focuses on the **shopping process** as well as provides you with the necessary **details** for making informed shopping choices in specific shopping areas, arcades, centers, department stores, markets, and shops.

Rather than just describe the "what" and "where" of travel and shopping, we include the critical **"how"** -- what to do before you depart on your trip as well as while you are in Singapore and Malaysia. We believe you and others are best served with a book which leads to both **understanding and action.** Therefore, you will find little in these pages about the general history, culture, economics, and politics of Singapore and Malaysia; these topics are covered well in other types of travel books. However interesting, such topics are not of particular importance to enhancing your shopping experience.

The perspective we develop throughout this book is based on our belief that traveling should be more than just another adventure in eating, sleeping, sightseeing, and taking pictures of unfamiliar places. Whenever possible, we attempt to bring to life the fact that Singapore and Malaysia are important centers of talented artists, craftspeople, traders, and entrepreneurs who offer you some wonderful opportunities to participate in their societies through their shopping processes. When you leave these countries, you will take with you not only some unique experiences and memories but also quality products that you will appreciate for years to come.

We have not hesitated to make qualitative judgments about shopping in Singapore and Malaysia. If we just presented you with shopping information, we would do you a disservice by not sharing our discoveries, both good and bad. While we know that our judgments may not be valid for everyone, we offer them as **reference points** from which you can make your own decisions. Our major emphasis throughout this book is on **quality shopping.** We look for shops which offer excellent quality and styles which we think are appropriate for Western homes and wardrobes. If you share our concern for quality shopping, you will find many of our recommendations useful to your own shopping.

Buying quality items does not mean you must spend a great deal of money on shopping. It means that you have taste, you are selective, you buy what fits into your wardrobe and home. If you shop in the right places, you will find quality products. If you understand the shopping process, you will get good value for your money. While shopping for quality may not be cheap, it need not be expensive. But most important, shopping for quality in Singapore and Malaysia is fun and it results in lovely items which can be enjoyed for years to come!

Throughout this book we have included "tried and tested" shopping information. We make judgments based upon our experience and research approach: visited many shops, talked with numerous people, and simply shopped.

We wish to thank the many individuals and organizations that made this trip possible. Japan Air Lines (JAL) took us safely to and from Asia and reconfirmed what we learned long ago -- this is one of the world's finest airlines for convenience, comfort, and service; it's one of the best ways to begin any Asian adventure. JAL's attention to detail and service and their exacting standards of excellence demonstrate what an outstanding airline can and should be.

The tourist associations in both countries -- the Malaysian Tourist Development Corporation (TDC) and the Singapore Tourist Promotion Board -- were extremely helpful in ensuring that this project be completed in a timely manner. Both headquarters and field personnel were gracious with their time, materials, and insights on shopping in each country. We are confident they will assist you in any way possible to ensure that your trip to their countries will be one of your most rewarding adventures. Through this book we include contact information on the tourist information offices found in each city. We urge you to visit these offices as soon as you arrive at your destinations. You will find they offer many informative maps, booklets, and brochures, and their personnel can answer many of your questions concerning local shopping, sightseeing, and touring opportunities.

We wish you well in your travel and shopping adventure to Singapore and Malaysia. The book is designed to be **used** on the streets of these two countries. If you **plan your journey** according to the first three chapters, **handle the shopping process** according to the next two chapters, and **navigate the streets** of Singapore and Malaysia based on the remaining seven chapters, you should have a marvelous time. You'll discover some exciting places, acquire some choice items, and return home with fond memories of these exotic places. If you put this book to use, it will become your passport to shopping in exotic Singapore and Malaysia!

Chapter One

SHOPPING IN EXOTIC PLACES

Welcome to two of Asia's most intriguing shopping and travel destinations. Situated at the crossroads of Southeast Asia, Singapore and Malaysia offer some of the best shopping and travel adventures in all of Asia. Here you can shop for exquisite antiques, handicrafts, tribal artifacts, fashionable clothes, electronic gadgetry, and souvenirs. These are places where collectors, home decorators, souvenir hunters, fashion lovers, and high-tech buyers can spend days and weeks discovering new products in Malaysia's and Singapore's many shopping centers, department stores, hotel shopping arcades, shophouses, markets, factories, and villages offering a whole new world of wonderful shopping and travel experiences.

AN EXOTIC WORLD OF WONDERS

Best of all, shopping in Singapore and Malaysia is both convenient and comfortable. You will be shopping and traveling in two of Asia's most modern countries. Hotels, restaurants, and transportation are simply outstanding. Standards of health and cleanliness are some of the best in

the world. Most people speak English and they are friendly, helpful, delightful, and interesting to meet.

While much of Singapore and Malaysia may look familiar to you, these are still exotic places for most travelers.
Both countries have a thick veneer of Western orderliness,
convenience, and comfort strapped to traditional societies
and cultures that continue to exhibit great ethnic and cultural diversity. The sights, sounds, service, and infinite
variety of people, places, and things make these two countries unique and colorful travel experiences. While the
hotels and restaurants may look familiar, it's the exceptional service, surroundings, and selections that make them
exotic. Cities, towns, and villages exhibit a kaleidoscope
of ethnic groups practicing colorful Malay, Chinese, Indian, European, and tribal customs and ceremonies. Concrete high-rise urban centers, bustling towns, quiet villages,
picturesque beaches, emerald seas, idyllic islands, misty
mountains, raging rivers, lush sun-drenched fields, and
inpenetrable jungles make for an unusual, varied, and
interesting landscape.

When you shop in Malaysia and Singapore, expect to
discover numerous surprises from the traditional and modern cultures of these two countries. Spend a few weeks
here and you will leave with a treasure-trove of purchases
and exciting memories of what may well become some of
the best shopping of a lifetime.

SURPRISING CITIES, TOWNS, AND VILLAGES

Shopping in Malaysia and Singapore primarily takes
place in urban settings. These are the centers for fashion,
design, trade, marketing, transportation, and communication. These are also the areas where you will find the best
travel amenities -- fine hotels, restaurants, entertainment,
and tourist sights. Occasionally, you may visit small
towns and villages where you can purchase local products
either not available in city shops or less expensive than
elsewhere. In general, however, the best shopping is found
in the cities. Very few towns and villages offer shopping
opportunities that would justify making trips into the
countryside.

Singapore is a shopper's paradise. Stroll down Orchard
Road, the city's "Golden Mile", and you will quickly discover why so many people come here to indulge their
shopping fancies. This is a city of outstanding hotels,
restaurants, and miles and miles of shopping centers, department stores, supermarkets, shophouses, and market
complexes selling an infinite variety of fashionwear, jewelry, electronic goods, antiques, handicrafts, and home decor-

ative items. In one moment you can be shopping in an ultra modern shopping center with hundreds of exclusive shops and the next moment -- just a few blocks down the street -- bargaining for antiques, handicrafts, gems, and fabrics in the shophouses of Singapore's traditional ethnic enclaves of Chinatown, Little India, and Arab Street as well as amongst the famous street vendors at Change Alley. But shopping doesn't stop in the highly touristed areas of downtown Singapore. There's even more shopping in the many suburban areas frequented by local Chinese, Malays, and expatriates.

While **Malaysia** is not a shopper's paradise on the par with Singapore, it is quickly making its mark on the Asian shopping scene, and even competing with Singapore in many respects. A relative newcomer to the international shopping scene, several Malaysia cities and towns offer excellent shopping opportunities for traditional arts, crafts, antiques, tribal artifacts, textiles, and home decorative items. The arts and crafts tradition in Malaysia remains very strong, and shopping in many areas of Malaysia is closely tied to the local cultures. But most important of all, Malaysia is beginning to produce a genre of arts and crafts that both reflect strong local traditions as well as appeal to the styles, designs, and color preferences of international travelers.

In Malaysia you will discover the cosmopolitan shopping centers, hotel shopping arcades, and department stores or **Kuala Lumpur**, one of Asia's most attractive and liveable cities. Intent upon competing with Singapore as one of Asia's major shopping centers, Kuala Lumpur offers a unique blend of traditional and modern shopping cultures where one can purchase the latest in Malay arts, crafts, and textiles. A colorful and culturally diverse city, Kuala Lumpur is always full of shopping surprises, be it inexpensive clothes, contemporary paintings, or exquisitely designed batik clothes, pewterware, jewelry, baskets, mats, and souvenirs.

Shopping outside Kuala Lumpur puts you in touch with several other Malaysias. Within two hours south of Kuala Lumpur you will come to the historic coastal town of **Malacca**, where the first Europeans settled and where today you will find numerous antique shops offering treasures from a by-gone era. Further north is **Penang**, a charming island and city (Georgetown) offering many shopping and travel attractions, from beach resorts to dusty antique stores, duty-free shops, and art galleries.

Malaysia's **East Coast** is a unique adventure into what remains of traditional Malay culture. Centered around the towns of Kota Bharu, Kuala Trengganu, and Kuantan, this is a mixed area of beach resorts, Malay fishing villages, town markets, and cottage industries. Here you will can observe the traditional rural Malay culture expressed in numerous ceremonies, festivals, market and cottage industry activities, and handcrafted products. Yet to be discovered by tourists, the East Coast is a delightful area where you can shop off the beaten tourist path.

East Malaysia, especially the Malaysia of **Sarawak** and its capital, **Kuching**, is a whole new travel and shopping world. This is truly adventure travel and shopping. Here you come into contact with some of the world's most interesting tribal artifacts that express the art, culture, and society of groups living along the rivers and in the jungles of Borneo. You'll discover some of the world's most interesting shopping for tribal artifacts and textiles in the quaint, colorful river town of Kuching.

Wherever you go in Singapore or Malaysia, you will find plenty of unique shopping opportunities and make numerous discoveries. If you are like others, shopping in these two countries will seem both familiar and exotic.

FOCUS ON QUALITY AND VALUE

Shopping in Exotic Singapore and Malaysia is designed to provide you with the necessary **knowledge and skills** to become an effective shopper in these two countries. We especially designed the book with two major considerations in mind:

- Focus on quality shopping
- Emphasis on finding unique items

This is not a book on how to find great bargains in inexpensive Singapore and Malaysia. Rather, this book primarily focuses on quality shopping for unique items. As such, we are less concerned with shopping in Malaysia and Singapore to save money and get great bargains than with shopping for unique local products that can be taken home, integrated with one's wardrobe and home, and appreciated for years to come. In fact, we have yet to find much bargain shopping in the world, especially given today's currency exchange rates that make our U.S. dollar less than the envy of the world! Rather than find a cheap tailor or purchase an inexpensive piece of jewelry or art, we prefer finding the best of what there is available and selectively choose those items we both enjoy and can afford. Buying, for example, one finely tailored suit, a piece of exquisite jewelry, or a valuable artifact or work of art that can be nicely integrated into your wardrobe and home will last much longer and you will appreciate it for many more years to come than to purchase several cheap pieces of jewelry or tourist kitsch that quickly loose their value and your interest.

Our general shopping rule is this: *A good buy is one that results in the exchange of money for something that has good value; when in doubt, go for quality because quality items will hold their value and you will enjoy them much more in the long run.*

Indeed, some of our most prized possessions from shopping in exotic places are those we felt we could not afford at the time, but we purchased them nonetheless because we knew they were excellent quality items and thus they had great value. Our decisions to buy quality items in the long run were wise decisions because these items are things we still love today.

We have learned one other important lesson from shopping abroad: *Good craftsmanship everywhere in the world is declining* due to the increased cost of labor, lack of interest among young people in pursuing the traditional crafts, and erosion of traditional cultures. Therefore, any items that require extensive hand labor and traditional skilled craftsmen -- such as ikat textiles, handcrafted jewelry, woodcarvings, and tribal artifacts in the case of Malaysia and Singapore -- are outstanding values today because many of these items are quickly disappearing as fewer craftsmen are trained in producing quality arts and crafts. As elsewhere in the world, the general trend in Malaysia and Singapore is to move from producing high quality traditional arts and crafts to mass producing contemporary handicrafts for tourists and export markets. Although many traditional handcrafted items may seem expensive, especially tribal artifacts and textiles, they are still good buys considering their labor content, workmanship, significance, and scarcity.

Throughout this book we have attempted to identify the best quality shopping in both Malaysia and Singapore. This does not mean we have discovered the cheapest shopping or best bargains. Our search for unique shopping and quality items that retain their value in the long run means many of our recommended shops may initially appear expensive. But they offer top value that you will not find in many other shops. So, for example, when we take you through the art and antique shops of Singapore, we take you to four of Singapore's finest quality shops in Tanglin Centre -- Tiepolo, Bareo, Mata-Hari, and Tatiana and one in Cuppage Terrace -- Babazar. We also visit three of our favorite home decorative and furniture shops: Classic Antique House, Renee Hoy Fine Arts, and Jessica.

In Kuala Lumpur we visit King's Art, 10 Kiapeng Art Gallery, A.P. Gallery, Lim Arts & Crafts, Karyaneka Handicraft Centre, Batik Permai, and Ahmed Toko Antik. In Kuching you will go with us into four shops offering tribal artifacts and textiles: Sarawak House, Thian Seng, Native Arts, and Borneo Art Gallery. We know these shops well because these are the places we have made some of our most important purchases. They offer both unique and quality items we will cherish for many years to come.

SELECTING AND ORDERING CITIES

Except for Singapore, which we visited at the very end of our trip, the cities and towns appearing in this book are in the sequence in which we visited them in our most recent trip to Singapore and Malaysia. The decision to do Penang first and then the East Coast, Kuala Lumpur, Malacca, Sarawak, and Singapore was purposeful.

Initially entering Malaysia at Penang via Southern Thailand, we felt our best shopping strategy would be to visit the smaller cities and towns first, stop in Kuala Lumpur half way through the trip, and then continue on to Malacca, back to Kuala Lumpur, and on to Kuching, Sarawak before ending our journey in Singapore. This proved to be a good decision because of our buying and shipping patterns. We expected to do the greatest amount of shopping in Kuala Lumpur, Kuching, and Singapore. By leaving these cities toward the end of our trip, we where able to consolidate our Penang, East Coast, Malacca, and Kuala Lumpur purchases in Kuala Lumpur, arrange to have them transhipped to Singapore where they would then be further consolidated with our new Kuching and Singapore purchases. Had we done Singapore first and Malaysia last, we would have lost some critical shipping advantages in Singapore.

Alternatively, you could begin your trip in Singapore or Kuala Lumpur, stop in the other cities, and then finish in Singapore. This might add two or more days to your trip, but it would give you an overview of your major shopping options at the very beginning of your trip. However you organize your trip, we strongly recommend completing your shopping adventure in Singapore where you will be in the best position to consolidate and arrange for shipping your purchases. You should have no problem doing so in some of the other cities, but it's much more convenient and shipping will be faster if done through Singapore.

Should you decide to include all the shopping locations included in this book, we strongly recommend starting with Penang on the West Coast and then drive or fly directly to

Kota Bharu on the East Coast. From Kota Bharu drive south to Kuala Trengganu and Kuantan before turning west to Kuala Lumpur and Malacca. After shopping in Kuala Lumpur and Malacca, fly from Kuala Lumpur to Kuching in East Malaysia and then fly from Kuching to Singapore for the conclusion of your exotic shopping adventure. While this may not be the normal sequence for traveling in Singapore and Malaysia, we found it to be the best for shopping purposes.

You should be able to include all of our shopping destinations into a fast-paced two to three week trip to Singapore and Malaysia. This amount of time will allow you to both shop and enjoy many of the major local sights. We recommend spending two to three days in Penang, three to five days along the East Coast, three to five days in Kuala Lumpur and Malacca, three days in Kuching, and four to five days in Singapore. If you have an additional week or two, you would be able to complete these areas at a more leisurely pace and enjoy more local sights.

APPROACHING THE SUBJECT

The chapters that follow take you into the best of shopping in Singapore and Malaysia. In so doing, we've attempted to construct a complete **user-friendly book** that first focuses on the shopping process and then offers extensive details on the "hows", "what", and "where" of shopping. It purposefully includes a sufficient level of redundancy to be informative, useful, and usable.

The chapters are organized like one would organize and implement a travel and shopping adventure to these two countries. Each chapter incorporates sufficient details, including names and addresses, to get you started in some of the best shopping areas and shops in each city or town.

Indexes and table of contents are especially important to us and others who believe a travel book is first and foremost a guide to unfamiliar places. Therefore, our index includes both subjects and shops, with shops printed in bold for ease of reference; the table of contents is elaborated in detail so it, too, can be used as another handy reference index for subjects and products. By using the table of contents and index together, you can access most any information from this book.

The remainder of this book is divided into three parts and 10 additional chapters which look at both the process and content of shopping in exotic Malaysia and Singapore. The next four chapters in Part I -- **"Traveling Smart"** -- assist you in preparing for your Singapore and Malaysian shopping adventure by focusing on the how-to of traveling and shopping in these two countries. Chapter Two, "Know Before You Go", takes you through the basics of getting to and enjoying your stay in each country, including international and domestic transportation and the promises and pitfalls of local travel. Chapter Three, "Major Shopping Choices", outlines the type of shopping you can expect to encounter, including products, shopping environment, and costs. Chapter Four, "Plan and Manage Your Adventure", examines how to best prepare for your trip to Singapore and Malaysia, including what best to pack as well as how to best manage your money, pack, identify your shopping needs, and ship your purchases home with ease. Chapter Five, "Shopping Rules and Bargaining Skills", prepares you for Singapore's and Malaysia's distinct shopping cultures where knowing important shopping rules, pricing practices, and bargaining strategies are keys to becoming an effective shopper.

The chapters in Part II -- **"Secrets of Exotic Singapore"** -- examine the how, what, and where of shopping in Singapore. Here you will discover Singapore's major shopping strengths and learn how and where to best shop for different products.

Part III -- **"Secrets of Exotic Malaysia"** -- focuses on the how, what, and where of shopping in five of Malaysia's major shopping and travel destinations: Penang, East Coast, Kuala Lumpur, Malacca, and Sarawak.

RECOMMENDED SHOPS

We hesitate to recommend specific shops since we know the pitfalls of doing so. Shops that offered excellent products and service during one of our visits, for example, may change ownership, personnel, and policies from one year to another. In addition, our shopping preferences may not be the same as your preferences.

Our major concern is to outline your shopping options in Singapore and Malaysia, show you where to locate the best shopping areas, and share some useful shopping strategies that you can use anywhere in Singapore and Malaysia, regardless of particular shops we or others may recommend. Armed with this knowledge and some basic shopping skills, you will be better prepared to locate your own shops and determine which ones offer the best products and service in relation to your own shopping and travel goals.

However, we also recognize the "need to know" when shopping in exotic places. Therefore, throughout this book we list the names and locations of various shops we have found to offer good quality products. In some cases we have purchased items in these shops and can also recommend them for service and reliability. But in most cases we surveyed shops to determine the quality of products offered without making purchases. To shop in all of these places would be beyond our budget, as well as our home storage capabilities! Whatever you do, treat our names and addresses as **orientation points** from which to identify your own products and shops. If you rely solely on our listings, you will miss out on one of the great adventures of shopping in exotic places -- discovering your own special shops that offer unique items and exceptional value and service.

EXPECT A REWARDING ADVENTURE

Whatever you do, enjoy your shopping and travel adventure to Singapore and Malaysia. These are two very interesting countries that are surprisingly easy and enjoyable to get around in -- moreso than most places in Europe. Better still, they offer many unique items that can be purchased and integrated well into many homes and wardrobes outside these countries.

So arrange your flights and accommodations, pack your credit cards and traveler's checks, and head for two of Asia's most delightful shopping and travel destinations. Three weeks later you should return home with much more than a set of photos and travel brochures. You will have some wonderful purchases and shopping tales that can be enjoyed and relived for a lifetime.

Shopping our exotic places only takes time, money, and a sense of adventure. Take the time, be willing to part with some of your money, and open yourself to a whole new world of shopping in exotic places. If you are like us, your shopping adventure will introduce you to an exciting world of quality products, friendly people, and interesting places that you might have otherwise missed had you just passed through these places to eat, sleep, see sights, and take pictures. When you go shopping in exotic places, you learn about these places through the people and products that define their urban and rural cultures.

PART I

TRAVELING SMART

Chapter Two
KNOW BEFORE YOU GO

Singapore and Malaysia are relatively small countries in terms of area and population. Malaysia, covering an area of 300,000 square kilometers, has a population of nearly 14 million. Singapore, occupying a small island of 620 square kilometers, boasts a population of 2.5 million.

POPULATION DIVERSITY

The populations in both countries are a diverse mixture of Chinese, Malays, and Indians who live in relative harmony. In Malaysia the Malays predominate with 54% of the population; other ethnic groups consist of the Chinese (35%) and Indians (10%). In Singapore these ethnic patterns are reversed with the Chinese predominating (76%) followed by the Malays (15%) and Indians and Pakistanis (7%).

In both countries the Chinese dominate the economy. Indeed, when you shop in Malaysia and Singapore, you will most likely deal with Chinese merchants whose families have been in business for decades. In Malaysia, the Malays primarily live in the rural areas where they farm, fish, and produce local crafts. Malays in the cities tend to be found in the government service or working as laborers.

13

LOCATION AND GEOGRAPHY

Both countries lie in the heart of Southeast Asia. Malaysia is divided into two parts -- Peninsular Malaysia and East Malaysia. Nearly equal in size, **Peninsular Malaysia** is both the smaller and larger half of the country with approximately 40% of the total land area and 85% of the total population. This is also the most highly developed and urbanized part of the country, the area where you will want to concentrate most of your shopping efforts. Starting at the southern border of Thailand and extending the length of the Malay Peninsula for nearly 900 kilometers, Peninsular Malaysia consists of an industrialized West Coast, a mountainous and densely jungled interior, and a less developed but attractive East Coast.

East Malaysia, boasting 60% of the country's land area but only 15% of its population, occupies the northern third of the densely jungled and mountainous island of Borneo. It is divided into the states of Sarawak and Sabah between which lies the independent Kingdom of Brunei. The remaining two-thirds of the island is part of Indonesia. **Singapore** is a speck on most maps. A small island of 620 square kilometers, it lies off the southern tip of the Malay peninsula where it faces both Malaysia and Indonesia.

CLIMATE AND WHEN TO GO

Malaysia and Singapore are hot and humid tropical countries located near the equator. Depending on the time of the year you go and where you plan to visit, expect these countries to be more or less hot and humid -- hot, hotter, and hottest! Light-weight natural fiber clothes and rain gear are traveling "musts" in this part of the world. When Singapore and Malaysia get hot and humid, especially in the months of June through September, they can be insufferable. During the wet months of November to January, rain can occur for short periods every day. While the rains are a nuisance to shoppers, they do bring some relief from the heat.

The climate can also vary greatly from one part of Malaysia to another. For example, when it's dry on the West Coast, it may be raining on the East Coast and in East Malaysia. Indeed, when we visited in November, the weather in Penang, Kuala Lumpur, and Malacca was excellent except for an occasional shower. But the East Coast was flooded from the incessant torrential monsoons that regularly lash this area during the wet season; Kuching was also rainy.

Given these major regional variations in climate, it is difficult to recommend any one "best time" to visit both Singapore and Malaysia. Our best guess would be the months of July, August, September, and October. However, July is one of the hottest months of the year even though it is also the driest. In October you take a chance of catching the rains early. If you plan to visit the East Coast and East Malaysia, avoid the rainy months of November to January.

INTERNATIONAL TRANSPORTATION

Both Singapore and Malaysia are easy to reach by major international carriers. We took Japan Air Lines from New York City to Bangkok; Thai Airways from Bangkok to Penang; Malaysian Air Service from Penang to Kota Bharu, Kuala Lumpur to Kuching, and Kuching to Singapore; and Japan Air Lines from Singapore to New York. All of our flights were excellent, but flights with Japan Air Lines were exceptional.

Japan Air Lines (JAL) has the reputation for being one of the top three airlines in the world. And it well deserves that reputation. JAL demonstrates the excellence for which the Japanese are so well noted. They do it by trying hard to please their passengers from the very moment they arrive at the departure gate to when they disembark at their final destination. Japan Air Lines simply performs like few other airlines in the world. The best way to characterize the JAL experience is service, service, and service. Indeed, JAL displays the very best of what one quickly learns to be one of the major attractions of Asia -- the service ethic. JAL departure lounges are the most orderly we have ever encountered. On-board service is five-star -- efficient, friendly, and courteous. When you finish a meal, for example, your tray is removed within just minutes -- something other airlines could well observe and emulate! The attention to detail is at times remarkable: the end paper on the roll of toilet paper in the restrooms is regularly hand-folded after others finish -- something only top hotels are noted for! Indeed, even after long trans-Pacific flights, the restrooms were still sparkling clean. JAL also offers an extensive on-board duty-free shopping service for name-brand items.

Many other international airlines also fly into Malaysia and Singapore. The national carriers, Singapore Airline and Malaysian Air System, both have regularly scheduled international flights from North America, Europe, and other parts of Asia into Kuala Lumpur and Singapore. Present round-trip economy fares from the U.S. West Coast to Kuala Lumpur or Singapore range from $1060 to $1463 depending upon the time of year. If you watch for special promotions, you can even fly round-trip for less. You will also find special seven-day package tours offering round-trip air, hotels, and a few tours for as little as US$1300. Asian Dreams (Tel. 1-800/628-0600), Four Winds Travel (Tel 1-800/248-4444), Pacific Bestours (Tel. 1-800/562-0208), TBI (Tel. 1-800/223-0266), and Visitours (Tel. 1-800/367-4368) are some of the better known such tours.

If, on the other hand, you want to travel deluxe class and money is no object, try the the tours offered by Abercrombie & Kent (Tel. 1-800/323-7308), Hemphill Harris (Tel. 1-800/421-0454), Lindblad (Tel. 1-800/243-5657), and Travcoa (Tel. 1-800/992-2003). Contact your local travel agent for information on special air fares as well as these and other package tours.

You can also arrive in Malaysia and Singapore by car, rail, or ship. One of the most delightful rail trips in the world is the 54-hour Singapore-Bangkok Express train which stops in Butterworth (Penang) and Kuala Lumpur on the way between Bangkok and Singapore. Along the way you will get a quick glimpse of rural and urban Southeast Asian life. The first-class accommodations are more than adequate, and although there is a dining car on some segments, you are well advised to take along some snacks and buy bottled drinks, unpeeled fruits, and well cooked foods from vendors at the various stops along the way. The trip is best enjoyed in the privacy of your own air-conditioned sleeping compartment. It's worth paying a little extra to really enjoy this wonderful rail trip.

You can also enter Malaysia and Singapore by car via southern Thailand. While we do recommend driving within Malaysia and Singapore, we strongly advise against doing so in Thailand. Thai roads are very dangerous due to the driving habits of the Thai. Even Malays fear driving in Thailand where only one rule of the road seems to operate -- the faster and more aggressive the better.

DOMESTIC TRANSPORTATION

Malaysian Air System (MAS) has regularly scheduled flights to all major cities in the country. We found their service be excellent, although their economy section is crowded and their seats can be uncomfortable for many long-legged westerners. After taking two uncomfortable flights, we discovered the magic of MAS: whenever possible, upgrade your seat to first-class. First-class is extremely comfortable and the service is outstanding. Best of all, the price difference between economy-class and first-class is minimal. Take, for example, our flight from Kuching to Singapore. First, we had accumulated so much that our luggage was over-weight by 20 kilos, which meant we would have to pay excess baggage charges. Second, we were tired of the uncomfortable and crowded flights. We decided to try first-class. To our delight we discovered the difference between economy-class and first-class was only US$27 per ticket which also gave us each an additional 20 kilos in baggage allowance. For US$27 we got the additional baggage allowance, a special departure lounge, wide seats, special meals, and simply outstanding service. Best of all, we had all 26 seats in the first-class section to ourselves. This was the best US$27 we spent in all of Malaysia! Our advice: whenever possible, pay a little extra and go first-class on MAS; you'll simply love this airline in first-class.

Book early and reconfirm your domestic flights at least 48 hours ahead of time. Many of MAS's flights are fully booked.

We also recommend **driving** in many parts of Malaysia and Singapore. The road system is excellent and driving habits in both countries are very orderly. The most dangerous and congested areas are the highways along Malaysia's heavily trafficked West Coast. With an international drivers license you can easily rent a car in most major cities at the airport or through one of the major car rental agencies in town. Avis, Hertz, Thrifty, and Budget rental car agencies are found throughout Malaysia and Singapore. A car is especially useful when traveling along Malaysia's East Coast, between Kuala Lumpur and Malacca, and in and around Kuching.

In East Malaysia you may also travel by **riverboat** between towns. These can be long but interesting trips which enable you to see a great deal of the countryside. When taking such trips, we recommend packing your own food and drinks as well as reading material to pass the time of day.

Within most large cities you will find plenty of taxis and buses. In most cities the **taxis** are metered, relatively inexpensive, comfortable, and convenient. We prefer taking taxis rather than buses since they are convenient and very inexpensive. In Penang and Kuching, however, taxi drivers do not use meters. You should set the price before entering the cab. Most short distance rides cost M$2 to M$3. In Kuching be prepared for taxi drivers who might overcharge you as well as get lost.

The **buses** in most cities are inexpensive and relatively easy to use. The local tourist office will usually have a bus map and provide information on how to use the bus system. Singapore offers an inexpensive one to three-day Singapore Explorer Bus Ticket which will take you to all of the major attractions on the island which are clearly marked on a special bus map and at all of the stops along the way.

Singapore has a new **subway** (MTR) which is both fast and convenient. Except for the Little India area, the MTR connects with most of the major shopping areas of interest to visitors. All tourist literature and maps now include information on using the MTR system.

Trishaws are found in cities and towns throughout Malaysia and Singapore. Taking these three-wheeled ped-dled vehicles are still charming ways to see Penang and Malacca. Be sure to bargain with the drivers before taking off to your destination. Expect to pay about M$6 to M$8 per hour for a trishaw. Some areas, such as Kuching, do not have trishaws. You will see few trishaws in the major shopping areas of Singapore since they are no longer a convenient and inexpensive form of transportation. A few operate along the side streets.

PLEASURES AND PITFALLS

We are happy to report that Malaysia and Singapore offer numerous pleasures and very few pitfalls for travelers to this part of the world. Unlike many other countries where standards of health and sanitation are questionable, traffic is chaotic, facilities are rudimentary, service shoddy and disorganized, cities unattractive, and touting and cheating rampant, Malaysia and Singapore have few if any such problems.

Comfort, Convenience and Service

The real strengths of these countries are **comfort, convenience, and service**. They are easy to get around in, facilities are excellent, and service is more often than not both friendly and efficient. Better still, the food in Malaysia and Singapore is outstanding. You can easily spend a few days just feasting in two of Asia's great food capitals - Penang and Singapore.

One of the first things to remember about Singapore and Malaysia is that these are not Third World countries with serious problems with poverty, underdevelopment, infrastructure, corruption, and organization. Malaysia, and to a greater extent, Singapore are relatively modern countries with a long history of excellent health standards, infrastructure, tourist facilities, organizational capabilities, enforced rules and regulations, and a relatively compliant and well educated population. Highly urbanized, they rank as two of Asia's top newly industrialized countries. Indeed, both Singapore and Malaysia surprise many visitors who expect to encounter the typical litany of Third World inconveniences. These are countries where the stamp of colonial orderliness, compliance, and tolerance have been readily accepted by the local cultures. Government tends to be efficient and effective, a help rather than a hinderance to international travelers.

Attractive Cities and Towns

If you are expecting another round of unattractive and inconvenient Asian cities in Malaysia and Singapore, you will be pleasantly surprised. **Cities and towns** in these countries tend to have character as well as display architectural creativity. Cities such as Penang and Malacca, as well as the ethnic enclaves (Chinese, Malay, Indian) and traditional markets in Singapore and Kuala Lumpur, have a great deal of character straight out of a W. Somerset Maugham or Noel Coward novel. Red tiled two-story shophouses, worn by a combination of age, tropical heat, and humidity and juxtaposed to modern high-rise office and hotel buildings, line the streets of these charming cities. Grand old colonial hotels, such as the E&O in Penang and the Raffles in Singapore, still testify to the fact that these cities played an important role in the history of 19th and 20th century Southeast Asia.

Singapore may even shock many visitors who find this city to be one of the cleanest, most convenient, well organized, efficient cities in the world -- moreso than any city we have encountered in North America or Europe. It's an urban planner's dream and a shopper's delight to discover this attractive city.

Kuala Lumpur is another great city with beautiful architecture, wide thoroughfares, spacious parklands, and colorful ethnic neighborhoods. Surprising Kuala Lumpur should rank as one of the great cities of Southeast Asia.

Food and Accommodations

Both Singapore and Malaysia have justly deserved reputations for offering some of the best foods in Asia. Singapore and Penang are famous food capitals of Southeast Asia. Indeed, many Asians travel to these cities just to sample their delicious foods. You will find everything from the most elegant Continental Restaurants (Compass Rose in Singapore and Suasa Brasserie in Kuala Lumpur) to the finest in Chinese, Malay, and Indian cuisine served in hawker stalls. Since health and sanitation standards are very high in both Singapore and Malaysia, the foods are safe to eat, including dishes served from most hawker stalls.

Singapore and Malaysia also offer fine hotels. The Shangri-La International Hotels predominate by offering the best hotels in three cities -- Penang, Kuala Lumpur, and Singapore. Other hotels, such as the Hilton and Regent in Kuala Lumpur, Ramada Renaissance in Malacca, Holiday Inn and Hilton in Kuching, Pantai Primula in Kuala Trengganu, and the Oriental, Marina Mandarin, Goodwood Park, and Sheraton Towers in Singapore are some of the finest hotels in the world, and they are relatively inexpensive compared to comparable accommodations in other major cities of the world.

Potential Problems

Nonetheless, you will find some inconveniences in the less developed regions of Malaysia, especially along the East Coast and in Sarawak. Most of these inconveniences, such as local transportation and communication, are relatively easy to adjust to and often become some of the more memorable and serendipitous travel and shopping experiences in Malaysia. In general we recommend that you avoid drinking tap water, although in most areas the public water supply should be safe. This is one area we always like to err on the side of being overly cautious. You will find plenty of canned soft drinks, fruit juices, beers, and bottled water throughout the cities and towns of Malaysia and Singapore.

Heat and Humidity

The major inconvenience in Malaysia and Singapore is the **heat and humidity**. It gets very hot and humid in these tropical and equatorial countries. If you arrive during the hottest and wettest seasons (July and November to January) you may feel frequently spent from the heat and depressed by the overcast and rainy days! However, you can and should adjust to the heat and humidity by wearing the proper clothes (light-weight natural fabrics), carrying appropriate rain gear (a collapsible umbrella is a practical necessity, and adjusting your walking habits to the local climate (slow down and avoid long walks in the heat of day). Best of all, Malaysia's and Singapore's modern air-conditioned hotels and shopping facilities enable you to frequently escape from the heat and humidity. We generally find the heat and humidity to be a problem during the first three days of our trip. Once we make a few adjustments with the proper clothing and walking patterns, the heat and humidity pose few problems.

Oppressive Crowds and Noise

Two other potential problems face some visitors who are not used to shopping and traveling in Asia: oppressive crowds and noise pollution. In many shopping areas of Malaysia and Singapore you will encounter large **crowds and noisy interiors** that can bother visitors who are used to more personal and peaceful space. Many shopping centers in Kuala Lumpur and Singapore are extremely crowded at night and on weekends. Some of these places also are very noisy with rock music blaring over huge speaker systems. The streets can also be very noisy as trucks, buses, cars, and motorcycles with questionable muffler systems ply the streets. At times you can hardly hear yourself talking. We have learned to quickly exit from such shopping centers and streets when the crowds and noise become too oppressive. Escape to a quiet restaurant or hotel lobby is an excellent remedy to these potential threats to your psychological and physical well being!

Touts and Cheating

Occasionally you will encounter **touts and cheating**. Touts hang around shopping areas to ostensibly assist you with your shopping by taking you to "recommended" shops. Some taxi drivers may also recommend certain shops. Avoid any such attempts to show you the local shopping ropes. In almost every case these individuals receive a 10 to 20% commission on every item you purchase at their recommended shops. Not surprising, the merchants add the commission on to the prices you pay for items in their shops. The tourist organizations in both countries attempt to rid themselves of such touts, but they exist nonetheless.

You may also become a victim of some form of **cheating**, be it overcharging for a taxi or other service, misrepresentation, scams, or being sold improper goods. If, for example, you are interested in purchasing a video camera, make sure the equipment is compatable with your system back home. Asian shops mostly sell electronic equipment -- videos and TVs -- that only operate on the Asian and European PAL systems. If you are from North America, videos and TVs only operate on NTSC systems. Since the various systems are incompatable, you must know your system. If in doubt whether you are purchasing PAL or NTSC, do not buy even though a salesperson may tell you "no problem". Many shoppers do have problems and only resolve them after lengthy hassles with the shops through their credit card companies -- should they have been so fortunate to have charged the purchase - or through the local tourist association.

If you are buying high-ticket items, such as expensive gems, jewelry, antiques, and artifacts, be sure you know what you are doing and have the ability to detect substitutes and fakes. There is a growing market of copied antiques and tribal artifacts that look like the real thing. Indeed, even some of the most honest and reputable dealers are occasionally swindled by clever middlemen who come up with excellent quality fakes that only the very best experts -- museum curators -- can detect as fakes. Therefore, you are well advised to shop only at reputable shops and even question the authenticity of items in these shops.

Disappointing Tailored Garments

A final pitfall of shopping in Malaysia and Singapore is **tailoring work**. Time and again visitors to Malaysia and Singapore -- like their brethren in Hong Kong, Korea, and Thailand -- come away with disappointing tailored clothes. The number one complaint tourist associations receive from travelers regards custom tailoring. Invariably tourists are disappointed with their tailored garments: they don't fit properly, they weren't delivered on time, or the final product was not what the buyer expected!

We know the many pitfalls that can trap the unwary shopper who, used to buying clothing off-the-rack at home, decides to indulge in this unique experience and have clothing custom tailored. Having heard from acquaintances who traveled through this part of the world years ago -- when wages were much lower than today -- about the great values in custom tailored goods, our traveler is easy prey for the unbelievable deals offered by many of the *"hey you mister"* hucksters.

Custom tailored clothing is no longer the bargain it once was in Singapore. The wages in Singapore have risen substantially over the past few years as Singapore now enjoys the second highest standard of living in Asia. (Japan is number one.) The cost of a well-made tailored suit has kept pace and increased as well. You can still find well tailored clothes at reasonable prices, but they won't be cheap. Yes, there are some shops of the *"hey you mister"* variety that will offer you unbelievable bargains. But you know the old adage, if it sounds too good to be true, it probably is! Some shops offer a man's suit, two extra pairs of slacks and three custom-made shirts at unbelievably low prices. You'll get what you pay for. In the end this experience could cost you plenty if the garments you pay for are so shoddily made that you seldom or never wear them.

First, consider whether you really want to have custom tailoring done. If you are hard to fit and can never find anything to fit properly at home, you may be a candidate for tailoring in Singapore. But if you have no trouble buying garments that fit well "off-the-rack", ask yourself if you really want to go through the hassle and risk of custom tailoring. The hassle involves effectively communicating your wishes to the tailor, returning to the shop for several fittings (don't even hope for a good fit without this), and possibly having to arrange for shipment of the garments to your home if the tailor fails to finish them on time. The risk is that you will have to pay for goods that are not satisfactory and that you would never have selected if you had found them hanging on the rack. There are beautiful ready-made clothes available in Singapore and you can try on the finished product and be sure it is for you before you put down your money. Generally you will find ready-made garments are also a better value.

TAILORING CONSIDERATIONS

If you do decide to go ahead with custom tailoring after our warnings, follow these guidelines:

TAILORING GUIDELINES

- **Don't expect to get something for nothing.** Quality fabrics and workmanship cost money anywhere in the world. Go to a good tailor and be willing to pay for quality work. The best tailors tend to be located in the arcades of the deluxe and first-class hotels.

- **Look at fabrics and examples of finished work carefully.** Are the fabrics of good quality? Are they soft and supple so they will lay smoothly in the finished garment? Go to the racks of completed sample garments. Check the general appearance of garments including topstitching, buttonholes, and button quality, smoothness of darts and pocket application. Hand sewing is one mark of quality custom tailoring. Turn up the collar and examine the underside for the slightly uneven hand stitches which indicate that it was partly hand sewn. Check the way hems are finished. Check women's jackets and coats to see that the chest area is not exces-

sively form fitted with darts which create a
fitted look not popular in the West -- especially if you plan to wear the jacket unbut-
toned and loose.

- **Check garments waiting for first or second
  fittings.** Next, go to the rack where other
  customers' unfinished garments are waiting
  for first or second fittings. Examine the inside construction of several garments to see
  how well each is constructed. Firm interfacing should be used inside the upper part of
  jackets and coats and inside the lapels and
  collar to give support and shape to the garment. Many tailors now use fusible (iron-on)
  interfacing to save time instead of the more
  supple woven interfacing which needs to be
  sewn into place. Fusible interfacing is fine
  when used in a limited way, but the exclusive use of fusible rather than woven interfacing results in stiff garments. If fabrics
  have a pattern check to see how well the
  pattern matches wherever seams meet.

- **Specify the right style for you.** Be prepared with photos showing the style or combination of styles you want. (Remember, these
  tailors are not working from pre-packaged
  patterns. You can select a collar from one
  photo, for example, to be combined with a
  jacket front from another) Know what looks
  best on you and avoid being swayed by the
  salesperson to go with the "latest fashion" if
  it won't fit your lifestyle back home or your
  shape.

- **Communicate every detail.** Don't assume
  your image is similar to the salesperson's
  image of the finished product. For example,
  if the fabric you've selected has stripes, specify the direction -- horizontal, vertical or
  diagonal -- for the stripes in the finished garment. The rule here is to: **assume nothing
  and explain everything.**

- **Give the tailor enough time to do a quality job.** Expect to have a minimum of two fittings -- three is better -- for garments in which fit is critical such as suits or slacks. One fitting might be acceptable for a loosely constructed garment such as a blouse. Expect a suit to take at least four days while a blouse might be completed in one or two days. Good work is not done overnight, and usually only *"Hey, you mister"* shops will make such rash promises.

- **Arrange to take delivery of your finished garments no later than the day before you leave.** Leave yourself a little extra time in case the tailor fails to make the scheduled deadline or time is needed to rectify problems you discover when picking up the completed garments and trying them on for the first time.

If you will be wary of potential pitfalls of custom tailoring and follow these guidelines, you will be a smart shopper for tailored garments. Like many other people, you may be pleased with the outcome of having tailoring completed during your stay in Singapore and Malaysia. The satisfied individuals are the ones the tourist associations never hear from.

We address custom tailoring at some length, including a separate chapter on how to ensure proper tailoring in our *Shopping in Exotic Hong Kong* and *Shopping in Exotic Places* volumes. You might want to refer to one of these books for more detailed "how-to" information on tailoring if you believe you need more specifics than outlined here.

Chapter Three

MAJOR SHOPPING CHOICES

Both Singapore and Malaysia offer an incredible number and variety of shopping choices from the latest in high-tech gadgetry and fashion clothes to traditional artifacts and handicrafts. We're convinced from our own shopping discoveries that any shopping trip to this part of the world would not be complete unless one visited both countries and focused on the shopping strengths of each.

Singapore's major product strengths are ready-made clothes, cameras, electronic goods, antiques, and home decorative items. Malaysia offers a vast array of hand-crafted items -- handicrafts, artifacts, and textiles. Differences in shopping strengths between these two countries are clearly reflected in the different roles, resources, and relationships developed by each country internally, with each other, and with other countries in the region. Singapore's shopping, for example, reflects its major role in Asia as an entrepreneurial entrepot that trades on the resources and artistic talents of neighboring countries as

27

well as the manufacturing skills and marketing know-how of its own population.

Malaysia's shopping choices express the traditional artistic talents of its various ethnic communities which only recently have been wedded to a new form of entrepreneurship partly motivated by the unexpected successes of its less developed northern neighbor, Thailand, and in competition with its always brash and flashy southern neighbor, Singapore.

CLOTHES, FOOTWEAR, AND ACCESSORIES

Shops, department stores, and markets in Singapore and Malaysia are filled with inexpensive to very expensive clothes ranging from T-shirts to designer fashion garments. Indeed, both Malaysia and Singapore are major clothes manufacturers and exporters of menswear and womenswear. Many of the garments, footwear, and accessories produced in these countries are found in department stores, shops, and markets. In addition, exclusive boutiques, such as those found in the Hilton Hotel, The Weld, and KL Plaza in Kuala Lumpur and Tudor Court, Me Shopping Gallery, and the Mandarin Hotel Shopping Arcade in Singapore, offer the latest in European, Japanese, and Australian fashion clothes and accessories.

You will also find plenty of inexpensive clothes -- T-shirts, jeans, shirts, slacks, dresses, jackets, pullovers, and under garments -- produced in Malaysia as well as imported from Thailand, Hong Kong, and Taiwan. The day and night markets, Chinatown's, and department stores of Penang, Kota Bharu, Kuala Lumpur, Kuching, and Singapore are filled with such clothes. Also look for inexpensive copies of name-brand clothes and accessories, such as Benetton, Yves St. Lauren, and Ralph Lauren. Most of these copies are imported from neighboring Thailand.

One problem you will find with much of the ready-made clothes and footwear in Malaysia and Singapore is the sizing. Most ready-made garments and shoes are sized for the locals who tend to be smaller in stature than Australians, Europeans, and North Americans. If you are a small size, you will find plenty of garments that fit. But large bodies will have few choices.

You will also find numerous tailors throughout Malaysia and Singapore. As we cautioned earlier, know what you are doing before contracting for tailoring services, and don't expect to get quality fabrics and wonderful tailoring work done inexpensively. Good quality tailored garments will cost you more than most ready-made clothes. If prices quoted seem too inexpensive, you should question the quality of your tailor!

JEWELRY

While the jewelry prices and selections in Singapore and Malaysia cannot compare to those found in Hong Kong and Bangkok, you will find numerous jewelry stores offering local jewelry and unique designs. Many of the jewelry stores in Malaysia specialize in 22-karat gold jewelry which is popular with local residents. Chinese and Indians prefer solid gold rings, bracelets, and necklaces. Malays have their own traditional gold jewelry consisting of beautifully handcrafted necklaces and bracelets used during ceremonial occasions.

Department stores, shopping centers, and hotel shopping arcades are the best places to find jewelry. In Singapore, for example, you will find many traditional gold shops in Little India and exclusive jewelers working with precious and semi-precious stones, such as Je t'aime, Larry Jewelry, and De Silva, in the city's major shopping centers. Kuala Lumpur has a few good jewelers but in general we find their designs and styles to be less appealing than those found in Singapore.

COMPUTERWARE, CAMERAS, AND ELECTRONIC GOODS

Singapore is one of Asia's major shopping centers for duty-free cameras and electronic goods as well as the latest in computer hardware and software. However, the duty-free status of cameras and electronic goods does not necessarily mean they are less expensive than in other countries. If you come from a country which places high duties on such goods, they will be good buys in Singapore. But if you come from the U.S. where such products are sold through discount houses, Singapore's cameras and electronic goods will be more expensive than in the U.S. Our best advice is to do comparative shopping for name-brand cameras and electronic goods at home prior to arriving in Singapore.

Malaysia, especially Penang, is quickly becoming a

major competitor to Singapore with its own range of duty-free cameras and electronic goods. Malaysia even claims their duty-free products are less expensive than in Singapore. In many cases this is true but in other cases the prices are the same or a little higher. Our best observation is that prices on such duty-free items in Malaysia are competitive with those in Singapore.

You will also find excellent prices on computer software in both Singapore and Malaysia. While most of the inexpensive software is pirated and the governments have declared it illegal in deference to political pressures from the U.S. to enforce copyright laws to protect U.S. intellectual property, the pirated software is readily available through most computer stores in Singapore and Malaysia. While two years ago you could purchase this software off the shelf, today the pirated software is no longer in public view. It has moved from the gray market to a black market. The difference is that today you must place an order for your desired software and then return to the store a few hours later to pick up the diskettes and manuals. Most of the software is for IBM or IBM-compatible computers. Programs that cost US$500 in the U.S., complete with diskettes and manuals, may cost less than US$25 in Singapore and Malaysia. Computer hardware is not a good buy unless you are from a country that places high import duties on such products.

ART

One of our favorite shopping discoveries was the contemporary works of art, primarily oils and watercolors, produced by Malaysia's and Singapore's many creative artists. While this art is primarily Western in orientation, in contrast to the more tradition handcrafted art forms, much of it incorporates local urban street and rural landscape themes reflecting their Singapore and Malaysian settings. Malaysia also has a strong abstract expressionist tradition that is clearly reflected in the paintings displayed at the National Art Gallery.

Shopping for contemporary art in Malaysia and Singapore can be a shopping adventure in itself. Except for a few famous batik artists who have their own galleries in Penang and Kuching, Malaysia has few art galleries and shops displaying this art. If your timing is right, you may be able to attend an occasional art exhibit held at a hotel or school. Art in Kuala Lumpur is beginning to be organized and marketed through a few shops, such as 10 Kiapeng Gallery and A.P. Gallery which offer some of the best oils and watercolors produced by both Malaysian and Singapore artists. In most cases you will have to contact artists directly to view their works and make purchases. In both Kuala Lumpur and Kuching the centers for contacting artists are the public galleries and a few key leaders in the artist community. While contacting artists directly can be a difficult and time consuming process, it is one of the most rewarding shopping experiences in Malaysia. You will discover some beautiful works of art few visitors to Malaysia ever have an opportunity to see and purchase.

Singapore's art is well organized around galleries and art shops in addition to exhibitions and direct purchases from artists. The paintings appearing in Singapore's galleries, shops, and exhibitions come from Singapore, Malaysia, China, and Europe. The major centers for art galleries are Orchard Point shopping center on Orchard Road and Tanglin Shopping Centre on Tanglin Road.

ANTIQUES AND FURNITURE

Both Singapore and Malaysia yield some wonderful antiques and furniture for collectors and home decorators alike. The major antique centers in Malaysia are Penang, Malacca, and Kuching, although you will also find a few nice antique shops in Kuala Lumpur and Kuantan. While many of these shops mix local and imported handicrafts amongst their antiques, for the most part you will find antique furniture and bric-a-brac.

Singapore is filled with antique shops primarily offering Chinese and Peranakan (Straits Chinese) furniture, ceramics, porcelain, carvings, and other collectibles from Singapore, China, Malaysia, Indonesia, Thailand, and Burma. Most of these shops are found in the Watten Estates area and in Tanglin Shopping Centre.

You will also find Korean chests and some lovely contemporary wicker and cane furniture in Malaysia's and Singapore's home decorative shops. Shops in Kuala Lumpur's Plaza Yaochuan and Singapore's Holland Road shopping area have very nice home decorative shops offering stylish cane furniture and home accessories.

TRIBAL AND PRIMITIVE ARTIFACTS

Malaysia and Singapore offer some of the best selections of tribal and primitive artifacts we have found anywhere in Asia. Most of these artifacts come from the islands of Borneo, Sumatra, Sulawesi, and New Guinea. They consist of masks, woodcarvings, staffs, weapons, hunting gear, headdresses, carved panels, house gables, baskets, drums, cooking utensils, boxes, and musical instruments which have both ceremonial and utilitarian significance. The quality of these artifacts can be outstanding with many pieces being of museum quality. Prices are also expensive since many of these artifacts are extremely scarce and the costs of acquiring them are high.

In general the tribal and primitive artifacts found in Malaysia come from the Dayak tribes in Sarawak. A few antique shops in Penang will carry Batak artifacts from the nearby Indonesian island of Sumatra. In Kuala Lumpur a few shops in the Hilton, Pan Pacific, Regent, Shangri-la hotel shopping arcades and the Sunday Market carry tribal and primitive artifacts from Sarawak and Indonesia; you may find an occasional piece from New Guinea. One shop in Kuantan also sells tribal artifacts.

But the real center for tribal artifacts in Malaysia is Kuching, Sarawak. Here, you will find at least five excellent shops offering a treasure-trove of artifacts for discerning shoppers. This is one of the most exciting cities to shop for such items. If you are a collector of tribal artifacts, Kuching is a "must go" city for such shopping.

Several shops in Singapore offer a wide range of tribal and primitive artifacts from throughout Southeast Asia and parts of the Pacific. Most of these shops are concentrated in the Tanglin Shopping Centre. Such shops as Tiepolo, Bareo, and Tatiana have some of the world's best collections of such artifacts.

TEXTILES AND FABRICS

If you collect textiles or wish to purchase fabrics for clothing and home decorative purposes, Malaysia and Singapore are excellent places to shop. While not as extensive as Indonesia, the textiles in Malaysia are nonetheless very impressive. If you have never thought of including textiles in your shopping plans, we urge you to acquaint yourself with textiles in Malaysia. You will learn a

great deal about Malaysian culture, society, art, craftsmanship, art, and women by just observing the different textile
traditions. Indeed, this could well become the shopping
highlight of your trip to Malaysia. And if you ever become "hooked" on Southeast Asian textiles, you will enter
into a whole new and exciting world of shopping and
traveling.

Malaysia has three major textile traditions which in-
trigue many visitors: **batik, songket, and pua kumbu.**
Additional textiles include **cottons and silks.** Like so
many other things in Malaysia, each textile tends to be
associated with the handcrafted and ceremonial traditions
of different ethnic groups found in Malaysian society as
well as in different regions of the country. Batik and
songket, for example, are Malay textiles most readily found
along the East Coast and in rural areas; the pua kumbu, or
warp-tie dyed ikats, are Iban textiles produced in the East
Malaysian state of Sarawak; and cottons and silks are the
preferred textiles of the Chinese and Indians who primarily
reside in urban areas. When you purchase these different
textiles, you buy into many important symbols of these
different societies and cultures in different areas of the
country.

The famous Malaysian **batik** is found throughout the
country, but especially in Penang, the East Coast, and
Kuala Lumpur. Batik is a reverse dye process involving
the application of various motifs and colors to cotton
fabric. It comes in three qualities involving different printing techniques. **Handmade batik** is produced by using a
waxing instrument. This is a small pen-like bamboo instrument with a reservoir for holding molten wax. Motifs
are hand-drawn on fabric and then certain sections of the
motif are covered with hot wax. The material is then dyed
in one color. Next, wax is removed from another section
of the motif, additional wax is applied to the newly dyed
area, and the material is dyed another color. The process
of waxing and dying is repeated until all the desired colors
in the motif appear. This is a very time consuming, labor-
intensive process in which the colorization of material is a
true art form.

Today much of the batik in Malaysia is **stamped batik**
produced with metal stamps. The motifs represented in the
stamps are repeated throughout the fabric.

Printed batik is the cheapest form of batik. For pur-
ists, this is not "real" batik. Batik motifs are printed only

on one side of the fabric. No waxing process in involved in making such imitation materials.

Most of the batik you find in Malaysia will be stamped batik. The Malay motifs tend to be small floral or geometric designs, although some of the handmade batik involves large floral patterns. Given the Islamic prohibition against the representation of human and animal motifs, you will only see floral and geometric designs in Malay batik. While many people are attracted to the Malay colors and designs, others -- including ourselves -- do not find it appealing. Much of the Malay batik lacks the innovation and creativity, as well as the attractive colors and designs, found in Indonesian batik. Indeed, in many parts of Malaysia, Malays prefer buying the Indonesian batik. However, you will find some beautiful designer batik in a few exclusive boutiques in Kuala Lumpur. This batik is very fashionable and made into attractive garments.

In both Penang and Kuala Lumpur you can visit large batik factories which also have factory shops from which you can purchase products. If you have never seen the batik process, a tour of these factories is well worth while.

Malaysia also produces **kain songket,** a unique hand-woven cotton fabric which has geometric patterns woven into it with gold and silver threads. This type of textile is popular among Malays who use it for weddings and ceremonial occasions. One of the major centers for producing kain songket is the East Coast. Village women weave these materials which are sold in the markets and shops of Kota Bharu, Kuala Trengganu, and Kuantan. You may find the colors and patterns of these textiles to be too traditional for your own use. However, kain songket colors and designs are undergoing some major changes as evidenced in the stunning fabrics and garments offered in several of Kuala Lumpur's major handicraft centers, such as Infokraf and Karyaneka.

Malaysia also produces its own form of **ikat** textiles called pua kumbu or simply **pua.** Produced by Iban women in the East Malaysian state of Sarawak, these warp-tie dyed textiles represent handwoven works of art that may well become the highlight of your Malaysian shopping adventure! If you are familiar with the fabulous world of Indonesian ikat textiles, you will appreciate these unique Malaysian textiles. Using natural dyes of muted ochre and tans, the intricate and powerful designs represent common themes found in Iban society, culture, and religion, such as animals, plants, and rivers. These textiles are the object of many collectors and art lovers who appreciate the workmanship, symbolism, and beauty of these one-of-a-kind pieces. Pua make wonderful home decorative items in the forms of wall hangings, framed textile displays, and coverings. The best place to shop for pua is in Kuching. Several antique, artifact, and handicraft shops sell a wide range of pua, from new to old pieces, and in a variety of price ranges. One shop in Kuala Lumpur at the City Market specializes in selling new pua. We find the pua to be the most interesting of all textiles produced in Malaysia, even though songket and batik remain the most popular textiles among Malays and tourists.

Other textiles found in Malaysia are imported and locally-produced silks and cottons. Malaysia has one company -- Suterasemai -- producing unique silk fabrics and clothes. Located just outside the East Coast town of Kuala Trengganu, this company has aspirations of becoming the silk king of Malaysia. Imported Chinese and Indian silks are found in numerous shops and markets of the large cities, such as Kuala Lumpur and Penang, and sold primarily by Indian cloth merchants.

Singapore is an excellent place to buy imported cottons, silks, and batik in the ethnic enclaves of Little India, Arab Street, and Chinatown. You will also find several shops selling attractive Thai, Chinese, and Indian silks which will also make fashionable tailored garments to your specifications. A few antique, artifact, handicraft, and home decorative shops, such as Babazar in Cuppage Terrace on Orchard Road, offer attractive textiles from all over South and Southeast Asia.

HANDCRAFTED ITEMS, HANDICRAFTS, AND SOUVENIRS

Both Malaysia and Singapore are shoppers' paradises for handcrafted items, handicrafts, and souvenirs. While there is often a fine line between antiques, artifacts, handicrafts, and souvenirs, many shops in Malaysia and Singapore mix these items into a big pot pourri of "handcrafted items". The general trend in many areas of Malaysia is to move from good quality antiques and artifacts to handicrafts and souvenirs. As antiques and artifacts increasingly disappear, they are replaced with copies or fakes, handicrafts, and souvenirs of various, and sometimes questionable quality.

Malaysia is a major producer of handcrafted items while Singapore is primarily an importer and exporter of handicrafts produced in other Asian countries. Singapore does not have a strong local handicraft production tradition whereas handicrafts are Malaysia's number one shopping strength. There you can purchase locally-produced handicrafts while watching craftspeople at work.

Malaysian handicrafts are produced throughout the country following both regional and ethnic patterns. The largest number of handicrafts are produced in Malay communities along the East Coast, especially in and around Kota Bharu in the far northeast. Many of these handicrafts are associated with local traditions, ceremonies, and annual festivals. Here you will find a vast assortment of handcrafted items and handicrafts which constitute traditional yet ongoing Malay art forms: kites, brassware, woven mats, knives (kris), silver objects, pottery, tops, baskets, and woodcarvings. If you consider textiles to be handicrafts, then batik and songket should also be included in any East Coast shopping list.

Other areas in Malaysia are also important centers for handicrafts. In Penang, for example, you will find many shops -- mainly antique shops and galleries -- selling a wide variety of handicrafts produced in Malaysia as well as imported from Thailand and Indonesia, especially from Bali. Thai handicrafts are also available in many shops along the East Coast and in Kuala Lumpur. Shops selling handicrafts and souvenirs in Kuching combine items from the East Coast with those produced in Sarawak -- woodcarvings, textiles, baskets, T-shirts, trays, blowpipes, pottery, masks, and bags.

Kuala Lumpur has the most shops offering well designed handcrafted items which best appeal to foreign visitors to Malaysia. Here you will notice a marked difference between the styles, designs, colors, and workmanship of handicrafts produced along the East Coast and those available the upmarket shops in Kuala Lumpur. The offerings in Kuala Lumpur are much more appealing to visitors interested in using handicrafts for home decorative purposes than those found in Kota Bharu and Kuala Trengganu. Such handicraft centers as Infokraf and Karyaneka as well as the City Market have outstanding handicraft selections and are "must" shopping stops for anyone visiting Kuala Lumpur.

Singapore is an excellent place to shop for handicrafts

produced throughout South and Southeast Asia. It will give you a good overview of the types of products you are most likely to find in other Asian countries. The ethnic enclaves of Little India, Arab Street, and Chinatown, for example, have numerous shops selling imported baskets, kites, textiles, leather goods, masks, toys, costumes, and pottery. But the major center for handicrafts is the Singapore Handicraft Centre on Tanglin Road. Here you can visit over 50 shops offering handcrafted items, handicrafts, and souvenirs from Malaysia, Indonesia, Thailand, Sri Lanka, India, Pakistan, the Philippines, and China -- everything from Oriental rugs to wayang puppets. Browse through this area and you will certainly find a treasure or two for your home or as a gift for a friend or relative. Other shops found in the major shopping centers and hotel shopping arcades in Singapore offer a wide variety of imported handicrafts and souvenirs.

SILVERCRAFT AND PEWTERWARE

Malaysia is especially well-noted for its handcrafted silver and pewterware. Malay craftsmen along the East Coast make lovely silver filigree and repousse items and jewelry, such as miniature knives and boats, bowls and tea sets, spoons, brooches, pendants, and earrings. Malaysia's major silvercraft cottage industry is centered in the State of Kelantan, in and around the town of Kota Bharu.

Pewterware is one of Malaysia's major shopping attractions. Several pewter companies produce an attractive range of handcrafted pewterware in the forms of mugs, cups, tea sets, clocks, boxes, pens, picture frames, and small figurines. Selangor Pewter is found in hundreds of shops throughout Malaysia and Singapore. It has the most attractive designs and the largest range of special pewter collections.

Many shops in Singapore also carry silver and pewterware produced in Malaysia. The Singapore Handicraft Centre is one of the best places to find these items.

DUTY-FREE GOODS

Both Singapore and Malaysia offer hundreds of duty-free items. Malaysia in particular has recently positioned itself as a shopper's paradise for duty-free items -- offering some of the best values on duty-free items in Southeast

Asia. Its airports shops are crammed with duty-free goods that are supposed to be as good -- and sometimes better -- buys as the duty-free goods found in Singapore. In general these claims are true. But our major concern is that the so-called duty-free items are not a good deal for many travelers who come from countries where the same goods can be purchased at the same or lower prices. Japanese cameras, for example, purchased in the duty-free shops of Penang and Kuala Lumpur may be the same price as those found in Singapore, but they are still higher than the same brands available through the major discount houses in New York City. And remember, the items are only duty-free in the country in which you purchase them. They may still be subject to duties in your own country.

We have yet to be convinced that duty-free shops anywhere in the world offer very good deals on items other than liquor and cigarettes. They are only good deals if you come from a country that places high duties on such items. Shoppers from India, Indonesia, Thailand, Australia, and Japan, for example, find Penang and Singapore to be shoppers' paradises for such duty-free items as sports goods, cameras, electronic goods, and European clothes and accessories. Indeed they are once you compare the high dutied prices for these same items in India, Indonesia, Thailand, Australia, and Japan with those found in these duty-free shops.

THE MORE YOU LOOK

You will find many of those and other products as you discover your own shopping pleasures in Singapore and Malaysia. Singapore in particular is filled with interesting items from all over the world. While its major shopping strengths are clothes, electronic goods, cameras, antiques, home decorative items, art, artifacts, and jewelry, you will be surprised by the sheer variety of shopping alteratives found in this incredible non-stop shopping city. Malaysia will also surprise you with its vast range of handicrafts and tribal artifacts. The Malay art forms expressed in textiles, pottery, silver, baskets, and woodcarvings as well as the tribal artifacts from Sarawak are each as exciting as they are exotic.

Our best advice is to take to the streets, enter the shops, look through their selections carefully, ask many questions, and focus on buying quality items that will make nice gifts or become unique additions to your wardrobe, collections or home decor. The more you look, the more you will discover the many shopping delights of these two exotic places.

Chapter Four

PLAN AND MANAGE YOUR ADVENTURE

While Singapore and Malaysia are relatively comfortable and convenient places to travel, they do require some basic pre-trip preparation if you plan to shop these places properly. You will especially want to anticipate the most important aspects of any trip to this part of the world by budgeting overall costs, gathering information, checking on Customs regulations, managing your money, gathering essential shopping information, packing right, and anticipating shipping alternatives and arrangements.

PREPARATION

Preparation is the key to experiencing a successful and enjoyable shopping adventure in Malaysia and Singapore. But preparation involves much more than just examining maps, reading travel literature, and making airline and hotel reservations. Preparation, at the very least, is a process of minimizing uncertainty by learning how to develop a shopping plan, manage your money, determine the value of products, handle Customs, and pack for the occasion. It involves knowing what products are good deals to buy in Singapore and Malaysia in comparison to similar items back home. Most important of all, preparation helps organize and ensure the success of all aspects of a shopping adventure in exotic places.

ANTICIPATE COSTS

Traveling and shopping in Malaysia and Singapore can be as inexpensive or expensive as you want them to be. You will find the cost of round-trip air transportation to be relatively inexpensive compared to costs 10 or 20 years ago or current costs of domestic airfares in the U.S. or international airfares from the U.S. to Europe. Indeed, Asia still has some of the most inexpensive airfares in the world. For example, you can fly round-trip from New York City to Kuala Lumpur or Singapore on major airlines for under US$1500, and many excellent package tours will include 10 days of hotels and some ground arrangements for that same price!

Hotels and local transportation in Malaysia and Singapore are also some of the best buys in the world. Kuala Lumpur, for example, is rated by many travel professionals as one of the cheapest cities in the world with excellent buys on first-class and deluxe hotels. Indeed, you may want to travel first-class in both Malaysia and Singapore given their price advantages and excellent service and facilities. The cost difference between a US$85 deluxe hotel in Penang, Kuala Trengganu, Kuantan, Kuala Lumpur, Penang, Kuching, and Singapore and a US$65 first or second class hotel in these same cities and towns is so minor as to justify pampering yourself in some truly fine deluxe hotels.

While Singapore and Malaysia offer some of the best foods in the world, they also do so at very inexpensive prices. You can easily get by on US$7 a day for excellent local foods or splurge at fine Continental restaurants for US$30 per person -- restaurants that might cost more than US$100 in other major cities of the world.

Your major traveling costs will most likely be the cost of shopping for local products. Here, we cannot give you specific guidelines other than the general observation that you should take enough cash, personal checks, and travelers' checks as well as sufficient credit limits on your credit cards in anticipation of finding plenty of treasures in these two countries. If you are a serious collector of antiques, tribal artifacts, and jewelry, you may quickly find yourself in financial trouble given the large number of quality items you will probably want to buy in both Malaysia and Singapore!

DEVELOP AN ACTION PLAN

Time is money when traveling abroad. The better you plan and use your time, the more time you will have to enjoy your trip. If you want to use your time wisely and literally hit the ground running, you should plan a detailed, yet tentative, schedule for each day. Begin by:

- Identifying each city you plan to visit.
- Blocking out the number of days you will spend in each area.
- Listing those places you feel you must visit during your stay.
- Leaving extra time each day for new discoveries.

Keep this plan with you and revise it in light of new information.

WELCOME SERENDIPITY AND GOOD LUCK

Planning is fine, but don't overdo it and thus ruin your trip by accumulating a list of unfulfilled expectations. Planning needs to be adapted to certain realities which often become the major highlights of one's travel and shopping experiences. Good luck is a function of good planning: you place yourself in many different places to take advantage of new opportunities. You should be open to unexpected events which may well become the major highlights of your travel and shopping experiences.

If you want to have good luck, then plan to be in many different places to take advantage of new opportunities. Expect to alter your initial plans once you begin discovering new and unexpected realities. Serendipity -- those chance occurrences that often evolve into memorable and rewarding experiences -- frequently interferes with the best-laid travel and shopping plans. Welcome serendipity by altering your plans to accommodate the unexpected. You can do this by revising your plans each day as you go. A good time to summarize the day's events and accomplishments and plan tomorrow's schedule is just before you go to bed each night.

Keep in mind that your plan should be a means to an end -- experiencing exciting travel and shopping - and not the end itself. If you plan well, you will surely experience good luck on the road to a successful trip!

CONDUCT RESEARCH AND
NETWORK FOR INFORMATION

Do as much research as possible before you depart on your Singapore and Malaysia adventures. A good starting place is the periodical section of your local library. Here you may find several magazine and newspaper articles on travel and shopping in Singapore and Malaysia.

You should also write, call, or fax the Singapore and Malaysian tourist associations for information on their countries. The Singapore Tourist Promotion Board (in the U.S. call 213/852-1901 or 212/687-0385), for example, puts together an excellent package of materials which outline the highlight of traveling and shopping in Singapore. The Malaysian Tourist Development Corporation (in the U.S. call 415/788-3344) also has several information booklets and brochures, including a listing of hotels, to help you plan your trip. Representatives of these offices are found in major North American and European cities.

We also recommend **networking for information and advice.** You'll find many people, including relatives, friends, and acquaintances, who have traveled to Singapore and Malaysia and are eager to share their experiences and discoveries with you. They may recommend certain shops where you will find excellent products, service, and prices. Ask them basic who, what, where, why, and how questions:

• What shops did you particularly like?
• What do they sell?
• How much discount could I expect?
• Whom should I talk to?
• Where is the shop located?
• How do I get what I want?
• Is bargaining expected?

Once you arrive in-country, be sure to contact the local tourist offices. In many Malaysian cities you will find two tourist information offices -- a state tourist office and a branch of the Tourist Development Corporation. While the state tourist office may have the most information, since it also includes the brochures and maps produced by the Tourist Development Corporation, you will get the most information by visiting both offices.

CHECK CUSTOMS REGULATIONS

It's always good to know Customs regulations before leaving home. If you are a U.S. citizen planning to return to the U.S. from Singapore or Malaysia, the United States Customs Service provides several helpful publications which are available free of charge from your nearest U.S. Customs Office, or write P.O. Box 7407, Washington, D.C. 20044.

- *Know Before You Go* (Publication #512): outlines facts about exemptions, mailing gifts, duty-free articles, as well as prohibited and restricted articles.

- *Trademark Information for Travelers* (Publication #508): deals with unauthorized importation of trademarked goods. Since you will find some copies of trademarked items in Singapore and Malaysia, this publication will alert you to potential problems with Custom inspectors prior to returning home.

- *International Mail Imports* answers many travelers' questions regarding mailing items from foreign countries back to the US. The U.S. Postal Service sends all packages to Customs for examination and assessment of duty before it is delivered to the addressee. Some items are free of duty and some are dutiable. The rules have recently changed on mail imports, so do check on this before you leave the U.S.

- *GSP and the Traveler* itemizes goods from particular countries that can enter the U.S. duty-free. GSP regulations, which are designed to promote the economic development of certain Third World countries, permit many products, especially arts and handicrafts, to enter the United States duty-free. Most items purchased in Malaysia will be allowed to enter duty-free. However, many items from Singapore will be dutiable since Singapore no longer enjoys full GSP status. In addition, most of Singapore's antiques, arts, and artifacts are imported from other countries. Therefore, they are not necessarily except from duties since they are not from the countries of origin -- a fine distinction Customs may make when enforcing the letter of the law. However, since ASEAN nations are treated as one country by U.S. Customs, many items

> originating in Thailand, Malaysia, Indonesia,
> or the Philippines could be purchased in
> Singapore and may enter the U.S. duty-free.

MANAGE YOUR MONEY WELL

It is best to carry traveler's checks, two or more major credit cards with sufficient credit limits, U.S. dollars, and a few personal checks. Our basic money rule is to take enough money and sufficient credit limits so you don't run short. How much you take is entirely up to you, but it's better to have too much than not enough when shopping in Singapore and Malaysia.

We increasingly find **credit cards** to be very convenient when traveling in Asia. We prefer using credit cards to pay for hotels and restaurants and for major purchases as well as for unanticipated expenses incurred when shopping. Most major hotels and stores honor MasterCard, Visa, American Express, and Diner's cards. It is a good idea to take one or two bank cards and an American Express card.

Take plenty of **traveler's checks** in U.S. denominations of $50 and $100. Smaller denominations are often more trouble than they are worth, but you may want a few. Most major banks, hotels, restaurants, and shops accept traveler's checks, although some do add a small service charge. Money-changers and banks will give the best exchange rates, but at times you'll find hotels to be more convenient because of their close proximity and better hours.

Personal checks can be used to obtain traveler's checks with an American Express card or to pay for goods to be shipped later – after the check clears your bank. Remember to keep one personal check aside to pay Customs should you have dutiable goods when you return home.

Use you own judgment concerning how much **cash** you should carry with you. Contrary to some fearful ads, cash is awfully nice to have in moderate amounts to supplement your traveler's checks and credit cards. But of course you must be very careful where and how you carry cash. Consider carrying an "emergency cash reserve" primarily in $50 and $100 denominations, but also a few 20's for small currency exchanges.

USE CREDIT CARDS WISELY

Credit cards can be a shopper's blessing. They are your tickets to serendipity, convenience, good exchange rates, and a useful form of insurance. Widely accepted throughout Asia, they enable you to draw on credit reserves for purchasing many wonderful items you did not anticipate finding when you initially planned your adventure. In addition to being convenient, you usually will get good exchange rates once the local currency amount appearing on your credit slip is converted by the bank at the official rate into your home currency. Credit cards also allow you to float your expenses into the following month or two without paying interest charges. Most important, should you have a problem with a purchase -- such as buying a piece of jewelry which you later discover was misrepresented or has fake stones, or electronic goods which are incompatible with your systems back home -- your credit card company can assist you in recovering your money and returning the goods. Once you discover your problem, contact the credit card company with your complaint and refuse to pay the amount while the matter is in dispute. Businesses accepting these cards must maintain a certain standard of honesty and integrity. In this sense, credit cards are an excellent and inexpensive form of insurance against possible fraud and damaged goods when shopping abroad. If you rely only on cash or traveler's checks, you have no such institutional recourse for recovering your money.

The down-side to using credit cards is that some businesses will charge you a "commission" for using your card, or simply not go as low in the bargaining process as they would for cash or traveler's checks. Commissions will range from 2 to 6 percent. This practice is discouraged by credit card companies; nonetheless, shops do this because they must pay a 4-5 percent commission to the credit card companies. They merely pass this charge on to you. When bargaining, keep in mind that shopkeepers usually consider a final bargained price to be a "cash only" price. If you wish to use your credit card at this point, you will probably be assessed the additional 2 to 6 percent to cover the credit card commission or lose your bargained price altogether. Frequently in the bargaining process, when you near the seller's low price, you will be asked whether you intend to pay cash. It is at this point that cash and traveler's checks come in handy to avoid a slightly higher price. However, *don't be "penny wise but pound foolish"*. You may still want to use your credit card if you suspect you might have any problems with your purchase.

A few other tips on the use and abuse of credit cards may be useful in planning your trip. *Use your credit cards for the things that will cost you the same amount no matter how you pay*, such as lodging and meals in the better hotels and restaurants or purchases in most department stores. Consider requesting a higher credit limit on your bank cards if you think you may wish to charge more than your current limit allows.

Be extremely careful with your credit cards. Be sure merchants write the correct amount and indicate clearly whether this is U.S. dollars, Singapore, or Malaysian dollars on the credit card slip you sign. It is always a good practice to write the local currency symbol before the total amount so that additional figures cannot be added or the amount mistaken for your own currency. For example, 192 Singapore dollars are roughly equivalent to 100 U.S. dollars. It should appear as "S$192" on your credit card slip. And keep a good record of all charges in local currency -- and at official exchange rates -- so you don't have any surprises once you return home!

SECURE YOUR VALUABLES

Malaysia and Singapore are relatively safe countries to travel in if you take the normal precautions of not inviting potential trouble. We have never had a problem with thieves or pickpockets but neither have we encouraged such individuals to meet us. If you take a few basic precautions in securing your valuables, you should have a worry-free trip.

Be sure to keep your traveler's checks, credit cards, and cash in a safe place along with your travel documents and other valuables. While money belts do provide good security for valuables, the typical 4" x 8" nylon belts can be uncomfortable in Singapore's and Malaysia's hot and humid weather. Our best advice is for women to carry money and documents in a leather shoulder bag that can be held firmly and which should be kept with you at all times, however inconvenient, even when passing through buffet lines. Choose a purse with a strap long enough to sling around your neck bandolier style. Purse snatching is not a common occurance in Singapore and Malaysia, but it is best to err on the side of caution than to leave yourself open to problems that could quickly ruin your vacation.

For men, keep your money and credit cards in your wallet, but always carry your wallet in a front pocket. If you keep it in a rear pocket, as you may do at home, you invite pickpockets to demonstrate their varied talents in relieving you of your money, and possibly venting your trousers in the process. If your front pocket is an uncomfortable location, you probably need to clean out your wallet so it will fit better.

You may also want to use the free hotel safety deposit boxes for your cash and other valuables. If one is not provided in your room, ask the cashier to assign you a private box in their vault. Under no circumstances should you leave your money and valuables unattended in your hotel room, at restaurant tables, or in dressing rooms. You may want to leave your expensive jewelry at home so as not to be as likely a target of theft.

If you get robbed, chances are it will be in part your own fault, because you invited someone to take advantage by not being more cautious in securing your valuables.

TAKE ALL NECESSARY SHOPPING INFORMATION

We recommend that you take more than just a copy of this book to Singapore and Malaysia. At the very least you should take:

- A prioritized "wish list" of items you think would make nice additions to your wardrobe, home decor, collections, and for gift giving.

- Measurements of floor space, walls, tables, and beds in your home in anticipation of purchasing some lovely home furnishings, tablecloths, bedspreads, or pictures.

- Photographs of particular rooms that could become candidates for home decorative items. These come in handy when you find something you think -- but are not sure -- may fit into your colors schemes, furnishings, and decorating patterns.

- Take an inventory of your closets and identify particular colors, fabrics, and designs you wish to acquire to complement and enlarge your present wardrobe.

- If you think you will have tailoring work done, be sure to take pictures or models of garments you wish to have made. If you have a favorite blouse or suit you wish to have copied, take it with you. It is not necessary to take a commercial pattern, because Asian tailors do not use these devices for measuring, cutting, and assembling clothes.

DO COMPARATIVE SHOPPING

You should also do comparative shopping before arriving in Singapore and Malaysia. This is particularly important in the case of cameras, computers, and electronic goods which are readily available elsewhere in the world. Once you arrive in Singapore and Malaysia, the only comparisons you can make are between various shops within and between cities, such as comparing duty-free shops in Penang with the duty-free airport shops in Kuala Lumpur and Singapore. Based on your comparative shopping, you may discover many so-called duty-free items are actually higher than the same products available back home. You'll never know unless you have done your homework.

If you are a true comparative shopper, you should first make a list of what you want to buy and then do some "window" shopping by visiting local stores, examining catalogs, and telephoning for price and availability information. If, for example, your list includes cameras or electronic equipment, you should compile a list of prices for comparable items found in stores and discount houses back home. In the U.S., call the toll-free numbers of reliable mail-order discount houses in New York City for phone quotes on cameras, film, computers, and electronic equipment: Bi-Rite (800/223-1970), 47st Photo (800/221-7774), Focus (800/331-0828), Executive (800/223-7323), and Olden Computer (800/223-1444). The Sunday and Wednesday editions of *The New York Times* include ads from these highly competitive firms. You will quickly discover their prices may be 10-30 percent cheaper than the best price you can find in your local discount houses. Some of these New York firms will even bargain over the phone when you inform them of a competitor's better price! You will also discover that most imported camera and electronic equipment purchased through these mail-order sources are 20 to 40 percent cheaper than in Singapore and Malaysia. So be sure to do your pricing research **before** you buy such items in Singapore or Malaysia. There's nothing worse to deflate your shopping enthusiasm than to return home with what appeared to be a terrific Singapore or Malaysian bargain and then discover you could have gotten the same item for less at home.

Jewelry is another item that begs comparative shopping and some minimal level of expertise in determining authenticity and quality. Read as much as you can on different qualities of jewelry and visit jewelry stores at home where you can learn a great deal by asking salespeople questions about craftsmanship, settings, quality, and discounts.

KEEP TRACK OF ALL RECEIPTS

Be sure to ask for receipts and keep them in a safe place. You will need them later for providing accurate pricing information on your Customs declaration form. Take a large envelope to be used only for depositing receipts. Organize it periodically by country and type of items purchased. List on a separate sheet of paper for each country what, where, and how much for each purchased item. When you go through Customs with your purchases organized in this manner, you should sail through more quickly since you have good records of all your transactions.

PACK RIGHT AND LIGHT

Packing and unpacking are two great travel challenges. Trying to get everything you think you need into one or two bags can be frustrating. You either take too much with you, and thus transport unnecessary weight around the world, or you find you took too little.

We've learned over the years to err on the side of taking too little with us. If we start with less, we will have room for more. Your goal should be to avoid lugging an extensive wardrobe, cosmetics, library, and household goods around the world! Make this your guiding principle for deciding how and what to pack: *"When in doubt, leave it out"*.

Above all, you want to return home loaded down with wonderful new purchases without paying extra weight charges. Hence, pack for the future rather than load yourself down with the past. To do this you need to wisely select the proper mix of colors, fabrics, styles, and accessories.

You should initially pack as lightly as possible. Remember, Singapore's and Malaysia's climates are hot and humid. Take only light-weight clothes made of natural fibers. Avoid any garments made of polyester or wool. Since dress in these countries is very casual, you need not take suits and coats. The very top restaurants and the gambling casino in Genting Highlands have dress codes, but they are very casual by Western standards: a coat and tie or a long-sleeve batik shirt for men and a dress or skirt and blouse for women. Plan to buy and wear additional clothes as you go, such as batik shirts, blouses, and skirts.

Items you are likely to pack but are also readily and inexpensively available in Singapore and Malaysia include clothes, suitcases, bags, books, maps, stationery, and audio-cassettes. Consequently, you may want to limit the number of such items you take with you since you can always buy more along the way. But do take all the shoes, specific medications, and makeup you will need on the trip. These items may be difficult to find in the brands you desire.

Since you will do a great deal of walking in Singapore and Malaysia, we recommend taking at least one pair of comfortable walking shoes and one pair of dress shoes. Break these shoes in before you take them on this trip. Wearing new shoes for lengthy periods of time can become quite uncomfortable.

CHOOSE SENSIBLE LUGGAGE

Whatever you do, avoid being a slave to your luggage. Luggage should be both **expandable and expendible**. Flexibility is the key to making it work. Get ready to pack and repack, acquire new bags along the way, and replace luggage if necessary.

Your choice of luggage is very important for enjoying your shopping experience and for managing airports, airplanes, and Customs. While you may normally travel with two suitcases and a carry-on, your specific choice of luggage for shopping purposes may be different. We recommend taking two large suitcases with wheels -- it's best when one can fit into another; one large carry-on bag; one nylon backpack; and one collapsible nylon bag.

If you decide to take hard-sided luggage, make sure it has no middle divider. With no divider you can pack some of your bulkier purchases. This type of luggage may appear safer than soft-sided luggage, but it is heavy, limited in space, and not necessarily more secure. A good soft-sided piece should be adequately reinforced.

Your **carry-on bag** should be convenient -- lightweight and with separate compartments and pockets -- for taking short trips outside major cities. For example, if you visit Dayak villages during a two to three day river safari in Sarawak, you can leave your large luggage pieces at a hotel in Kuching and travel only with the carry-on bag.

We also recommend taking a small nylon **backpack** in lieu of a camera bag. This is a wonderfully convenient bag, because it can be used as a comfortable shoulder bag as well as a backpack. It holds our cameras, film, travel books, windbreakers, umbrella, drinks and snacks and still has room for carrying small purchases. We take this bag with us everywhere. When we find our hands filled with purchases, our versatile backpack goes on our back so our hands are free for other items.

A collapsible **nylon bag** also is a useful item to pack.

Many of these bags fold into a small 6" x 8" zippered pouch. You may wish to keep this bag in your backpack or carry-on for use when shopping.

SHIPPING WITH EASE

One of the worst nightmares of shopping abroad is to return home after a wonderful time to find your goods have been lost, stolen, or damaged in transit. This happens frequently to people who do not know how to ensure against such problems. Failing to pack properly or pick the right shipper, they suffer accordingly. This should not happen to you in Singapore or Malaysia.

On the other hand, you should not pass up buying lovely items because you feel reluctant to ship them home. Indeed, some travelers only buy items that will fit into their suitcase because they are reluctant to ship larger items home. But you can easily ship from Malaysia and Singapore and expect to receive your goods in excellent condition within a few weeks. We seldom let shipping considerations affect our buying decisions. We know we can always get our purchases home with little difficulty. For us, *shipping is one of those things that must be arranged*. We have numerous alternatives from which to choose, from hiring a professional shipping company to hand carrying our goods on board the plane. Shipping may or may not be costly, depending on how much you plan to ship and by which means. It is seldom a hassle in Singapore and Malaysia.

Before leaving home you should identify the best point of entry for goods returning home by air or sea. Once you are in Singapore and Malaysia, you generally have five alternatives for shipping goods home:

- Take everything with you.
- Do your own packing and shipping through the local post office (for small packages only).
- Have each shop ship your purchases.
- Arrange to have one shop consolidate all of your purchases into a single shipment.
- Hire a local shipper to make all shipping arrangements.

Taking everything with you is fine if you don't have much and you don't mind absorbing excess baggage charges. If you are overweight, ask about the difference been "Excess Baggage" and "Unaccompanied Baggage". Excess baggage is very expensive while unaccompanied baggage is much less expensive, although by no means cheap.

Most major shops are skilled at shipping goods for customers. They often pack the items free and only charge you for the actual postage or freight. Many of these shops use excellent shippers who are known for reasonable charges, good packing, and reliability. If you choose to have a shop ship for you, insist on a receipt specifying they will ship the item and specify that you want the shipment insured.

If you have several large purchases -- at least one cubic meter -- check with local shippers since it is cheaper and safer to consolidate many separate purchases into one shipment which is well packed and insured. Choose a local company which has an excellent reputation among expatriates for shipping goods. Consult the Yellow Pages under the headings "Shipping" or "Removers". Do some quick research. If you are staying at a good hotel, ask the concierge about reliable shippers. He should be able to help you. Personnel at the local embassy, consultate, or international school know which companies are best. Call a few expatriates and ask for their best recommendations.

Sea freight charges are usually figured by volume -- either by the cubic meter or a container. **Air freight** charges are based on a combination of size and weight. For a sea shipment there is a minimum charge -- usually one cubic meter -- you will pay even if your shipment is of less volume. There are also port fees to be paid, a broker to get the shipment throught Customs, and unless your hometown is a major seaport that handles freighters, you will also pay to have your shipment trucked from the port of entry to your home. On air freight you pay for the actual amount you ship -- there is no minimum charge. You can usually have it flown to the international airport nearest your home and avoid port fees altogether. However, there will be a small Customs fee.

If you buy any items that are less than three feet in length and you don't wish to hand-carry them home, consider sending them by **parcel post**. This is the cheapest way to ship and parcel post tends to be reliable, although it may take four to six months for final delivery. Most shops will take care of the packing and shipping for parcel post.

If you have items that are too large for parcel post, but nonetheless are small and relatively lightweight, air freight may be a viable option. Consider air freight if the package is too large to be sent parcel post, but much smaller than the minimum of one cubic meter, and does not weigh an excessive amount relative to its size. Air freight is the transportation of choice if you must have your purchase arrive right away. Sea freight is the better choice if your purchase is large and heavy and you are willing to wait several weeks for its arrival. When using air freight, contact a well established and reliable airline. It will be most cost effective if you can select one airline, i.e., the same carrier flies between your point of shipping and your hometown airport.

We have tried each of these shipping alternatives with various results. Indeed, we tend to use these alternatives in combination. For example, we take everything we can with us until we reach the point where the inconvenience and cost of excess baggage requires some other shipping arrangements. We plan to be in Kuala Lumpur and Singapore at key points during our trip so we can consolidate shipments with shops where we know we will probably be making purchases. We then arrange to have a shipment sent by truck from Kuala Lumpur to another consolidation point in Singapore. If we don't know which shop will be the consolidation point in Singapore, we inform the Kuala Lumpur shop to hold our shipment until we call them from Singapore with instructions. Such an approach requires trusting a few key shops, making a long distance telephone call or two, and using Kuala Lumpur as a intermediate consolidation point and Singapore as the final consolidator and shipper. While it may seem complicated at first, in practice this approach works very well and we receive our goods with little or no problem.

When you use a shipper, be sure to examine alternative shipping arrangements and prices. The type of delivery you specify at your end can make a significant difference in the overall shipping price. If you don't specify the type of delivery you want, you may be charged the all-inclusive first-class rate. For example, if you choose door-to-door delivery, you will pay a premium to have your shipment clear Customs, moved through the port, transported to your door, and unpacked by local movers. On the other hand, it is cheaper for you to just have the shipment arrive at your door; you do your own unpacking and carting away of the trash. We don't recommend trying to pick up your shipment at the designated sea port. For $75 to $100 a local broker will save you the hassle of clearing Customs and moving the shipment out of the port and onto a truck for transport to your home.

We simply cannot over-stress the importance of finding and establishing a personal relationship with a good local shipper who will provide you with services which may go beyond your immediate shipping needs. A good local shipping contact will enable you to continue shopping in Singapore and Malaysia even after returning home!

Chapter Five

SHOPPING RULES AND BARGAINING SKILLS

Shopping in Singapore and Malaysia is as much a cultural experience as it is a set of buying and selling transactions in unique urban and commercial settings. While many of the shops, department stores, and markets may look similar to ones you shop in back home, they do have important differences you should know about prior to starting your Singapore and Malaysian shopping adventures. Most of these differences relate to certain shopping and pricing traditions that constitute an important set of shopping rules and bargaining skills you can and should learn before you begin making purchases in these countries.

SHOPPING BY THE RULES

The structure of shopping in Singapore and Malaysia is such that you should make a few adjustments to the way you normally approach shopping if you are to best enjoy your shopping adventure. The most important adjustments constitute a set of shopping rules that are applicable in most shopping situations:

KNOW THE SHOPPING RULES

- **The most important shopping areas are concentrated in the central business districts and a few outlying suburban areas of major cities.** The best products in terms of quality, designs, and colors are found in shopping centers, hotel shopping arcades, department stores, and shophouses concentrated along one or two major streets in the central business districts of most major cities. In Penang, it's Penang Road; in Kuala Lumpur, go to Jalan Tuanku Abdul Rahman and "The Golden Triangle"; in Kuching, stroll down Jalan Main Bazaar; and in Singapore, Orchard Road is the shopping street. The major cities also have some good suburban shopping. However, don't expect to find much shopping in rural areas other than at factory shops and cottage industry houses on the outskirts of some cities such as Kuching, Kota Bharu, and Kuala Trengganu. Knowing these shopping patterns, it's a good idea to stay at a hotel in close proximity to the main downtown shopping streets. Except for an occasional trip to visit a few factories and shops outside the central business district, expect to do 90 percent of your shopping along only a few downtown streets.

- **Concentrate your shopping on a few shopping areas within close proximity of each other each day.** While it is relatively easy to get around in Singapore and Malaysian cities, it's best to focus your shopping in particular shopping areas rather than continuously travel from one shop to another between areas. Compile a list of shops or areas you wish to visit, locate them on a map, and each day try to visit those close to one another.

- **Prepare to do a great deal of walking within and between shopping areas.** While most shops, shopping centers, and department stores are located along a few streets in the central business district, these are often very long streets requiring a considerable amount of walking. Take a good pair of walking shoes, slow down your pace of walking, and take public transportation whenever possible.

● **Use public transportation when going between shopping areas or even within some
shopping areas.** Public transportation, such
as taxis, buses, and trishaws, are inexpensive
and convenient for shoppers in both Malaysia
and Singapore. Given the high heat and humidity as well as the long distance walking
involved in shopping, avoid extensive walking. Our rule of thumb: if we must walk
more than one kilometer, we take a taxi or
bus.

● **Pack your rain and sun gear whenever
you go out.** Unless you know for certain the
weather forecast for the day, it's always a
good ideal to take an umbrella -- a small
collapsible one is perfect -- sunglasses, and
hat when you go out during the day and an
umbrella at night. Singapore and Malaysia
have hot and humid climates that can be unpredictable at times. The umbrella keeps
both the rain and sun off our heads. When
we forget to take our umbrella, invariably it
rains!

● **Expect to shop in two very different shopping cultures.** The first world is the most
familiar one for visitors -- shopping centers,
department stores, and hotel shopping
arcades. Shops in this culture tend to have
window displays, well organized interiors,
and fixed prices which may or may not be all
that fixed, depending on your ability to get
discounts. The second shopping culture consists of the traditional shophouses, markets,
and hawkers which tend to be somewhat
disorganized and involve price uncertainty
and bargaining skills. You will most likely
be able to directly transfer your shopping
skills to the first culture, but you may have
difficulty navigating in the second shopping
culture.

● **The day and night markets can be fun
places to shop, but only if you are open to
new sights, sounds, and smells not normally found in other shopping sites.** Many of

the markets combine fresh fruits, vegetables, and meats with hawker food stalls and shop stalls selling household goods. Usually clean and well organized, although seemingly chaotic, these markets can be very interesting and colorful places to visit. They tend to cater to a different class of local resident -- lower to lower-middle -- than the department stores and shopping centers. Many of the markets also have distinct ethnic characters as they are predominately Malay, Chinese, Indian, or Dayak markets. Locals especially love to shop in the Chinese markets because the prices appear cheap compared to their other shopping alternatives. Shopping may be limited to a few handcrafted items, but it's the cultural experience and photo opportunities that make these places so interesting for visitors. Other markets primarily offer inexpensive clothes, accessories, and household goods along with exotic dishes prepared by the ubiquitous hawker food stalls. These, too, are great places to experience the more traditional buying and selling culture. While you will seldom find good quality products in these markets -- the emphasis is on buying cheap goods -- there are exceptions and you will find plenty of inexpensive clothes, souvenirs, and fake products to make the trip to these markets worthwhile. Bargaining, with discounts ranging from 20 to 70 percent, is the only way to buy in these markets. You will be foolish to pay the first asking price.

• **Shopping centers tend to be crowded, noisy, and multi-level buildings filled with small shops.** Except for the indoor pedestrian mall concept incorporated in the new Marina Square shopping arcade in Singapore, shopping centers in Malaysia and Singapore are not shopping malls where shoppers can leisurely browse. Given the high costs of urban land, most shopping centers are high density buildings occupying very little land. Instead, they are built up with shops occupying as much interior area as possible. Levels are connected by several escalators and one or two elevators. Given the structure of such buildings, they tend to look and feel very crowded, especially on weekends when most locals do their shopping. These centers are also very noisy and many are social centers for young people who enjoy window shopping, eating, and meeting friends. If you are not used to such types of shopping centers, they may feel unfamiliar to you at first.

- **Most shopping centers and department stores cater to the shopping preferences of local residents rather than to foreign tourists.** Don't expect to find a great deal of quality local products in shopping centers and department stores. Most of these places orient their product lines to the local middle-class with numerous average quality consumer products and imported goods. However, you will find a few exceptional quality shopping centers -- primarily in Singapore -- that are "must visit" places for most visitors. In Penang, its the Komtar shopping center; in Kuala Lumpur, The Weld, KL Plaza, Plaza Yow Chuan, and The Mall are the upscale places to visit; and in Singapore, look for Tudor Court, Tanglin Shopping Centre, Wisma Atria, The Promenade, and Paragon Shopping Centre.

- **The best quality products are invariably found in the major hotel shopping arcades and a few shopping centers with reputations for quality.** There is nothing surprising to discover that the best quality shops tend to congregate near the best quality hotels which cater to the more affluent business travelers and tourists. The shops in these places will offer a mix of expensive imported products -- designer label clothes, jewelry, luggage, shoes, and accessories -- as well as excellent quality local products, especially antiques, artifacts, textiles, and tailored clothes. The prices in such shops can seem high, but they offer good quality products. The "best buys" will be on high quality local products rather than the usual mix of upscale imported goods that are available in many other cities and duty-free shops around the world.

- **Expect to get the best prices on locally produced items that use inexpensive labor.** Imported goods will be expensive regardless of their duty-free status. But any products that use inexpensive local labor -- textiles, woodcarvings, woven handicrafts -- are excellent buys because the cost of labor is going up and many of the handcrafting skills are quickly disappearing with the onslaught of inexpensive plastic materials and machine labor.

- **Don't expect to get something for nothing.** If a price seems too good to be true, it probably is. Good quality products, especially jewelry, antiques, and artifacts, may not seem cheap in Singapore and Malaysia. But they are bargains if you compare their prices to similar items found in the shops of Tokyo, Sydney, Paris, London, or New York City.

- **Expect the design and color selections of many locally produced items to be different from your design and color preferences.** This is an especially valid observation in the more traditional handicraft production areas of Malaysia, such as along the East Coast. The designs and colors of traditional handicrafts may appeal to Malay villagers, but they have a long way to go before they will catch the eyes of westerners who have a very different sense of what constitutes good quality in design and color in their own cultural settings. Nonetheless, many changes are underway in Malaysia to "modernize" the designs and colors of traditional Malay handicrafts. Major government handicraft centers in Kuala Lumpur, such as Infokraf and Karyaneka, display the very best of this new thrust toward redesigning traditional forms to appeal to a larger international audience. Clothes of local designers in Malaysia and Singapore also have their own unique styles and colors which may or may not appeal to your wardrobe tastes.

- **Ask for assistance whenever you feel you need it.** While Malaysia and Singapore are in reality easy to get around, at times you may feel lost and have difficulty finding particular shops or products. Whenever this happens, just ask for assistance from your hotel, tourist office, shopkeepers, and people you meet on the street. Malaysians and SinSingaporians are friendly and will assist you if they can.

• **Don't be surprised if some shopkeepers take a great deal of your time in developing a personal and long-term relationship with you.** Business in Singapore and Malaysia is still a personal set of relations, regardless of all the symbols of impersonal efficiency and effectiveness. While some merchants may initially appear distant and suspicious, most are generally inquisitive if you will initiate a conversation that involves their family, work, or country. Many merchants in Singapore and Malaysia, for example, are extremely friendly, enjoy learning more about visitors, willing to share their knowledge about their country and products, and prefer cementing personal relationships with their customers. The lines between buyer and seller may quickly fade as you develop a friendship with the shopkeeper. You may even find some shopkeepers inviting you to lunch, dinner, or their home as well as giving you special gifts. You may even feel you are being adopted by the family! This is usually a genuine expression of interest, concern, and friendship rather than a sales tactic. In fact, you may find such personal encounters to be the highlights of your shopping adventure in Singapore and Malaysia and they may lead to lasting friendships with these individuals.

You will also learn other shopping rules as you proceed through the many shophouses, shopping centers, hotel shopping arcades, department stores, and markets in Singapore and Malaysia. Many of these relate to pricing policies and bargaining practices that you can and should learn if you want to become an effective shopper in Singapore and Malaysia.

PRICING PRACTICES AND BARGAINING

Bargaining still remains the way of shopping life in most parts of Singapore and Malaysia. While the Singapore Tourist Promotion Board is attempting to end the practice of bargaining, it still goes on nonetheless. Therefore, if you want to become an effective shopper in Singapore and Malaysia, you need to know something about the basics of bargaining.

Most North American and European tourists come from fixed-price cultures where prices are nicely displayed on items. The only price uncertainty may be a sales tax added to the total amount at the cash register. Only on very large-ticket items, such as automobiles, boats, houses, furniture, carpets, and jewelry, can you expect to negotiate the price. If you want to get the best deal, you must do comparative shopping as well as wait for special discounts and sales. Bargain shopping in such a culture centers on comparative pricing of items. Shopping becomes a relatively passive activity involving the examination of printed advertisements in newspapers and catalogs.

Expert shoppers in fixed-price cultures tend to be those skilled in carefully observing and comparing prices in the print advertising media. They clip coupons and know when the best sales are being held for particular items on certain days. They need not be concerned with cultivating personal relationships with merchants or salespeople in order to get good buys.

Like a fish out of water, expert shoppers from fixed-price cultures may feel lost when shopping in Singapore and Malaysia. Few of their fixed-price shopping skills are directly transferable to the Singapore and Malaysian shopping environments. Except for department stores and some ads in the monthly tourist literature as well as local newspapers announcing special sales, few shops advertise in the print media or on TV and radio.

COPING WITH PRICE UNCERTAINTY

Goods in Singapore and Malaysia fall into three pricing categories: **fixed, negotiable, or discounted.** The general trend in Singapore is toward fixed prices on more and more goods. In the meantime, **price uncertainty** -- negotiable or discounted prices -- is the standard way to sell most goods and services in Singapore and Malaysia. The general pricing guideline is this: *Unless you see a sign stating otherwise, you can expect prices of most goods in small shops to be negotiable.* You can safely assume that all stated prices are the starting point from which you should receive anything from a 10 to 60 percent discount, depending upon your haggling skills and level of commitment to obtain reduced prices.

Discount percentages in Singapore and Malaysia will vary for different items and from one shop to another. In general, however, expect to receive at least a 10 to 20 percent discount on most items in shops willing to discount. Many will discount as much as 50 or 60 percent.

The structure of prices on certain goods and services varies. The prices on items in department stores are fixed. Prices for tailors, hairdressers, some taxis, and medical personnel are fixed. Hotel prices are subject to a variety of discounts for different categories of travelers -- VIP, business, government, weekend, and tourist.

When in doubt if a price is fixed, negotiable, or subject to discounts, *always ask for a special discount.* After the salesperson indicates the price, ask one of two questions: *"What kind of discount can you give me on this item?"* or *"What is your best price?"* If the person reveals a discount, you can either accept it or attempt to negotiate the price through a bargaining process.

While skilled shoppers in fixed-price cultures primarily compare prices by reading ads and listening to special announcements, the skilled shopper in bargaining cultures is primarily engaged in face-to-face encounters with sellers. To be successful, the shopper must use various interpersonal skills. Once you know these and practice bargaining, you should become a very effective shopper in Singapore and Malaysia.

ESTABLISH VALUE AND PRICE

Not knowing the price of an item, many shoppers from fixed-price cultures face a problem. *"What is the actual value of the item? How much should I pay? At what point do I know I'm getting a fair price?"* These questions can be answered in several ways. First, you should have some idea of the value of the item, because you already did comparative shopping at home by examining catalogs and visiting discount houses, department stores, and specialty shops. If you are interested in a camera, for example, you should know what comparable quality cameras sell for back home.

Second, you have done comparative shopping among the various shops you've encountered in Singapore and Malaysia in order to establish a price range for positioning yourself in the bargaining process. You've visited a department store in Singapore to research how much a similar item is selling for at a fixed price. You've checked with a shop in your hotel and compared prices there. In your hotel you might ask *"How much is this item?"* and then act a little surprised that it appears so expensive. Tell them that you are a hotel guest and thus you want their *"very best price"*. At this point the price usually decreases by 10 to 20 percent as you are told this is *"our very special price"*, *"our first-customer-of-the-day price"*, or *"our special hotel guest price"*.

Once you initially receive a special price from your first price inquiry, expect to get another 10 to 20 percent through further negotiation. But at this point do not negotiate any more. Take the shop's business card and record on the back the item, the original price, and the first discount price; thank the shopkeeper, and tell him or her that you may return. Repeat this same scenario in a few other shops. After doing three or four comparisons, you will establish a price range for particular items. This range will give you a fairly accurate idea of the going discount price. At this point you should be prepared to do some serious haggling, playing one shop off against another.

Effective shoppers in Singapore and Malaysia quickly learn how to comparative shop and negotiate the best deal. In learning to be effective, you don't need to be timid, aggressive, or obnoxious -- extreme behaviors frequently exhibited by first-time practitioners of the Asian art of bargaining. Although you may feel bargaining is a defensive measure to avoid being ripped-off by unscrupulous merchants, it is an acceptable way of doing business in many Asian cultures. Merchants merely adjust their profit margins to the customer, depending on how they feel about the situation as well as their current cash flow needs. It is up to you to adapt to such a pricing culture.

One problem you may soon discover is that every situation seems to differ somewhat, and differences between items and shops can be significant. You can expect to receive larger discounts on jewelry than on shoes. For example, discounts on jewelry may be as great as 50 to 60 percent whereas discounts on home furnishings may only be 10 to 20 percent.

The one major exception to bargaining concerns tailors. Tailors normally quote you a fixed-price subject to little or no negotiation; you merely trust that you are getting a fair price and, after all, it is not a good idea to make your tailor unhappy by bargaining when he doesn't want to. He may *"get even"* by cheapening the quality of your clothes. Only in tailor shops do we avoid forcing the price issue by bargaining. At best ask for *"your best price"*, use a common friend's name as reference, or ask for an extra shirt, but don't risk being short-changed on quality just to save a few dollars. If you comparative shop among a few tailor shops, you will quickly identify what should be the *"fair market rate"* for tailoring services assuming the use of comparable quality materials.

Our general rule on what items to bargain for is this: *bargain on ready-made items you can carry out of the shop*. If you must have an item custom-made, be very careful how you arrive at the final price. In most cases you should not bargain other than respond to the first price by asking *"Is this your best price?"* Better still, drop a few names, agree on a mutually satisfactory price, and then insist that you want top quality for that price.

Except for custom-made items, department stores, and shops displaying a *"fixed prices"* sign, *never accept the first price offered*. Rather, spend some time going through our bargaining scenario. Once you have accepted a price and purchased the item, be sure to *get a receipt* as well as *observe the packing process*. While few merchants will try to cheat you, some tourists have had unpleasant experiences which could have been avoided by following some simple rules of shopping in unfamiliar places.

GET THE BEST DEAL POSSIBLE

Chances are you will deal with a Chinese merchant who is a relatively seasoned businessman; he or she is a family entrepreneur who thrives on status and personal relationships. As soon as you walk through the door, most merchants will want to sell you items then and there.

The best deal you will get is when you have a personal relationship with the merchant. Contrary to what others may tell you about bargains for tourists, you often can get as good a deal -- sometimes even better -- than someone from the local community. It is simply a myth that tourists can't do as well on prices as the locals. Indeed, we often do better than the locals because we have done our comparative shopping and we know well the art of bargaining -- something locals are often lax in doing. In addition, some merchants may give you a better price than the locals because you are *"here today and gone tomorrow"*; you won't be around to tell their regular customers about your very special price.

More often than not, the Singapore and Malaysian pricing systems operate like this: *If the shopkeeper likes you, or you are a friend of a friend or relative, you can expect to get a good price.* Whenever possible, drop names of individuals who referred you to the shop; the shopkeeper may think you are a friend and thus you are entitled to a special discount. But if you do not have such a relationship and you present yourself as a typical tourist who is here today and gone tomorrow, you need to bargain hard.

PRACTICE THE 12 RULES OF BARGAINING

The art of bargaining in Malaysia and Singapore can take on several different forms. In general, you want to achieve two goals in this haggling process: *establish the value of an item and get the best possible price*. The following bargaining rules work well.

┌─ **EFFECTIVE BARGAINING PRINCIPLES** ─┐

1. **Do your research before initiating the process.** Compare the prices among various shops, starting with the fixed-price items in department stores. Spot-check price ranges among shops in and around your hotel. Also, refer to your research done with catalogs and discount houses back home to determine if the discount is sufficient to warrant purchasing the item abroad rather than at home.

2. **Determine the exact item you want.** Select the particular item you want and then focus your bargaining around that one item without expressing excessive interest and commitment. Even though you may be excited by the item and want it very badly, once the merchant knows you are committed to buying this one item, you weaken your bargaining position. Express a passing interest; indicate through eye contact with other items in the shop that you are not necessarily committed to the one item. As you ask about the other items, you should get some sense concerning the willingness of the merchant to discount prices.

3. **Set a ceiling price you are willing to pay.** Before engaging in serious negotiations, set in your mind the maximum amount you are willing to pay, which may be 20 percent more than you figured the item should sell for based on your research. However, if you find something you love that is really unique, be prepared to pay whatever you must. In many situations you will find unique items not available anywhere else. Consider buy-

ing now since the item may be gone when you return. Bargain as hard as you can and then pay what you have to -- even though it may seem painful -- for the privilege of owning a unique item. Remember, it only hurts once. After you return home you will most likely enjoy your wonderful purchase and forget how painful it seemed at the time to buy it at less than your expected discount. Above all, do not pass up an item you really love just because the bargaining process does not fall in your favor. It is very easy to be *"penny wise but pound foolish"* in Singapore and Malaysia simply because the bargaining process is such an ego-involved activity. You may return home forever regretting that you failed to buy a lovely item just because you refused to "give' on the last $5 of haggling. In the end, put your ego aside, give in, and buy what you really want. Only you and the merchant will know who really won, and once you return home the $5 will seem to be such an insignificant amount. Chances are you still got a good bargain compared to what you would pay elsewhere if, indeed, you could find a similar item!

4. **Play a role.** Shopping in Singapore and Malaysia involves playing the roles of buyer and seller. Asians tend to be terrific role players, moreso than westerners. In contrast to many Western societies, where being a unique individual is emphasized, high value is not placed on individualism here. Rather, Asians learn specific sets of behaviors appropriate for the role of father, son, daughter, husband, wife, blood friend, classmate, superior, subordinate, buyer, seller. They easily shift from one role to another, undergoing major personality and behavioral changes without experiencing mental conflicts. When you encounter a Chinese businessperson, you are often meeting a very refined and sophisticated role player. Therefore, it is to your advantage to play complementary roles by carefully structuring your personality and behavior to play the role of buyer. If you approach sellers by just *"being yourself"* -- open, honest, somewhat naive, and with your

own unique personality -- you may be quickly walked over by a seasoned seller. Once you enter a shop, think of yourself as an actor walking on stage to play the lead role as a shrewd buyer, bargainer, and trader.

5. **Establish good will and a personal relationship.** A shrewd buyer also is charming, polite, personable, and friendly. You should have a sense of humor, smile, and be lighthearted during the bargaining process. But be careful about eye contact which can be threatening to Asians. Keep it to a minimum. Asian sellers prefer to establish a personal relationship so that the bargaining process can take place on a friendly, face-saving basis. In the end, both the buyer and seller should come out as winners. This can not be done if you approach the buyer in very serious and harsh terms. You should start by exchanging pleasantries concerning the weather, your trip, the city, or the nice items in the shop. After exchanging business cards or determining your status, the shopkeeper will know what roles should be played in the coming transaction.

6. **Let the seller make the first offer.** If the merchant starts by asking you *"How much do you want to pay?"*, avoid answering; immediately turn the question around: *"How much are you asking?"* Remember, many merchants try to get you to pay as much as you are willing and able to pay -- not what the value of the item is or what he or she is willing to take. You should never reveal your ability or willingness to pay a certain price. Keep the seller guessing, thinking that you may lose interest or not buy the item because it appears too expensive. Always get the merchant to initiate the bargaining process. In so doing, the merchant must take the defensive as you shift to the offensive.

7. **Take your time, being deliberately slow in order to get the merchant to invest his or her time in you.** The more you indicate that you are impatient and in a hurry, the more you are likely to pay. When negotiating a

price, **time** is usually in your favor. Many shopkeepers also see time as a positive force in the bargaining process. Some try to keep you in their shop by serving you tea, coffee, soft drinks, or liquor while negotiating the price. Be careful; this nice little ritual may soften you somewhat on the bargaining process as you begin establishing a more personal relationship with the merchant. The longer you stay in control prolonging the negotiation, the better the price should be. Although some merchants may deserve it, **never** insult them. Merchants need to *"keep face"* as much as you do in the process of giving and getting the very best price.

8. **Use odd numbers in offering the merchant at least 40 percent less than what he or she initially offers.** Avoid stating round numbers, such as 60, 70, or 100. Instead, offer $62.00, $73.50, or $81.00. Such numbers impress upon others that you may be a seasoned haggler who knows value and expects to do well in this negotiation. Your offer will probably be 15 percent less than the value you determined for the item. For example, if the merchant asks $100, offer $62.50, knowing the final price should probably be $75.00. The merchant will probably counter with only a 10 percent discount -- $90. At this point you will need to go back and forth with another two or three offers and counter-offers.

9. **Appear disappointed and take your time again.** Never appear upset or angry with the seller. Keep your cool at all times by slowly sitting down and carefully examining the item. Shake your head a little and say, *"Gee, that's too bad. That's much more than I had planned to spend. I like it, but I really can't go that high."* Appear to be a sympathetic listener as the seller attempts to explain why he or she cannot budge more on the price. Make sure you do not accuse the merchant of being a thief! Use a little charm, if you can, for the way you conduct the bargaining process will affect the final price. This should be a civil negotiation in which you nicely

bring the price down, the seller "saves face", and everyone goes away feeling good about the deal.

10. **Counter with a new offer at a 35 percent discount.** Punch several keys on your calculator, which indicates that you are doing some serious thinking. Then say something like *"This is really the best I can do. It's a lovely item, but $67.25 is really all I can pay"*. At this point the merchant will probably counter with a 20 percent discount - $80.

11. **Be patient, persistent, and take your time again by carefully examining the item.** Respond by saying *"That's a little better, but it's still too much. I want to look around a little more."* Then start to get up and look toward the door. At this point the merchant has invested some time in this exchange, and he or she is getting close to a possible sale. The merchant will either let you walk out the door or try to stop you with another counteroffer. If you walk out the door, you can always return to get the $80 price. But most likely the merchant will try to stop you, especially if there is still some bargaining room. The merchant is likely to say: *"You don't want to waste your time looking elsewhere. I'll give you the best price anywhere -- just for you. Okay, $75. That's my final price."*

12. **Be creative for the final negotiation.** You could try for $70, but chances are $75 will be the final price with this merchant. Yet, there may still be some room for negotiating "extras". At this point get up and walk around the shop and examine other items; try to appear as if you are losing interest in the item you were bargaining for. While walking around, identify a $5-10 item you like which might make a nice gift for a friend or relative, which you could possibly include in the final deal. Wander back to the $75 item and look as if your interest is waning and perhaps you need to leave. Then start to probe the possibility of including extras while agreeing on the $75: *"Okay, I might go $75, but only if you include this with it".* The

"this" is the $5-10 item you eyed. You also might negotiate with your credit card. Chances are the merchant is expecting cash on the $75 discounted price and will add a 2-5 percent "commission" if you want to use your credit card. In this case, you might respond to the $75 by saying, *"Okay, I'll go with the $75, but only if I can use my credit card"*. You may get your way, your bank will float you a loan in the meantime, and you have a form of insurance in case you later learn there is a problem with your purchase, such as misrepresentation. Finally, you may want to negotiate packing and delivery processes. If it is a fragile item, insist that it be packed well so you can take it with you on the airplane or have it shipped. If your purchase is large, insist that the shop deliver it to your hotel or to your shipper. If the shop is shipping it by air or sea, try to get them to agree to absorb some of the freight and insurance costs.

This slow, civil, methodical, and sometimes charming approach to bargaining works well in most cases. However, merchants do differ in how they respond to situations. In some cases, your timing may be right: the merchant is in need of cash flow that day and thus he or she is willing to give you the price you want, with little or no bargaining. Others will not give more than a 10 to 20 percent discount unless you are a friend of a friend who is then eligible for the special "family discount". And others are not good businessmen, are unpredictable, lack motivation, or are just moody; they refuse to budge on their prices even though your offer is fair compared to the going prices in other shops. In these situations it is best to leave the shop and find one which is more receptive to the traditional haggling process.

Bargaining in traditional markets requires a different approach and may result in larger discounts. In contrast to the numerous polite middle-class merchants you encounter in shops, sellers in open-air markets tend to be lower-class, earthy, expressive, pushy, persistent, and often rude as they attempt to sell you many things you cannot use or have no desire to even inspect. They may joke a great deal, shout at you -- *"Hey, you mister"* -- push and shove, and pester you. These markets are similar to a great big carnival.

In contrast to our previous bargaining rules, successful

bargaining in open-air markets should involve **little time** and a great deal of **movement**. If you are interested in an item, ask the price, counter with a price you are willing to pay, and be relatively firm with this price. Since there is a great deal of competition in these markets, it is to your advantage to spend very little time with any one vendor. State your offer and slowly move on to the next vendor. Sellers know they will probably lose you to the competition, so they need to quickly conclude a deal before someone else gets to you; they are motivated to give you large discounts. You also can be a little more aggressive and obnoxious and less charming in these places. If, for example, an item is quoted at $10, offer $4 and move on toward the next vendor. Chances are the seller will immediately drop the price to $7. If you counter with $5 and are moving while stating your offer, the seller will probably agree to your offer. But be sure you want the item. Once your offer is accepted, you are expected to carry through with the purchase. Open-air stalls are great places to accumulate junk while successfully practicing your bargaining skills!

BARGAIN FOR NEEDS, NOT GREED

One word of caution for those who are just starting to learn the fine art of Asian bargaining. *Be sure you really want an item before you initiate the bargaining process.* Many tourists learn to bargain effectively, and then get carried away with their new-found skill. Rather than use this skill to get what they want, they enjoy the process of bargaining so much that they buy many unnecessary items. After all, they got such "a good deal" and thus could not resist buying the item. You do not need to fill your suitcases with junk in demonstrating this ego-gratifying skill. If used properly, your new bargaining skills will lead to some excellent buys on items you really need and want.

EXAMINE YOUR GOODS CAREFULLY

Before you commence the bargaining process, carefully examine the item, being sure that you understand the quality of the item for which you are negotiating. Then, after you settle on a final price, make sure you are getting the goods you agreed upon. You should carefully observe the handling of items, including the actual packing process. If at all possible, take the items with you when you leave the shop. If you later discover you were victimized by a switch or misrepresentation, contact the national tourist association as well as your credit card company if you charged your purchase. You should be able to resolve the problem through these channels. However, the responsibility is on you, the buyer, to know what you are buying.

BEWARE OF SCAMS

Although one hopes this will never happen, you may be unfortunate in encountering unscrupulous merchants who take advantage of you. This is more likely to happen if you wander away from recommended shops in discovering your own "very special" bargains or enter the *"Hey, you mister"* shops. The most frequent scams to watch out for include:

POTENTIAL SCAMS

- **Switching the goods.** You negotiate for a particular item, such as a watch, camera, or blouse, but in the process of packing it, the merchant substitutes an inferior product.

- **Misrepresenting quality goods.** Be especially cautious in jewelry stores and antique shops. Sometimes so-called expensive watches are excellent imitations and worth no more than $15 -- or have cheap mechanisms inside expensive cases. Precious stones, such as rubies, may not be a precious as they appear. Synthetic stones, garnets, or spinels are sometimes substituted for high quality rubies. Some substitutes are so good that experts even have difficulty identifying the difference. Accordingly, you may pay $2,000 for what appears to be a ruby worth $10,000 back home, but in fact you just bought a $25 red spinel. Pearls come in many different qualities, so know your pearls before negotiating a price. Real jade and ivory are beautiful, but many buyers unwittingly end up with green plastic, soapstone, or bone at jade and ivory prices. The antique business is relatively unregulated. Some merchants try to sell "new antiques" at "old antique" prices. Many of the fakes are outstanding reproductions, often fooling even the experts. Better still, there is a reputable business in fakes. You may want to just shop for fakes!

● **Goods not shipped.** The shop may agree to ship your goods home, but once you leave they conveniently forget to do so. You wait and wait, write letters of inquiry, and receive no replies. Unless you insured the item and have all proper receipts, you may not receive the goods you paid for.

Your best line of defense against these and other possible scams is to be very careful wherever you go and whatever you do in relation to handling money. A few simple precautions will help avoid some of these problems:

─── TAKE ADEQUATE PRECAUTIONS ───

● **Do not trust anyone with your money** unless you have proper assurances they are giving you exactly what you agreed upon.

● **Do your homework** so you can determine quality and value as well as anticipate certain types of scams.

● **Examine the goods carefully,** assuming something may be or will go wrong.

● **Watch very carefully how the merchant handles items** from the moment they leave your hands until they get wrapped and into a bag.

● **Request receipts** that list specific items and the prices you paid. Although most shops are willing to *"give you a receipt"* specifying whatever price you want them to write for purposes of deceiving Customs, avoid such pettiness because Customs know better, and you may need a receipt with the real price to claim your goods or a refund. If the shop is to ship, be sure you have a shipping receipt which also includes insurance against both loss and damage.

● **Patronize shops which are affiliated with the local tourist associations.** They are more likely to treat you honestly since the parent organization does somewhat police its members.

Protect yourself against scams by using credit cards for payment, especially for big ticket items which could present problems, even though using them may cost you a little more.

If you are victimized, all is not necessarily lost. You should report the problem immediately to the local tourist association, the police, your credit card company, or insurance company. While inconvenient and time consuming, nonetheless, in many cases you will eventually get satisfactory results.

PART II

SECRETS OF
EXOTIC SINGAPORE

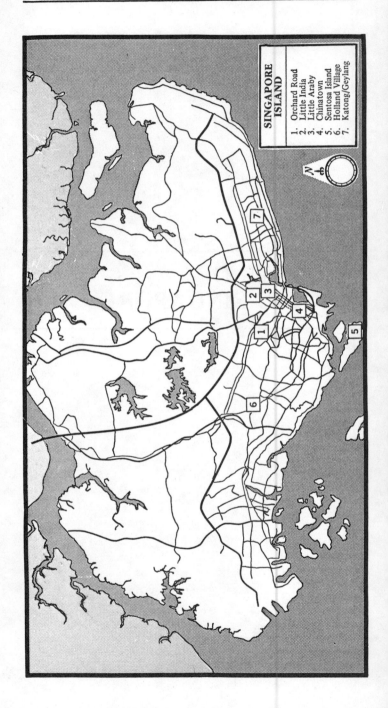

SINGAPORE
ISLAND

1. Orchard Road
2. Little India
3. Little Araby
4. Chinatown
5. Sentosa Island
6. Holland Village
7. Katong/Geylang

Chapter Six
SINGAPORE

Singapore is one of Asia's most delightful surprises. It's a shopper's paradise offering wonderful shopping opportunities not found in other cities. If you already visited Hong Kong, you will be tempted to compare it with Singapore. If you have journeyed to Thailand, Indonesia, and Malaysia, you will notice an immediate difference between shopping in Third World and newly emerging industrialized countries versus clean, green, modern, high-tech, and efficient Singapore. In fact, Singapore may give you a quick case of "reverse culture shock."

SURPRISING SINGAPORE

Singapore is unlike any other country you will visit. A small city-state of only 620 square kilometers (238 square miles), occupied by 2.7 million people and visited by nearly 4 million travelers each year, it is one of the world's major trading and financial powerhouses. It boasts the world's second busiest port, the second largest oil refinery center, and the fourth largest financial center.

Singapore is a story of survival against numerous odds.

In many respects, this small city-state defies the logic of national survival and prosperity. A small area with no natural resources, Singapore gained independence in 1965 during a period of high unemployment and low per capita income. Within a decade, however, it rose like a phoenix as it surprised everyone -- including Singapore's dynamic leader Lee Kuan Yew -- with a remarkable record of economic development. Using its major resource -- a hard working and relatively compliant population -- Singapore's leadership helped propel this country into the status of the second most developed country in Asia, following Asia's other remarkable performer, Japan. Today, Singapore stands as a shining example of economic success far beyond its wildest dreams!

Singapore is one of Asia's most westernized, comfortable, and convenient countries as well. English, one of Singapore's official languages, is spoken everywhere. The standard of living is exceptionally high. The city is ultra-modern, displaying some of the best tourist facilities found anywhere and some of the loveliest gardens in Asia. Except for its high heat and humidity, you will feel right at home in Singapore. This country could well receive an award for being the most clean, orderly, predictable, convenient, and comfortable place in the world!

Singapore is an excellent place to shop. Similar to Hong Kong, it offers a wide variety of electronic, photo, and computer goods as well as clothes, jewelry, and accessories at duty-free prices. But unlike Hong Kong, Singapore draws from the economies and societies of its neighboring South and Southeast Asian countries. Its multi-racial society is situated at the crossroads of one of the world's most diverse cultural regions.

Singapore offers/ shoppers a wide range of goods from all over the world, but with particular emphasis on the arts and crafts from all South and Southeast Asian countries. In Singapore you discover the shopping wonders of India, Pakistan, Sri Lanka, Burma, Thailand, Indonesia, the Philippines, Papua New Guinea, and Iran. No other country or city in Asia can claim such a central role in bringing together so many of the region's and world's shopping delights.

GETTING TO KNOW YOU

Singapore is a pleasant and easy country to visit. Variously dubbed the "Lion City," "Garden City," "Instant Asia," and the "Emporium of the East," Singapore is a mighty little wonder to behold. From the moment you step off your plane at the super efficient Changi International Airport to when you are courteously escorted to your room, you are impressed with this marvelous place called Singapore. It is so familiar, yet so unreal. If one were to plan the ideal city -- neat, clean, efficient, and modern -- it would probably look and feel like Singapore. In fact, many leaders from other Asian countries visit Singapore to see how they might create a little bit of Singapore back home. It is the model of what should go right in any city that claims to be civil, modern, and progressive.

We highly recommend Singapore for several reasons. First, it is one of the most **convenient and comfortable** countries to travel and shop. Singapore actively promotes itself as a travel and shopping paradise by offering some of the best transportation, hotels, restaurants, shopping centers, and travel services in Asia. Having started later than Hong Kong, Singapore's hotels and shopping centers have the advantage of being newer than those in Hong Kong. Most shopping takes place in the air-conditioned comfort of shopping centers and arcades. You can easily travel to neighboring countries by making arrangements through any of several agents who offer a wide variety of itineraries and tours. And the Singapore Tourist Promotion Board (STPB) does an outstanding job in providing self-directed materials for easily visiting this city on your own.

Second, as a truly **international shopping city**, Singapore offers many items not found in other Asian cities. Here you will discover fine Persian carpets, unique designer clothes, and local paintings as well as fabulous antiques, arts, and crafts from neighboring India, China, Burma, Thailand, Malaysia, and Indonesia. If you have little time to visit these other countries, Singapore's shops will provide you with an abbreviated version of what to shop for in these other exotic places.

Third, Singapore is **not an expensive city** to visit, but neither is it cheap. Having over built first-class and deluxe hotels in the 1980s, today Singapore is still experiencing the effects of a recession brought on by falling oil prices as well as increased competition from Indonesian oil refineries. In the meantime, Singapore is trying to remain competitive on the tourist front by offering good hotel prices and special discounts to visitors. For example, comparable deluxe hotels costing $130 a night in Hong Kong, Seoul, Jakarta, or Bali go for $90 in Singapore. Transportation also is inexpensive as are many of the restaurants outside the major hotels. Nonetheless, prices in Singapore are on the increase; they are likely to catch up with those in other major Asian cities within the very near future.

Fourth, Singapore is an **extremely interesting city** in

terms of its peoples, cultures, and sights. A truly multi-racial society living in remarkable harmony, you will encounter the colorful traditional cultures of the Chinese, Indians, Arabs, and Malays in the midst of modern high-rise buildings, luxury hotels, and superhighways. While Singapore is not noted for being steeped in history, nor does it honor well what history it claims, it does offer a living museum of diverse peoples and cultures.

Fifth, if you also enjoy treating your stomach to the finer things in life, Singapore is a **gastronomic delight**. Of all cities in Asia, Singapore offers the widest variety of international foods ranging from elegant French restaurants to street stalls selling wonderful noodle dishes and *satay*. All the major East Asian, Southeast Asian, and South Asian cuisines are well represented in Singapore along with the standard western fare. In addition, Singapore produces a unique Chinese-Malay cuisine called *Nonya* food. And the foods and drinks in Singapore are among the safest in the world. You can drink the tap water and consume the ice.

Sixth, Singapore is a **totally integrated travel and shopping experience**. In addition to offering shopping opportunities, it boasts fine recreational facilities, many sites worth visiting, good entertainment, and numerous excursions and trips to neighboring countries. The down-side to Singapore is a comparative one of minor propor-tions. Singapore reminds many visitors of Taiwan -- -somewhat over-rated and hyped. Compared to many other exotic Asian countries, Singapore lacks character, color, location, and reverence for the past to complement its traveling and shopping delights. It does not, for example, have gorgeous harbor views, breath-taking commercial skylines, towering hills and mountains, glittering neon signs, charming ferry rides, and a mysterious giant in its hinterland (China) that give Hong Kong its character -- unusual sights and experiences that make traveling so interesting and enjoyable. Singapore also lacks the impres-sive exotic temples, palaces, and museums of Thailand and Indonesia which verify that these countries had glorious indigenous histories. It does have a character of its own-- be it the bustling shopping centers or colorful ethnic encla-ves--but this is not the same as the more exotic character of neighboring countries.

Singapore is a flat island in hot pursuit of the present and future. Whatever past identity it lacks, Singapore makes up in terms of its identity with the future. The name of the game in Singapore is to be disciplined and work hard at making more money and creating more secur-ity for one's self and one's family. Except for preserving a few examples of its colonial past and ethnic heritage, Singapore is obsessed with being modern. If it has any character, it is to be more modern than the most modern countries in the world. Deliberately casting off its past as if it were an impediment to its future, Singapore has a very good idea where it is going. When you shop in Singapore, you contribute to its on-going character by helping to sustain the mighty money machine that is so critical to keeping this place running at such a high level of performance.

This obsession with modernity and the future initially impresses most visitors. But after a while you might find Singapore a little bit boring. It is too neat, too tidy, too efficient, and too regulated -- a caricature of a planner's textbook image. It's an antiseptic city where happiness is defined as orderliness, cleanliness, efficiency, and air-conditioning. If you have become captivated by the charm of Thailand's and Indonesia's living chaos, the diversity of Malaysia's culture and the mystery of its tribal peoples, the spontaneity of other Southeast Asian peoples, the serendipity of Third World travel, and the adventure of discovering unique items by digging through disorganized shops, Singapore may not be your type of city. For some people, this city is much too easy and convenient to be called an exotic place -- especially if you spend most of your time confined to air-conditioned shopping centers. At best, in Singapore you shop for things produced in **other** exotic places.

However, if you have just come from Thailand, Malaysia, or Indonesia, you might appreciate returning to a world according-to-Singapore. It's a wonderful place to pamper yourself with the finer things in life and literally *"shop 'til you drop"!*

Singapore is always a surprising place for visitors. Its diversity means that Singapore can be different things to different people. While it is a shopper's paradise for some visitors, it is a memorable city of the Raffles Hotel, Singapore Sling, W. Somerset Maugham, trishaws, Change Alley, and sailors to others. The process of continuously layering more modern office buildings, hotels, shopping centers, restaurants, and subways onto Singapore's current stock of buildings and transportation arteries gives this city-state its own unique character. Only after visiting the city many times does one come away with a sense of never really knowing the "real Singapore". For the real Singapore is what is happening today and probably tomorrow. Visit one year and come back the next, and you will discover a new Singapore in the process of being transformed into yet a another new Singapore -- which will surprise you again next year!

Singapore is an exotic place if you go beyond its exterior textbook image and symbols of modernity. After visiting the hotels, restaurants, shopping centers, museums, and parks, be sure to walk the ethnic enclaves of Chinatown, Little India, and Arab Street -- especially at night -- and observe a festival or two. These areas and events have all the character of exotic places. They quickly remind you that you still are not home. You will discover the other side of Singapore that remains very Asian, despite its wonderful veneer of westernization which entices you and millions of others to its shores. Singapore, too, has its pockets of color, spontaneity, and chaos that give this city-state an interesting character absent along the clean green streets of Singapore's major shopping areas.

THE BASICS

Location and People

Singapore is an island nation located just off the tip of the Malay Peninsula. It consists of the main island and 57 smaller islands. At 1 degree latitude and 140 kilometers (87 miles) north of the equator, Singapore looks and feels like it's on the equator. The main island is connected to Malaysia by a causeway which conveniently links Singapore by road and rail to Malaysia and Thailand.

Singapore's 620 square kilometer area is constantly being enlarged due to reclamation efforts. This is home to 2.7 million people who primarily reside in the city proper. Singapore is one of the world's most multi-racial societies. Its population consists of Chinese (77%), Malay (15%), Indian and Pakistani (6%), and numerous other groups (2%). The Chinese primarily run this country but in remarkable harmony with the other groups.

Historically, Singapore developed due to its excellent location and management. Situated at the confluence of the Indian and Pacific Oceans, ships passing through the Straits of Malacca used Singapore as a convenient port and trading center. Today, Singapore continues to play a central shipping role in Asia as well as to serve as one of the world's most important trading and financial centers. Strategically located at the center of South and Southeast Asia, Singapore also is a convenient place from which to embark to other Asian countries. Above all, Singapore is managed extremely well in the areas of oil refining, ship building, high-tech industries, finance, and tourism.

Climate, Seasons, and When to Go

The weather in Singapore is similar to that in Jakarta. Being a tropical country situated almost on the equator, it is more or less hot and humid year round. The rainy season hits full force during December and January. July is the driest month. The ideal time to visit Singapore is between **July and September** -- the period of least heat and humidity. Whenever you go, you will appreciate the fact that Singapore has moved most of its shops into air-conditioned quarters. You will not "shop 'til you drop" because of Singapore's shopping climate!

Singapore is a **walking city** with ample opportunities to escape into air-conditioned hotels, restaurants, and shopping centers. Wherever you go, you will spend a great deal of time walking. While much of this is indoor walking, much of it also is outdoors. Be sure to take it easy when outdoors. Wear lightweight cotton clothes and take comfortable shoes, an umbrella, sunglasses, a hat, and handkerchief.

Getting There

Singapore is easy and convenient to get to by air, rail, road, or ship. Over 40 major **airlines** fly into Singapore from major cities around the world. Many of them, such as Japan Air Lines, Singapore Airline, United Airlines, Korean Air, and China Air, offer excellent roundtrip airfares from major cities in the United States, Canada, and Europe. For example, you can fly roundtrip from New York City to Singapore during much of the year for as little as $1069 as well as arrange stops in Seoul, Hong Kong, and Bangkok for an additional $50 per stop. Special 8-day "Singapore Dream" packages go for as little as $998 per person, including first-class hotels and roundtrip airfare from the West Coast in the United States (contact a travel agent or call 800/628-0600 for information).

The **rail** trip into Singapore remains one of the world's most interesting. You can take a train from Bangkok, through Malaysia, and into Singapore. While the trip takes about 54 hours, it is relatively comfortable, and you will have a chance to see a great deal of urban and rural southern Thailand and Malaysia along the way.

The **roads** connecting Malaysia to Singapore are excellent. In fact, you could take buses all the way from Bangkok to Singapore. It is a grueling trip, especially through southern Thailand. Many bus seats are built for smaller bodies than that of the average American, Australian, or European. But it is an inexpensive way to go, and you

can see the colorful countryside. Better still, you can rent
a car in Malaysia, drive to Singapore, and drop it with a
Singapore agency.

It is easy to drive in Malaysia given the excellent road
system, maps and signs in English, sane driving habits of
the Malaysians, and the ease of entering Singapore. However, do not drive through Thailand into Malaysia unless
you are extremely adventuresome or foolish -- or both.
The Thai side is even too dangerous for Malays! It would
be best to either fly or take a train into Penang/Butterworth
or Kuala Lumpur in Malaysia and then rent a car to drive
the rest of the way to Singapore.

Singapore's Keppel Harbour is a major port for freighter,
container, and cruise **ships**. Over 150 shipping lines regularly dock in Singapore. Several major cruise ships, such
as the QE2, Pearl of Scandinavia, Royal Viking, Holland
America, and Cunard Line, include Singapore on their
Asian ports of call. Contact these cruise lines for information on their tours.

Documents

Singapore encourages tourists to visit their city-state by
making Immigration procedures relatively easy. Most
nationalities only need to present a valid passport at the
various air, sea, and land entry points to receive permission
to stay for several weeks. Tourists from the United States
and most European countries, for example, can stay up to
90 days without a visa; Canadians need a visa if they plan
to stay longer than two weeks. An international certificate
documenting an appropriate vaccination is needed only if
one comes from a yellow fever infected area.

Arrival

Singapore has cornered the market on airport efficiency. The Changi International Airport is one of the world's
most impressive airports. Normally one can pass through
Immigration, retrieve baggage, clear Customs, change
money, and be off in a comfortable taxi within 30 minutes
of arrival. We've done this whole process in an amazing
15 minutes! It's so fast you have to think twice about
whether you forgot something. Look on the wall ahead as
you exit Immigration and you'll spot a sign with your
flight number indicating the carousel where you can claim
your luggage. Be sure you observe all the "No" signs
awaiting you in the taxi and along the streets: *"No Smoking, No Spitting, No Stopping, No Littering, No Crossing"*.
Violations are punishable with stiff fines: up to S$500.

Watch what you do, and get rid of any bad habits you may have picked up along the way in more lax Thailand or Indonesia! Welcome to the land obsessed with creating order and the culture of "No."

The trip by taxi into the city is even more impressive. The taxis are metered, and most drivers speak English. They may even point out some of the wonders along the way -- or be so audacious as to complain that Singapore needs to be even more efficient; visitors are really perplexed when the complaint is directed toward the marvelous airport! Wide boulevards lined with trees and flowers initially greet you, and then the symbols of modernity hit you as you see hundreds of sparkling high-rise apartment buildings, hotels, banks, and shopping centers. Everything looks new or freshly painted. Except for a few ethnic enclaves, there's nothing worn or makeshift about this Asian city. Here's a place that appears to have everything under control. It visually invites you to enjoy your stay. Nice streets, nice sidewalks, street lights, traffic flowing in a straight line, no litter, no beggars, no cigarette butts -- just a nice clean and orderly place.

Entry by rail, road, or ship is equally efficient. Unless you look like a hippie or druggie, with passport in hand, you should be whisked through the Customs and Immigration lines and on to your destination in very little time.

Customs and Immigration

Singapore Customs allows you to bring in the usual allowances -- 200 cigarettes and one liter of liquor. Bringing illegal drugs into the country results in long prison sentences and possible execution. Singapore also prefers granting entry to neat and tidy people. Should you have long hair or look somewhat unkempt, you may not make it through the process as quickly as others.

Departure Tax

The departure tax on international flights is S$12. If you leave Singapore for Malaysia by land, you will be assessed a S$5 tax. Before departing for the airport, ask at your hotel front desk about paying the departure tax there. In many hotels you can purchase the departure tax coupon at the front desk and thus save time at the airport.

Currency and Credit Cards

The Singapore dollar is equivalent to US$.52, or S$1.93 equals US$1. The Singapore dollar comes in 1, 5, 10, 20,

50, 100, 500, 1,000, and 10,000 denominations. Each dollar is divided into 100 cents. Coins are issued in 1, 5, 10, 20 and 50 cent denominations.

You can easily exchange your money at the airport bank windows or among the numerous licensed money-changers found in the shopping complexes, Raffles Place, and Change Alley. Most display a "Licensed Money Changer" sign. They usually give the best exchange rates. You should receive a better exchange rate on traveler's checks than on currency. As in most cities, hotels in Singapore give the lowest exchange rates and some add a small service charge.

Most major credit cards are widely accepted in Singapore. Some shops, however, may try to add a surcharge to cover their costs of accepting credit card purchases. Like other Asian countries, this most often happens when you bargain for a price and then try to charge the purchase. Remember, bargained prices generally are "cash" prices. However, if you buy expensive items which could possibly present problems later on, such as camera or electronic goods, consider charging them even though it will cost you a bit more. Should you later have a problem -- such as the VCR unit you bought is incompatible with U.S. systems even though you specified you would be using it in the U.S. -- your credit card company can help you get a refund.

Security

Singapore is one of the world's safest cities to visit. You can walk around with little fear of having your pockets picked or getting mugged. You may occasionally encounter a tout in tourist shopping areas, but they are out to make a fast buck on commissions rather than physically harm you. Even women traveling alone will feel safe here. Nonetheless, take normal precautions concerning your valuables. The airport also is very safe. Singapore simply doesn't have the political and criminal problems found in many other countries.

Tipping

Tipping in Singapore is close to being declared an official sin. The government is trying to discourage tipping. You can help rid Singapore of this decadent practice by not tipping anyone except those from whom you ask special favors. Singapore's wages are the second highest in all of Asia, and hotels and restaurants add a 10 percent service charge and a 3 percent government tax. Taxi drivers enjoy receiving tips, and some will conveniently forget to give you change, especially if it is a small amount. Help them break this habit by requesting your change and then count it in full; they sometimes forget to give you all your change.

On the other hand, should you need special assistance, asking for help will eventually get help in service-oriented Singapore. However, a tip may get you even better service. Money still talks when it comes to getting things done quickly. If, for example, you need a taxi in a hurry but your hotel taxi queue is long, press a few small bills in the hand of the doorman or porter and you may discover how to by-pass the line altogether.

Language

Singapore recognizes four official languages: English, Mandarin, Malay, and Tamil. English is by far the preferred language of business, government, and tourism. You will have no problem communicating wherever you go. Even many taxi drivers speak English.

Business Hours

Banks are open from 10am to 3pm, Monday through Friday. They also are open from 9:30am to 11:30am on Saturday. Branches of the Development Bank of Singapore at Bukit Timah, Katong, Orchard, Thomson, and Toa Payok remain open until 3:00pm on Saturday. However, many banks do not exchange foreign currency on Saturdays.

Offices are normally open from 9/9:30am to 5/5:30pm, Monday through Friday. Some are open on Saturday. Shopping hours vary. Most department stores and shops in the large shopping complexes are open every day from 10am to 6pm. Some shops stay open later. The Chinese Emporiums, for example, remain open until 10pm. While many stores in the large shopping complexes will remain open on Sunday, some open late or not at all. Many small shops will be closed on Sunday.

Transportation

The easiest ways to get around Singapore are by taxi or subway. Taxis are air-conditioned and metered and relatively inexpensive since you normally will not have to travel far from one shopping area to another. Each cab has a list of "don'ts", fares, and additional charges clearly posted for your convenience. However, you might want to check a map before getting into a cab. Cab drivers will take you where you tell them to go, even though it may be only one block!

Singapore's new **subway**, the MRT (Mass Rapid Transit system), is quickly becoming the favored mode of transportation for local residents. Air-conditioned underground stations are conveniently located in and around all of Singapore's major shopping areas and hotels. Fares range from 50 cents to S$1.40. Most maps and tourist literature now include information and maps on how to use this convenient system.

Singapore's **buses** also are convenient, comfortable, and inexpensive. Fares range from 40 to 80 cents. For details on the various routes, pick up a free copy of *This Week in Singapore* or purchase the *Singapore Bus Guide* which is available at most bookstores or newstands.

The best transportation deal of all is to purchase a 1-Day (S$5) or 3-Day (S$12) **Singapore Explorer Bus Ticket** which permits you to travel anywhere on the island using the Singapore Bus Service (red and white buses) or the Trans Island Service (orange and yellow buses). With this ticket you receive a color-coded Explorer Bus Map for stopping at most of the major points of interest on the island. Individual bus stops have special signs indicating nearby attractions for individuals using the Explorer ticket.

You can also rent **self-drive cars** from several rental agencies throughout the city. The traffic is sane, maps are excellent, and signs are plentiful. Be sure you have an international driver's license.

Tours, Travel Agents, and Information

Travel in and around Singapore is extremely well organized and convenient for either individual or group approaches. The Singapore Tourist Promotion Board has developed excellent tour literature to assist individuals in conducting their own walking and bus tours. Most of this literature is available at the airport or through two STPB offices: first floor of the Singapore Handicraft Center (131 Tudor Court, Tanglin Road, Tel. 2356611) and in the new Raffles City Tower #37-00 (250 North Bridge Road, Tel. 339662).

Numerous private tour companies, such as Tour East, Singapore Sightseeing, World Express, Siakson Tours, Gray Line, and RMG Tours, offer several excellent and relatively inexpensive tours of the city, islands, harbor, and southern Malaysia. Tour East, for example, offers a 3 1/2 hour daily shopping tour of Orchard Road, Arab Street, and Change Alley. Most companies have brochures of their tours at the front desks of major hotels. Their air-conditioned buses or vans with English-speaking guides will pick you up and drop you off at your hotel.

Singapore has hundreds of travel agents to help you plan your trip. Singapore Airlines, Garuda, and Thai International offer special packages to Sumatra, Java, and Bali from Singapore. Other special tours to neighboring countries can be arranged through most travel agents.

Food and Drink

Singapore is a true gastronomic delight where you can feast to your heart's content. The variety of cuisines is overwhelming. You can find just about any type of food you might want, and then some -- European, American, Mexican, Middle Eastern, Chinese, Indian, Pakistani, Indonesian, Malay, Thai, Korean, or Japanese. A local cuisine, called *Nonya* or *Peranakan,* is a special blending of Chinese and Malay cooking.

Your range of eating establishments include elegant and expensive hotel restaurants as well as colorful and inexpensive open-air food stalls. The major international fast-food chains are well represented here. Several hotels offer set breakfasts and lunches as well as the ubiquitous noon buffet -- the Belvedere at the Mandarin Hotel reputed to be the best buffet at present. Wherever you eat in Singapore, you will be eating well.

You will find plenty of popular soft drinks, excellent local beers, and the famous Singapore Sling at its place of origin -- the Long Bar in the Raffles Hotel.

Accommodations

A population of 2.7 million hosting nearly 4 million guests a year is very experienced in the hotel business. Singapore offers a wide range of excellent accommodations and services for travelers. But the best news of all these days is that Singapore still offers excellent accommodations at reasonable prices. During the past seven years Singapore went through a hotel building boom which resulted in an over-supply of hotel rooms. The boom continues with the opening of even more new hotels in anticipation of continual growth in the tourist industry and increased business travel. Accommodations in first-class and deluxe hotels in Singapore are now some of the best dollar values in all of Asia. However, the outstanding buys of the 1986-1987 recession period, when some deluxe hotels offered rooms for S$60 a night, have all but disappeared. As occupancy rates have increased, hotel prices have gone up accordingly.

Most of the major hotels are conveniently located near the major shopping areas along Orchard Road, Scotts Road, Bras Basah Road, and Raffles Boulevard. Many visitors with a sense of history stay at the grand old Raffles Hotel. Although it is expensive compared to the prices and amenities offered by some of the new first-class and deluxe hotels, and a bit worn, the Raffles has the character of the by-gone British colonial era. Renovation of the Raffles is beginning; when completed, she should once again be able to hold her own against the 20th century newcomers to the hotel scene.

Singapore has numerous first-class and deluxe hotels that rank as some of the world's finest. The hotels along Orchard and Scotts roads are the most convenient for walking to the numerous shopping complexes along this street. You can choose from many fine hotels, such as the **Pavilion Inter-Continental, Hilton International, Hyatt Regency, Royal Holiday Inn, Dynasty Hotel,** and the **Mandarin Hotel.** Just as convenient to Orchard Road is the **Boulevard Hotel.** The **Ladyhill** and the **Shangri-La** are located nearby as is the **Sheraton Towers Hotel.**

We have stayed at the Mandarin, the Hilton International, and the Boulevard and thoroughly enjoyed our stay at each hotel. The Mandarin and the Hilton both house Singapore's two best shopping arcades -- an added bonus to their excellent accommodations and service. The Boulevard's location on a hill overlooking Orchard Road and Orchard Boulevard affords a wonderful view of a park-like setting with the high-rise hotels and shopping complexes as a backdrop. It is also very convenient to some of our favorite shopping haunts.

Marina Centre, a relatively new area of hotels as well as shops has been open nearly two years. This area's hotels include the **Oriental Singapore, Marina Mandarin,** and the **Pan Pacific** in the Marina Square, and the **Westin Stanford** and **Westin Plaza** in Raffles City across from the Raffles Hotel. Both Marina Square and Raffles City include sizeable shopping malls. Clothing and jewelry stores predominate in these malls. Although not as convenient to the more specialized and diversified shopping in the Orchard Road area, these hotels do allow the visitor to appreciate Singapore's waterfront. The view from the pool deck of the Oriental Mandarin is breathtaking.

Unless you are getting a "special promotion price", you might ask for discounts at the hotels. During low occupancy periods many hotels are willing to extend discounts or they offer special weekend prices.

You will also find numerous middle-range and inexpensive hotels in Singapore. Try, for example, **Hotel Asia, Dai-Ichi Hotel, Hotel Equatorial, Hotel Mirama, Peninsula Hotel, President Merlin Singapore** for moderate accommodations. **Hotel Bencoolen, Metropole Hotel, New Seventh Storey Hotel,** and **Hotel Royal** are relatively inexpensive.

Electricity and Water

Electricity in Singapore is 220-240 volts, 50 cycle AC power. Some hotels have 110-volt outlets. Most hotels have transformers to convert your 110-120 volt, 60 cycle AC appliances. Tap water and ice are safe to consume in Singapore.

Resources

A great deal of information is available on Singapore. The best source is the Singapore Tourist Promotion Board (STPB). It publishes several guide books, brochures, and maps to assist you in getting around Singapore with relative ease. Their *Singapore Official Guide, Singapore Tour It Yourself, Surprising Singapore,* and *Singapore Shopping* booklets are excellent self-directed guides to the city. The STPB also publishes a set of useful brochures on various aspects of visiting Singapore--eating out, Chinatown, Little India, Arab Street, Sentosa Island, museums, monuments, gardens, zoo, handicrafts. Most of this literature is available at Changi International Airport. Be sure to stop at one of the STPB stands to pick up this literature just before you exit from the airport.

Several guide books also provide good coverage of Singapore. Two APA Insight Guides entitled *Singapore* -- a country and a city guide -- give excellent overviews of this island republic. Similar in format to other volumes in the APA series, these books survey the history, culture, and sights of Singapore as well as include useful travel sections. Fodor's city guide -- *Fodor's Singapore* -- provides one of the most extensive treatments of topics of most interest to tourists -- history, sights, accommodations, restaurants, recreation, and entertainment.

Since Singapore is one of the major publishing centers in the world, you will find a great deal of literature on Singapore in the local bookstores. One of the best resources is the Ropion, Miowe, and Hunt's illustrated shopping and sightseeing map: *The Secret Map of Singapore.* Similar to other maps for Rangoon, Bangkok, Chiengmai, Kuala Lumpur, and Sydney, the map examines each major section of the city in terms of products found in individual shops and interesting sights to visit. This map is available in many hotel sundry shops. Another useful book is *Papineau's Guide to Singapore*. It provides a good overview of the setting, culture, shopping, sightseeing, accommodations, and restaurants as well as includes a nice fold-out map of Singapore.

Should you wish to do some background reading on the history, society, and politics of Singapore, try some of the following books: Noel Barber's *The Singapore Story* and *Sinister Twilight: The Fall of Singapore*; James Clavell's *King Rat*; and Alex Josey's *Singapore: Its Past, Present, and Future*. The evolution of Singapore since World War II remains a fascinating story of how a small city-state has managed to regularly transform itself into a major economic force in Asia under the brilliant, yet always controversial authoritarian, leadership of President Lee Kuan Yew. If you are interested in shopping for Singapore's many antiques, arts, and crafts, be sure to pick up a copy of Anne Jones' *A Guide to Buying Antiques, Arts & Crafts in Singapore*.

THE STREETS OF SINGAPORE

We have little other than praise for the streets of Singapore. The streets are clean, orderly, and easy to navigate; you may even wish to do your own driving. There is nothing disorienting about this city other than perhaps the initial shock of seeing a place that may even look better than back home. After that, you should be able to get around easily in this city.

A few rules for navigating Singapore's streets will help you get around to shop efficiently:

1. **Get ready to walk since this is a walking city.** Singapore is a compact city where the major shopping complexes are confined to stretches of road no more than one mile in length. You can easily walk from one shopping complex to another in the same area. Most of your walking, however, will be confined to the interior floors and levels of the air-conditioned shopping complexes. Take a good pair of walking shoes for Singapore.

2. **Take public transportation whenever possible.** Since Singapore is very hot and humid, do not try to walk too much outdoors. A one mile walk in the heat of the day can be very debilitating. Even though shopping

areas, such as Chinatown and Little India, may look close to each other on a map, they are not once you start walking. Take taxis, buses, or the subway (MRT) if you must walk for more than one kilometer at a time. You can drive your own car, but it is still more convenient to take taxis, buses, and the subway. When you drive, you will need to find and pay for parking.

3. **Carry your rain and sun gear.** Umbrella, sunglasses, and a hat may come in handy, given Singapore's hot, humid, and wet climate.

4. **Observe the local rules.** The Singapore government is very strict about regulating its streets. This means no jay-walking, no littering, no cigarette butts, and no smoking in many public places. Cross at the street lights.

5. **Orient yourself to two distinct shopping cultures.** Singapore offers two separate styles of shopping -- complexes and department stores versus Third World shops. The modern shopping complexes and department stores are most heavily concentrated along Tanglin, Orchard, and Scotts Roads. These are best approached like any air-conditioned shopping mall -- walk in and browse. Their goods are nicely displayed, salespeople speak English and are polite, and your purchases are processed through cash registers and deposited in plastic shopping bags. The Third World shopping culture is found in the ethnic enclaves of Chinatown, Little India, and Arab Street, and in such places as Change Alley. Lined with rows of small shophouses selling in bazaar fashion, these areas have the look, sound, and smell of similar shops found in many parts of Thailand and Indonesia. Shops have a worn and cluttered look to them. You must bargain for everything. Shopkeepers probably speak some English. And your purchases are likely to totaled on an abacus or handwritten on a piece of paper. You will feel more comfortable shopping in the first culture, but the second culture is much more exotic and can be a great deal of fun.

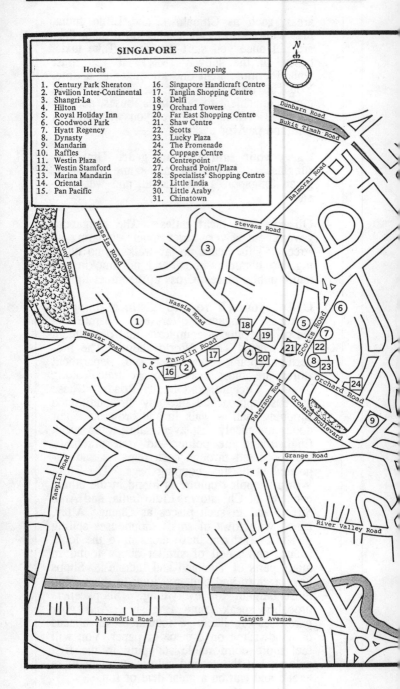

SINGAPORE

Hotels	Shopping
1. Century Park Sheraton	16. Singapore Handicraft Centre
2. Pavilion Inter-Continental	17. Tanglin Shopping Centre
3. Shangri-La	18. Delfi
4. Hilton	19. Orchard Towers
5. Royal Holiday Inn	20. Far East Shopping Centre
6. Goodwood Park	21. Shaw Centre
7. Hyatt Regency	22. Scotts
8. Dynasty	23. Lucky Plaza
9. Mandarin	24. The Promenade
10. Raffles	25. Cuppage Centre
11. Westin Plaza	26. Centrepoint
12. Westin Stamford	27. Orchard Point/Plaza
13. Marina Mandarin	28. Specialists' Shopping Centre
14. Oriental	29. Little India
15. Pan Pacific	30. Little Araby
	31. Chinatown

Becoming oriented toward Singapore is relatively easy. The major destination for most visitors is the city proper, located on the southern section of Singapore Island. The city is laid out on a grid system. Most of the hotels, restaurants, shopping complexes, and shops front on the main streets. Unlike Thailand and Indonesia, in Singapore you need not explore many back lanes or residential areas for shopping opportunities. Just go to the main streets and walk down block after block of shops and explore various levels of shopping complexes.

Take, for example, Orchard Road, which is Singapore's most famous shopping street. Lined with fine shops and shopping complexes on both sides of the street, you shop this area by walking up one side and down another. When you come to Scotts Road, which intersects Orchard Road, you'll discover even more shops and shopping complexes to explore. The same is true for the ethnic shopping areas: Chinatown, Little India, and Arab Street. Crowded and congested, these areas, too, must be explored on foot, going from shop to shop, block after block.

To do the streets of Singapore properly, you need four things: a good map, comfortable shoes, a lot of time, and persistence. You are in luck in the case of the map. The shoes, time, and persistence are up to you. The problem with Singapore is that there is too much to do in such a small place. Like Hong Kong, you will be assaulted by shop after shop offering wonderful selections of goods. After your first day in Singapore, you wonder how in the world you will ever have time to shop this city as well as find time to see the many interesting sights. Where do I start, and when do I finish? The sheer volume of shopping complexes and shops presents you with a formidable task as you feel your way through your Singapore shopping adventure.

WHAT TO BUY

Singapore is often compared to Hong Kong as if the two cities were in competition to attract international shoppers. This is unfortunate, because the two cities have different shopping strengths. It is true that both Hong Kong and Singapore offer similar electronic and camera equipment, but such items are questionable bargains in either city if you come from a country which places few duties on electronic and camera equipment. In the United States, for example, you are better off making the same purchases through a New York City mail-order house or a discount store than buying the items in Singapore or Hong Kong.

So what does Singapore have that Hong Kong doesn't? Plenty. Singapore's most important shopping strengths are in the areas of Asian antiques, arts, crafts, carpets, fashion goods, ready-made clothes, pewterware, computerware, and imported luxury items from Europe. When comparing prices between Hong Kong and Singapore, similar goods are priced about the same. Singapore has some price advantage on cameras, watches, liquor, tobacco, household appliances, costume jewelry, toys, games, and perfume. Hong Kong has some price advantage on mens' clothing, cosmetics, and leather goods. Although some claim Singapore is cheaper than Hong Kong, don't believe them. Whatever differences that do exist are minor; they don't justify the additional expense of visiting the other city just to try to save a little money.

Antiques, Curios, Tribal Art

While Hong Kong serves primarily as a conduit for Chinese goods, Singapore offers a wonderful collection of antiques and curios from all over Asia as well as the South Pacific. Most shops specialize in particular types of antiques. Some, for example, only carry local (Straits) Chinese antiques (**Petnics's** on Cuppage Road) whereas others focus on tribal art and textiles (**Bareo, Tiepolo,** and **Tatiana** in Tanglin Shopping Centre). The three shops in Tanglin Shopping Centre are "must" stops if tribal art is one of your interests. Each shop has excellent quality and a range of goods often not found in their country of origin -- primarily Indonesia and Malaysia.

Several shops have central or branch offices in Hong Kong, Bangkok, and Australia. Linked to these other countries through an intricate web of family, professional, and friendship ties, they regularly make buying trips to neighboring countries or have their friends and relatives supply them with new items to replenish their collections. When you visit these shops, ask if they have a branch in other cities. You may want to browse in these other shops when in Bangkok or Hong Kong.

Chinese, Burmese, and Thai antiques are particularly popular at present. Several shops also carry primitive art pieces from Indonesia and Papua New Guinea. Most of the Indonesian tribal art is from the nearby Batak area in Sumatra. Singapore is the only place in Southeast Asia where we have found primitive art pieces from the Sepik River area in Papua New Guinea. The art work is gorgeous and tempts one to add a Sepik River leg to one's Asian and Pacific shopping adventures!

Many of the shops and department stores stock Chinese,

Thai, Burmese, Indonesian, and Indian antiques and curios. The Chinese antiques include the usual assortment of items: porcelain, carpets, snuff bottles, incense burners, paintings, jade and ivory carvings, and jewelry. The Thai antiques are similar to those found in Bangkok's River City Shopping Complex: Buddha images, ceramics, gilded wood carvings and gables. Burmese antiques include lacquerware, gilded panels, woodcarvings, and tapestries. Indonesian collections tend to specialize in masks, puppets, woodcarvings, and small chests. And the Indian antiques and curios are primarily oil lamps, brass and bronze figures, and jewelry.

One major advantage of buying Asian antiques in Singapore is that you can take them out of the country without special export permits. Indeed, many of the Burmese and Thai antiques found in Singapore have already been smuggled out of these countries. Thai Buddha images, which can be difficult to export from Thailand, are plentiful in Singapore. However, be very careful about fakes. Some shops may claim the newly carved Thai "antiques" are indeed old and charge you accordingly. Many of the bronze Buddha images claimed to be from the Sukhothai and Ayuthaya periods may have similar age and price claims.

Prices for antiques, curios, and primitive art in Singapore are high compared to their countries of origin. For example, Batak house gables selling for S$200 in Parapat, Lake Toba (Sumatra, Indonesia) may cost over S$1500 in Singapore. The same is true for Burmese and Thai antiques. Nonetheless, we have found many lovely Burmese and Thai antiques and curios in Singapore which we could not find in either Burma or Thailand. On the other hand, if you have been to Indonesia -- especially Jalan Kebon Sirih Timur Dalam in Jakarta and along Kuta Beach on Bali -- you will be disappointed with the Indonesian selections found in Singapore. Many of the items are the ubiquitous Balinese woodcarvings. You would do much better on selections and save a great deal of money by making a quick trip to Medan, Lake Toba, Jakarta, or Bali than to make your Indonesian purchases here in Singapore. Special tour packages from Singapore make such trips inexpensive and worthwhile. Savings on your purchases will more than make up for the expense of such trips into Indonesia from Singapore.

Shops selling antiques, curios, and primitive art are primarily found in the shopping complexes, department stores, and hotels in and around Orchard Road. The largest concentration of good quality shops is found in the Watten Estate area (try **Unique Antique House, Young**

Antique Co., Tomlinson Antique House, Shanghai, D'Antiquemart, and Red House Carved Furniture Co.) and throughout the Tanglin Shopping Centre (try **Funan, Moon Gate, Ju-I Antiques, Tiepolo, Bareo, Tatiana, Mata-Hari, Antiques of the Orient** for starters). Other good shops are found in the Holland Road Shopping Centre (**E&E Antiques** and **The Pagoda House**), the Mandarin Hotel Shopping Arcade (**Mandarin Galleries**), Far East Shopping Centre (**China Crafts** and **Kwok Gallery**), Cuppage Road (**Babazar, Della Butcher Gallery,** and **Petnic's**), Paya Lebar Road (**Just Anthony**), and Changi Road (**Changi Junk Store**). One of our favorite shops for antique furniture is **Classic Antique House** at 42 Lorong Mambong, just down the street from Holland Road Shopping Centre. *may be open Sun.*

Art

Several art galleries are located in the major shopping areas and hotel shopping arcades. While much of the art is imported from other Asian countries, as well as from Europe, many shops also offer oils, watercolors, and sculptures produced by Singapore's and Malaysia's local artists. We have been very pleased with the overall quality of this art--some of the best in all of Asia. Famous local artists such as Tan Swie Hian, Chen Wen-Hsi, Tay Bak Toi, Tan Oe-Pang, Ong Kim Seng, Tong Chin Sye, Tan Leong Kheng, Thomas Yao, Anthony Poon, Wan Soon Kam, Teng Juay Lee, Nai Swee Leng, James Tan, Ang Ah Tee, and Gog Sing Hoi are producing everything from Chinese brush paintings to abstract landscapes. Much of this art reflects a creative blending of traditional Asian and contemporary Western motifs and styles. You may find much of this art will go well in your home.

Works of art are often found in the antique and curio shops. The largest concentration of art galleries is found in the Orchard Point shopping center on Orchard Road. Here you will find several art galleries on the third floor: **Central Arts Place, Sin Hua Gallery, Kuo Fong Gallery, Orchard Gallery,** and **Liufa Gallery.** The **Mandarin Galleries** in the Mandarin Hotel Shopping Arcade includes high-quality traditional Chinese brush paintings, antique Buddhas, and ceramics. Other shops offering good quality art include **Art Forum** in The Promenade; **Della Butcher Gallery** in Cuppage Terrace; **Tzen Gallery, Sun Craft, The Old & New Gallery, Antiques of the Orient,** and **Contemporary Art** in Tanglin Shopping Centre; **The Collector's Gallery** in Raffles City; **Gallery Fine Arts** in Orchard Towers; **Raya Gallery** in Specialist's Centre;

Guenter Lienau Decor in the Marina Square shopping
arcade; **D'Artist Gallery** in the Holland Road Shopping
Centre; and **Arbour Fine Art** on Lorong Mambong **Road.**
We've also found some lovely watercolors at **Jessica** in
The Promenade at 300 Orchard Road (also has shops **at**
Cold Storage Jelita and Holland Road Shopping Centre).

Carpets

More than any other city in Asia, Singapore offers **an**
excellent selection of new and antique Chinese, Pakistani,
Afghan, Persian, and Turkish carpets. Several shops specialize in such carpets. If your timing is right and you
make a point to survey announcements in the local newspapers, you may have a chance to attend a carpet auction.
  You will find carpet shops in several shopping areas.
The **Oriental Carpet Palace** at the Singapore Handicraft
Centre (Tanglin Road) has a good selection of Persian and
Turkish carpets and rugs. Nearby, on the corner of Tanglin and Tomlinson roads, is the famous **Tai Ping Carpets
and Rugs** which produces custom-made hooked carpets.
Several shops along **Orchard Road** and **Arab Street**
specialize in Persian carpets. The **Peninsula Shopping
Centre** on Coleman Street offers Chinese carpets. For
good copies of Chinese Tai Ping carpets, go to the **Singapore Carpet Manufacturers** (Haw Par Centre, Clemen-
ceau Avenue). Other places to explore are **Chinese Carpets** and **Oriental Carpet Palace** in the Singapore Handicraft Centre; **Kashmir Carpet House** in Wisma Atrium;
Amir & Sons in Lucky Plaza; **Hassan's** in Tanglin Shopping Centre; **Eastern Carpets** in Raffles City; **Tabriz and
Qureski's** in Centrepoint; and **Uzma Carpets & Handicrafts** in Forum Galleria.
  Wherever you shop for carpets, be sure to bargain hard.
Buying carpets in Singapore is like buying carpets anywhere else in the world. Bargain, bargain, bargain. As
with many of the antiques found in Singapore, be sure you
know your carpets before buying.

Jewelry

Singapore is a good place to buy jewelry. Workmanship is excellent, and prices are comparable to those in
Hong Kong. In fact, several of the jewelry stores along
Orchard Road are actually branches of Hong Kong shops.
Family enterprises, the brothers, sisters, sons, and daught-
ers of these establishments regularly move back and forth
between Hong Kong and Singapore.

The range of jewelry in Singapore is excellent. You will find Chinese gold and jade everywhere, but especially in Chinatown and the Chinese Emporiums. You will also find excellent quality pearls, diamonds, sapphires, rubies, emeralds, topaz, coral, turquoise, and ivory as well as inexpensive Indian jewelry.

Jewelry designs in Singapore range from traditional to modern. In Chinatown, for example, you will find 22-carat gold jewelry made in traditional designs. Most of these shops are concentrated in **People's Park** and along **South Bridge Road**. Several shops in the shopping complexes along **Orchard Road** offer exquisite designer jewelry using diamonds, precious and semi-precious stones, and pearls. You also will find shops selling loose stones, jewelry in Italian designs, and antique jewelry. Many shops offer average quality necklaces, earrings, bracelets, pins, and rings.

Excellent quality jewelry at reasonable prices can be found in Singapore. Visit enough shops to get an accurate feel for the quality, designs, and prices. Again, be sure to bargain hard in all the shops. Expect to receive as much as a 50 percent discount off the asking price in some shops.

One of the best jewelry stores in Singapore is **Je t'aime** on the second floor of Wisma Atria (#02-10) at 435 Orchard Road. This well established jeweler with a preference for Italian craftsmanship, creates exquisite designs in gold and diamonds. Prices start at S$2000 and go up. The owner, Regina Wong, also recently opened a branch shop in Reno, Nevada.

Other excellent jewelers include **Larry Jewelry** with shops at Orchard Towers, Lucky Plaza, and Raffles City; **Minh Anh** and **Marina Diamond Centre** in the Marina Square shopping arcade; **Monette** in Colombo Court; **Franc** in the Promenade Shopping Centre; **Mikimoto** in the Pavilion Inter-Continental; **Chap Mai Jewelry** in Raffles City; **C.T. Hoo** on Tanglin Road for pearls; **Kevin-'s** in the Shangri-La Hotel; **Pierre Jewellery** and **Prestige Jewellery** in the Mandarin Hotel Shopping Arcade; **House of Hung** at the Far Eastern Shopping Centre; and **Pat Jewellers** in Orchard Towers. When in Tanglin Shopping Centre, stop at **S.P.H. De Silva** and **Eramanis Jewellers**.

Handicrafts and Souvenirs

Singapore is filled with handicrafts from all over Asia. Department stores, emporiums, and shops carry woodcarvings, basketware, rattan and cane goods, lacquered goods, copper and brass items, pewterware, batik, and all types of knickknacks. Like so many handicrafts found in other countries, many of the ones in Singapore have that distinct "Made for Tourists Only" look. Nonetheless, you will be able to find some good quality handicrafts amidst the tourist kitsch.

If you are interested in Chinese handicrafts, the best place to shop are the **Chinese emporiums** in People's Park Complex (New Bridge Road) and along Orchard Road as well as in several shops in the Chinatown area. Offering a large variety of handicrafts from China, the emporiums are similar to the ones in Hong Kong -- packed with a large assortment of items, including large pieces of furniture. They are especially well stocked with inexpensive -- although not fashionable -- clothes from China. In **Chinatown**, explore the shops along Trengganu, Temple, and Smith streets. These three streets are full of discoveries. Just walk into the cluttered shops and look everywhere for handcrafted items. Shophouses along these streets sell a large variety of baskets, kites, ceramics, dolls, costumes, pottery, and fans. You will find plenty of nice gift items amongst the many Chinese handicrafts at such shops as **Chop Nam Jo, Chua Guan Hong Kee, Tow Huat Heng Kee, Toh Foong,** and **Thye Nam & Co.** Don't forget to stop at the famous **Rising Arts & Crafts** in the old Thong Chai Medical Institution on Wayang Street, just north of People's Park Centre on Eu Tong Sen Street, for Chinese paintings, papercuts, plates, vases, embroidered silk cushions, tablecloths, fans, carvings, soapstone figurines, chops, and seals. If you are interested in some of the most unique Chinese folk art, look for funeral items in the shops on Sago Street.

Along **Arab Street** you will find numerous Malay and imported handicrafts. Several shops are crammed with attractive and inexpensive baskets, carpets, cloth, batik, lamps, leather goods, hats, fans, and much more. Many of the handicrafts are imported from India, the Philippines, Indonesia, and even Kenya. We especially like the selections at **Habib Handicraft, B&K Textile,** and **Jothi Palayakat Co.**

Little India, which begins at the corner of Sarangoon and Sungei roads, has several shops selling Indian handcrafted items: brass, flowers, brocades, paintings, and batik.

One of the best places to shop for local and international handicrafts is the **Singapore Handicraft Centre** just off Tanglin Road near the Tanglin Shopping Centre. Once a thriving and popular center for handicrafts, this area had declined in recent years. However, we are pleased to find that the Centre is once again offering some of best selections of handicrafts in Singapore -- if not all of Southeast Asia. This area is once again on our "must visit" shopping list in Singapore. The shops here present handicrafts from 16 Asian countries.

Some of our favorite shops at the Singapore Handicraft Centre include **Natraj's Arts & Crafts** for Indian carvings, brass, and jewelry; **Chu's Jade Centre** for jade and neckpieces; **Indonesia Handicrafts** for wayang puppets and fashionable clothes from the Sarinah Jaya company in Jakarta; **Nayong Pilipino Handicraft** for shell work, woodcarvings, placemats, and lamps; **Treasures of Siam** for Thai handcrafted items; **Selangor Pewter** for beautifully crafted pewterware; **Ying Fatt Trading** for cloisonne, ivory, and jade; **Sri Lanka Trading** for jewelry, batik paintings, and woodcarvings; **Kraftangan Malaysia** for an unusual mix of Burmese tapestries, batik shirts, T-shirts, wayang puppets, woodcarvings, and pewter; **Henley Souvenirs & Gifts** for Chinese masks, ivory, batik paintings, pewter, butterflies, and T-shirts; **Lee Ming** for pewter, Chinese masks, and batik paintings; and **Waldon Arts Souvenir Industries** for umbrellas, fans, batik paintings, pewter, woodcarvings, kites, and ceramics.

You also may want to visit the Singapore Handicraft Centre on Wednesday, Friday, Saturday, and Sunday evenings at which time a special outdoor bazaar is held for tourists. Vendors set up small tables to display handicrafts, souvenirs, clothes, and knickknacks. While not offering many quality goods, the vendors are fun to talk to and, of course, to bargain with. This also is a good opportunity for an unusual look at Singapore by night. One of the more interesting aspects of this visit may be the adjacent open-air food stalls. They serve excellent Chinese and Nonya food at inexpensive prices, and are always crowded -- usually a sign of good food and value!

Some of the best shops offering Asian handicrafts include **Babazar** at Cuppage Terrace; **Borobudur Arts & Crafts** in the Far Eastern Shopping Centre; **Lim's Arts & Crafts** and **Visual Dharma** at the Holland Road Shopping Centre; **Legaspi** in Wisma Atria; **Sin Kee Arts & Crafts** and **Royal Pewter House** in the Mandarin Hotel Shopping Arcade; **Chinese Cloisonne Ware** and **Chinese Embroidery House** in Raffles City; and **Jessica** and **Renee Hoy Galleries** at Cold Storage Jelita on Holland Road.

Be sure to look for handicrafts and souvenirs in **department stores** as well as in the aerial **Change Alley** located on the air-conditioned pedestrian bridge crossing Collyer Quay, **Tanglin Shopping Centre, Mandarin Shopping Arcade, Lucky Plaza, Raffles City,** and **Marina Square Shopping Arcade.**

Clothes

Singapore is a good place to buy fashionable **ready-made clothes.** Many department stores and boutiques offer the latest imported as well as locally produced European fashion clothes -- produced in Singapore under licensing arrangements with Europe's top designers. You will also find some unique styles designed by such famous Singapore designers as Bobby Chang, Peter Kor, Kelvin Choo, Esther Tay, Arthur Yen, Rest & Relax, Tan Yoong, and Benny Ong as well as the latest Japanese fashions. Most of the department stores and small boutiques offering such clothes are found in the shopping complexes along the Tanglin-Orchard-Scotts Road shopping corridor as well as in several hotel shopping arcades.

The best place to view and buy clothes designed by local fashion designers is **Studio** designer showcase at Scotts shopping center on Scotts Road. On this one floor you will find the fashion designs of Singapore's major designers: Bobby Chang, Rest & Relax, Chapters, Peter Kor, Kelvin Choo, Esther Tay, and Arthur Yen.

For the best quality imported fashion clothes, visit the new Tudor Court on Tanglin Road, Me Shopping Gallery at the Hilton Hotel, Mandarin Hotel Shopping Centre, The Promenade, Paragon Shopping Centre, Forum Galleria, and Galeries Lafayette. All the major department stores and shopping centers are filled with fashionable ready-made clothes.

Tudor Court is Singapore's latest upscale fashion center. Located on Tanglin Road, between the Singapore Handicraft Centre and Tanglin Shopping Centre, this small two-story shopping arcade is packed with Singapore's most exquisite and expensive fashion shops offering a wide variety of the latest imported clothes and accessories. Most shops offer European, Japanese, Hong Kong, and Australian designer fashion. Look for the top brand names in fashionwear: **Luciano Soprani, Ermenegildo Zegna, Maxim's de Paris, Diane Freis, Roberta De Camerino, Mariella Burani, Gianfranco Lotti, Kwanpen, Louis Quatorze, Loris Azzaro, Ken Done, Vienna Bijou,** and **R. Martegani.** Risis Singapore, a local firm, offers a unique collection of gold orchids and chicken eggs.

Me Shopping Gallery at the Hilton Hotel on Orchard Road is Singapore's finest upscale hotel shopping arcade. Here you will find numerous exclusive clothing and accessory shops offering the latest in international fashions. Look for such quality shops as **Daks, Gianfranco Ferre, Fendi, Jaeger, Gottex, Lanvin, Ad Hoc, L'ultimo, Singora, Maud Frizon, Georgio Armani, A. Testoni, Valen-**

tino, Alfred Dunhill, Loewe, Davidoff Boutique, Gucci, and Louis Vuitton.

The Mandarin Hotel Shopping Arcade also has several upscale boutiques, clothing, and accessory stores. Look for Miss Ming, Club 21, Sonia Rykiel, Djien Boutique, Moda Italiana, Casa Moda, La Donna, and A. Testoni.

Other shopping centers offering exclusive womenswear and menswear are The Promenade and the Paragon Shopping Centre on Orchard Road. At the Promenade look for Ralph Lauren, Charles Jourdan, Tyan, Man & His Women, Ayers Design, Apricot Design, or Matsudu. At the Paragon Shopping Centre you will find numerous trendy boutiques and such exclusive brand names as Emanuel Ungaro and Gucci. Next door your will also find the Esprit building offering the latest in European fashion clothes.

Several other shopping centers offer exclusive fashionwear. Try, for example, the shops at Wisma Atrium, Specialists' Shopping Centre, and Raffles City. We especially like the selections offered by China Silk House which has shops at Tanglin Shopping Centre, Lucky Plaza, Scotts Shopping Centre, Centerpoint, and Marina Square shopping arcade. They have beautiful silk fabrics and ready-made clothes, and they will custom-make garments at their Tanglin Shopping Centre shop. Look for Amour Silk & Batik in the Marina Square shopping arcade and Jin T, Designer Labels, MayeeLok, and St. Ives Collection in Wisma Atria. Department stores, such as Galeries Lafayette, Tangs, John Little, Metro Far East, Metro Grand, Isetan, Sogo, Tokyu, Robinson's, and Yaohan.

Singapore used to be a good place to buy tailor-made clothes. Promotional literature may still tell you that one of the great shopping treats and buys in Singapore is tailor-made clothes. We and others don't believe it. More often than not, one of the greatest shopping disappointments in Singapore is tailoring. While you can still have good tailoring done here, it simply is no bargain compared to the quality and prices of Singapore's ready-made clothes. The cost of labor in Singapore has risen greatly during the past five years to the point where tailors are now competing with the ready-made clothes market. And they can't compete successfully. Nonetheless, should you need a good tailor, one of Singapore's best is Ed Kwan at the Westin Stamford and Westin Plaza of Raffles City (Hotel Shop #9, Level 3, Tel. 3380819). Several other tailors are located in Tanglin Shopping Centre (CYC and Justmen for men) and in the Specialist Centre (Bagatelle Shoppe and Hawaiiana for women and Rewas for men).

The large concentration of tailors in Lucky Plaza and the Far Eastern Shopping Centre on Orchard Road offer inexpensive tailored garments. However, you normally get what you pay for in tailored clothes. If the price is cheap, expect your garments to look cheap. Indeed, tailored clothes are the number one shopping complaint for tourists in Singapore. The complaint is usually the same: they didn't get what they expected, workmanship was poor, and the garments weren't delivered on time. This is not surprising. These are the same problems we find in Hong Kong, Korea, and Thailand. The basic problem, however, is the buyer: he or she tries to get something for nothing, does not know how to communicate with a tailor, and had little time to do the proper number of fittings. The combined results of being cheap, inexperienced in dealing with tailors, and out of time result in poorly tailored garments that are largely a waste of time and money.

There are exceptions to our general tailoring observations, but our experience is that time and again tourists will make this their number one shopping mistake in Singapore and other countries where they will be tempted to purchase tailored garments. Our advice: if you are determined to have tailoring work done, go to a reputable tailor, be willing to pay for quality fabric and workmanship, and get it done right. Reputable tailors are more expensive than the *"Hey, you mister"* tailors who are found throughout many of Singapore's shopping centers. They are expensive because they use the best fabrics and spend the proper amount of time on cutting, assembling, and fitting the garments. The best tailors invariably are found in the shopping arcades of Singapore's best hotels.

A final word of advice: In most cases you will be much better off buying ready-made clothes which are less expensive and more fashionable than much of the tailoring work produced by the small tailor shops in Singapore. You also get to try on the finished product before you put down your money.

Textiles

Singapore offers a large variety of fabrics from all over Asia. You will find Chinese and Thai silks, Malay and Indonesian batiks, Malay *kain songket* (silk interwoven with gold thread from Kelantan), Filipino *jusi* or *pina* (a fine nearly transparent silk), Indian cottons and silks, and European, American, and Japanese fabrics in all types of colors and designs.

For **Chinese** fabrics, browse through the Chinese emporiums as well as the shops in the Tanglin Shopping Centre

and along Smith Street in Chinatown. We especially like
the silk fabrics and designs available at the **China Silk
House** which has branches located in Tanglin Shopping
Centre (main shop that also does tailoring), Lucky Plaza,
Scotts Shopping Centre, Centrepoint, and Marina Square.
For **European, American, Japanese,** and **Indonesian**
fabrics, try department stores, People's Park Centre, North
Bridge Road, Arab Street, High Street Plaza, Sultan Plaza,
High Street, and Katong Shopping Center. **Indian** silks
are found along Serangoon Road and High Street as well
as in the Singapore Handicraft Centre. You will find **Thai**
silk in the Singapore Handicraft Centre and hotel shopping
arcades, along Arab Street, and in several shopping complexes. The noted Bangkok-based Design Thai has a shop
in Tanglin Shopping Centre; their selections here are better
than in Bangkok -- offering colors, designs, and styles
more appropriate to Singapore's Western audience. For
Malay *kain songket* and **Filipino** *jusi* or *pina*, visit the
shops at the Singapore Handicraft Centre and along Arab
Street. One of the oldest batik shops in Singapore, offering good quality Javanese batik, is **Chop Yeo Hong Seng**
at 63 Arab Street.

Computers, Electronic Goods, and Cameras

Many shops in Singapore are filled with the same types
of computer and electronic goods and cameras found in
Hong Kong. They overflow with calculators, stereo equipment, cassette players, radios, televisions, video recorders,
35mm and video cameras, appliances, and the latest gadgetry. Much of this produced in Singapore as well as imported from Japan, Hong Kong, Korea, and Taiwan.
Unless you are from a country which places high duties
on imported items, you are not likely to find any great
deals on electronic goods and cameras in Singapore.
Similar to Hong Kong, you may be able to get better buys
on such goods through direct-mail in the United States --
thanks to Asian dumping practices and the volume sales of
U.S. discount houses. However, you may find some items
not available back home. In many cases, new products are
first introduced in Hong Kong and Singapore and only
later appear in U.S. and European markets. These products
may be the ones of greatest interest to you.
Be cautious when buying electronic goods and cameras. You should always get a receipt and an international
guarantee as well as test the product. Make sure items are
compatible with your systems back home. Be especially
careful about televisions and video cameras. Most are
designed for the Asian and European PAL systems; they

will not work on NTSC systems found in the U.S. and some other countries. While you should bargain hard for all of these goods, consider using your credit card even if it means your bargained price isn't quite as low as a cash price. Should you have a problem with your purchase after returning home, your credit card company can assist you as long as you have your credit card charge slip and receipt.

Computer software is a particularly good buy in Singapore. Like electronic goods, computer hardware in Singapore is no longer the great bargain it used to be since hardware prices have fallen dramatically in the U.S. since 1986. But software is a fantastic buy -- the best of any buy in all of Asia. However, be forewarned that you are entering a market of pirated computer software which does not sit well with U.S. software companies and may present some problems when passing through U.S. Customs. Indeed, the Singapore legislature passed a law to protect U.S. copyrights. Implemented in June, 1987, this law prohibits the sale of pirated software. The practical results of this law have been to move software purchases from a "gray market" to a "black market" and to make such purchases more inconvenient and time consuming. Rather than buy pirated software "off-the-shelf" in full public view, you must now "put-in-an-order". Within a few hours you can return to the store to pick up your purchase. Without naming specific shops, let's just say that most computer shops will accommodate such requests. All you need to do is walk into a shop and ask them *"Can you get me this program, including the manuals?"* In general, the quality of the software and manuals is good, but by no means guaranteed. A software package costing US$500 in the U.S. can be purchased in Singapore -- complete with diskettes and manuals -- for approximately US$50!

You will find several computer shops in the Funan Centre on North Bridge Road, between High and Coleman streets; in Chinatown at the **People's Park Centre** (Eu Tong Sen Street at Upper Cross Street) and **Fook Hai Building** (South Bridge Road and Upper Hokien Street); **Lucky Plaza** on Orchard Road; and the **Far East Plaza** on Scotts Road.

Most of the software found in Singapore is for IBM or IBM compatible computers. Shops carry only a limited selection of Apple software. Most programs cost S$5 per diskette and about S$10 for each book. They will give you a discount -- perhaps 20 percent -- if you ask for one and are paying cash.

Furniture, Wickerware, and Caneware

Singapore offers a good selection of locally-produced and imported furniture, wickerware, and caneware. One of Singapore's best furniture companies is **Fefco Fine Furniture** at the Meridien Shopping Centre (100 Orchard Road). The furniture and antique shops at **Watten Estates** (Tomlinson Antique House, Young Antique Co., Unique Antique House, and Red House Carved Furniture Co.) offer good selections of traditional furniture. We especially like the selections available at **Classic Antique House** at 42 Lorong Mambong, located behind the Holland Road Shopping Centre.

A few shops in the Holland Road area offer excellent quality Korean chests, Chinese cabinets, and wicker and cane furniture. **Lim's Arts & Crafts** in the Holland Road Shopping Centre has two floors of Korean chests and other home furnishings. Behind the Centre, look for **Excel Caneware** at 38 Lorong Mambong for cane and ratten furniture. **Avant Garde Design** on the corner at 21 Lorong Mambong is a nice home decor shop with some beautifully designed cane and rattan furniture. You will also find a few shops along Lorong Mambong selling wicker baskets. At Cold Storage Jelita on Holland Road you will find two nice shops offering selections of tastefully designed furniture: **Jessica** and **Renee Hoy Fine Arts**.

Other shops offering good quality furniture include **Babazar** (Cuppage Terrace) for Indian, Korean, Indonesian, and Chinese furniture; **Chin Yi Antique House** (117 Upper Paya Lebar Road) for Chinese lacquer and blackwood furniture; **Da-Ching Fine Arts** in Centrepoint (176 Orchard Road) for Korean chests; **Just Anthony** (379 Upper Paya Lebar Road) for Chinese lacquer and blackwood furniture;

Wickerware in the form of baskets, hats, mats, birdcages, fans, and chests is readily available in the shops along **Arab Street**. We especially like the selections at **Habib Handicraft, Jothi Palayakat Co.,** and **B&K Textile** on Arab Street. Caneware in the form of cane and rattan furniture is best found in several shops along **Joo Chiat Road**.

Silverware and Pewterware

Silverware in Singapore comes primarily from the Malaysian states of Trengganu and Kelantan where it is handmade into intricate styles. Many gift and curio shops in the shopping complexes along Orchard Road as well as in the Singapore Handicraft Centre offer this silverware as well as pewterware. For simple and modern styles of silverware, visit **Georg Jensen** at the Mandarin Hotel.

Pewterware is a specialty of both Malaysia and Singapore. You will find pewterware in the form of candlesticks, decorative plates, tankards, cups, bowls, and tableware. The quality is generally good, and the designs are unique to Malaysia and Singapore. Try **Selangor Pewter** in the Singapore Handicraft Centre and **Orient Crafts** at 31 Cuppage Road for good quality pewterware.

The More You Look

The longer you stay in Singapore, the more you will discover to buy. Among many other things, Singapore is well noted for its abundant supply of good quality **watches, sports equipment** (from fishing to golf), **carved ivory figures, furs, optical products,** and **reptile skin goods** (shoes, handbags, wallets, and belts made from lizard, crocodile, alligator, and snake skins). The list goes on and on. Similar to Hong Kong, but different in terms of particular shopping strengths, Singapore is indeed a shopper's paradise.

WHERE TO SHOP

This is one of the easiest cities in the world to shop. The maps are outstanding, the streets are convenient, most shops are found in air-conditioned shopping complexes, most people speak English, and you need not travel far from one shop to another, and from one shopping complex to another.

Singapore seems to have been designed with the international shopper in mind. The Singapore Tourist Promotion Board actively promotes an on-your-own, self-service approach to enjoying your stay in Singapore. Their literature and maps make shopping in Singapore easy. The special Singapore Explorer Bus Ticket makes getting around Singapore both convenient and inexpensive.

Not All Is Guaranteed

However, all is not perfect in Singapore's 20,000 retail shops. You must be careful about pricing, exaggerated claims of authenticity and quality, and service. Some merchants are still out to make a fast buck from unsuspecting tourists. If you stay near department stores and recommended quality shops, you can expect the merchants to be honest and give you the expected quality and price advantages. If you wander off into the *"Hey, you mister"* shops and stalls that claim to give you the *"best deal in town"* or are taken to a shop by a tout, don't expect to walk away with much of a deal. There is no such thing as a free lunch in either Singapore or New York City. Many small stalls have a fly-by-night mentality. Be careful in spending your money in such places.

The **Singapore Tourist Promotion Board** plays an important role in ensuring that your Singapore shopping adventure will be most rewarding. During the past few years it has tried to improve the image of shopping in Singapore by responding to complaints and setting standards among shops. Unfortunately, some tourists have reported a combination of rude behavior, poor workmanship, misrepresentation, and other unscrupulous practices among some merchants. In 1985 the STPB stepped in by creating a new Associate Membership Scheme. Replacing the old Associate Membership Scheme of 1973, this new one sets strict standards and good business practices among its members. Shops that apply and are accepted for membership prominently display a red decal with the gold Merlion (a lionhead figure). Known as "Good Retailers", these shops agree to put price tags on all their merchandise and thus eliminate the need to bargain -- a practice which STPB feels inhibits visitors from buying as well as encourages dishonesty. These shops promise to issue receipts, guarantee their products, and provide good service. The STPB, in turn, lists these shops in their promotional literature. Should you have any complaints against their member shops, the STPB will take action to assist in resolving your complaint. As the STPB puts it, *"Shoppers can patronise these 'good retailer' shops . . . without fear of being taken for a ride."*

It would be to your advantage to patronize such places, especially for big ticket items, such as jewelry and video equipment, which could be subject to misrepresentation. While few in number at present (135 out of 20,000 retailers), the number of STPB approved shops should steadily increase in the coming years. Keep an eye open for shops displaying the red decal.

Before starting your shopping adventure in Singapore, we strongly recommend that you purchase a copy of *The Secret Map of Singapore*. This map will take you quickly into each of the major shopping areas and will identify various shops and products -- a "must" resource for any serious shopper in Singapore. Your hotel sundry shop should sell copies of the map.

Shopping Areas

Singapore has seven major shopping areas of primary interest to international shoppers: Orchard Road, Chinatown, Little India, Arab Street, Change Alley, Holland Village, and Katong. The first five are located within close proximity to each other in the downtown area whereas the last two are located in suburban areas. All are within 20 minutes of each other by taxi.

Orchard Road is Singapore's fashionable "Golden Mile." Bordered on the north by Tanglin Road and intersected by the popular Scotts Road shopping extension, Orchard Road's broad tree-lined sidewalks lead to Singapore's major department stores, shopping complexes, and hotels. Most of the better quality art, fashion, and jewelry shops are located in this area alongside the more traditional shops selling electronic goods, appliances, clothes, gifts, and curios. Shopping in this area takes place in air-conditioned comfort. You only need to go outside for a few minutes on your way to the next department store, shopping complex, or hotel shopping arcade.

You can easily spend two days shopping the thousands of stores on both sides of this street. For many shoppers, Orchard Road is the shopper's heaven of Asia. It is New York's Fifth Avenue, London's Oxford Street and Knightsbridge, and Hong Kong's Nathan Road and Queen's Road Central rolled into one.

Chinatown, in addition to Little India and Arab Street, is one of three traditional ethnic enclaves which also functions as a distinct shopping area. Consisting of small cluttered shops and Chinese emporiums, this is a colorful area of traditional craftsmen and temples. Chinatown's major shopping streets are Trengganu, Temple, and Smith. It's best to start shopping this area at the **Chinatown Complex**, a large covered market bounded by New Bridge Road, Smith Street, and Sago Street where you will find several stalls selling fruits, vegetables, and meats as well as household goods and handcrafted items. A good time to come here is between 11am and noon when the commercial shops open, although the fresh market area on the lower level opens at 6:30am. Nearby the Complex you will find rows of old Chinese shophouses offering a variety of standard Chinese household goods, fresh produce, handicrafts, funeral objects, medicine, jade, silk, and bonsai trees. We especially like the handicraft selections at **Chop Nam Jo** and **Chua Guan Hong Kee** on Smith Street and **Toh Foony Curios, Tow Huat Heng Kee,** and **Thye Nam & Co.** on Temple Street. Bargaining in these Chinatown shops will normally get you a 10 to 20 percent discount.

Two of Singapore's largest Chinese emporiums are located just one block east of Trengganu Street on Eu Tong Sen Street near Upper Cross Street -- **People's Park Complex** and **People's Park Centre**. Both of these shopping centers are packed with small shops selling everything from the latest in electronic goods to inexpensive clothes, fabrics, footwear, and luggage. You will find a popular department store between these two emporiums -- **OG Building**.

Other streets in Chinatown tend to be noted for particular items. South Bridge Road, for example, is Chinatown's goldsmith street. Sago Street is Chinatown's street for funeral objects. On Wayang Street you can visit **Rising Arts and Crafts** which is housed in the architecturally interesting old Thong Chai Medical Institution building. Here you can browse for Chinese woodcarvings, porcelain, screens, paintings, cloisonne, and kites. The night market centers around Pagoda and Trengganu Streets.

Many visitors may find Chinatown more interesting as a cultural experience than as a worthwhile shopping adventure. Most products found in Chinatown are foods, medicines, clothes, and household goods for the local Chinese community. Except for the Rising Arts and Crafts shop and a few handicraft shops along Trengganu, Temple, and Smith streets, the most interesting international shopping is found in the **People's Park Complex** and **People's Park Centre**. Each emporium is filled with small shops and stalls selling textiles, clothes, luggage, watches, footwear, jewelry, appliances, cameras, embroideries, and computerware. Just behind People's Park Complex is the **Old People's Park Complex**. Filled with textiles, this is good place to buy lengths of fabric by the meter. **Fook Hai Building** on the corner of South Bridge Road and Upper Hokien Street is a good place to purchase computerware, modeling kits, and remote control equipment for cars, planes, and boats.

The **Arab Street** section, which begins just north of Beach Road, across the street from the Plaza Hotel, is filled with many shopping surprises. Shops along the streets are especially noted for offering Malay and Indonesia batiks, textiles, dress trimmings, braids, batik, basketware, luggage, jewelry, loose stones, lace, carpets, prayer rugs, brassware, and leather goods.

It's best to begin your Arab Street shopping adventure at the corner of **Arab Street** and **Beach Road**. Walk northwest on Arab Street and turn right onto **Baghdad Street**. You will find all types of interesting little shops selling traditional items in this area. When you come to the corner of **Bussorah Street**, take a left; you will see the famous Sultan Mosque in the distance. If you are interested in Malay crafts, stop at **Haija Asfiah** (#43 Bussorah Street). At the end of Bussorah Street, take a left or right onto **Muscat Street**. While most of the shops are concentrated along the Arab-Baghdad-Bussorah-Muscat streets area, you will find numerous shops selling other items on nearby streets. Of particular note are the inexpensive clothes and junk shops supposedly selling antiques in **The Golden Mile Food Centre** -- not our idea of a good shopping time. The **Textile Centre** and **Sultan Plaza** on Jalan Sultan have a good selection of traditional Arab, Indonesian, Malay, and Indian textiles, including batik.

Some of our favorite shops along Arab Street include **Habib Handicraft** (#18 & 20), **B&K Textile** (#40), **Jothi Palayakat Co.** (#42), and **Chop Yeo Hong Seng** (#63).

Little India is an ethnic area beginning at the corner of Serangoon and Sungei roads. Another cultural experience, complete with aromas from Indian spices, this is an area of goldsmiths, textile merchants, money-changers, fortune tellers, and food stores. The major shopping streets in this area are Serangoon Road, Campbell Lane, Clive Street, Dunlop Street, and Buffalo Road. Little India is noted for its **Zhu Jiao Centre** (also called the Kandang Kerbau Market) and **Thieves' Market** at the corner of Serangoon and Buffalo roads. This area is filled with *sari* shops and stores selling inexpensive clothes, musical instruments, antiques, copy watches, electronic goods, brassware, porcelain, and an assortment of knickknacks. Several shops along Serangoon Road and the adjacent side streets specialize in textiles, porcelain, antiques, Vietnamese vases, Filipino shirts, jade, carvings, brassware, Indian gold jewelry, luggage, joss sticks, birds and birdcages, medicines, and food stuffs.

Your best approach to exploring the Little India area is to walk the streets and poke into the various shops. Start just north of the juncture of Serangoon Road and Buket Timah Road (adjacent to Rochor Canal Bridge), near Buffalo Road and Campbell Lane. If you walk north along both sides of Serangoon Road for about 700 feet, you will be in the midst of the major shopping area. Of special interest are **Si Hu Art Studio** (#347 Serangoon Road) to see photo transfers on porcelain plates, and **P.Govindasamy Pillai** (opposite the Zhu Jiao Centre) for the largest collection of Indian fabrics and costumes.

Change Alley is located just off Clifford Pier. A famous bazaar-style shopping area for sailors and tourists leaving their cruise ships, Change Alley retains its traditional crowded and dark atmosphere. It is filled with money-changers offering good exchange rates and merchants selling footwear, costume jewelry, textiles, copy Rolex and designer watches, and all sorts of junk you probably don't need or want. Bargain hard here, and prepare to be taken for a ride if you are not careful about pricing and checking the quality of goods.

An upscale version of Change Alley is found in the nearby **Change Alley Aerial Plaza**. Shops lining this overhead bridge at Shenton Way sell clothes, pewterware, tablecloths, and a large assortment of tourist knickknacks. As with Change Alley, watch yourself here; bargain hard and expect to be taken for another ride.

Holland Village is a favorite shopping area for Singapore's expatriate community. Located to the west within a 15-minute taxi ride from downtown Singapore and along Holland Road, this area offers a wide selection of antiques, gifts, souvenirs, and curios from China, Japan, Korea, the Philippines, Sri Lanka, and India, clothes from the Philippines, and ceramics, porcelain, caneware, basketry, and earthenware. Be sure to visit the shops in **Holland Road Shopping Centre**, especially **Lim's Arts and Crafts**, **E&E Antiques**, **Jim Art**, **Visual Dharma**, **D'Artist Gallery**, and **The Pagoda House** for good quality antiques, arts, crafts, furniture, and home decorative items.

Just around the corner on Lorong Mambong Road are several art, antique, furniture, and home decorative shops. We especially like **Classic Antique House** (#42) for excellent quality antique Chinese furniture, porcelain, carvings, and beds as well as new locally produced furniture; **Avant Garde Design** (#21) for tastefully designed cane and rattan furniture and accessories; and **Excel Caneware** (#38) for cane and rattan furniture. Also look for **Holland Village Gallery** (#40), **Merlin Frame Maker** (#36), and **Chong Hwa Arts & Frame Makers** (#34-B) for a large variety of arts and crafts.

For a good selection of furniture, art, antiques, home decorative items, crafts, curios, and gifts, visit **Cold Storage Jelita** (293 Holland Road), a five-minute taxi ride from Holland Road Shopping Centre. Here you will find two excellent shops: **Renee Hoy Fine Arts** and **Jessica**.

Katong is a suburb located on the East Coast. If you take the expressway, you can get to Katong in about 20 minutes from downtown Singapore. Katong is a Chinese and Malay area. The major shopping area -- **Geylang Road** --is also reputed to be the center for the Chinese Mafia. Here, as well as on **Sims Avenue, Changi Road, and Joo Chiat Road**, you will find clothes, antiques, leather goods, furniture, toys, baskets, lanterns, Chinese and Malay style jewelry, Malay costumes and bridal accessories, and the usual assortment of household goods, medicines, spices, and fresh produce. You will need a good half-day to explore the streets and shops of Katong.

Shopping Centers

Singapore's large number of air-conditioned shopping centers makes shopping both comfortable and convenient. Most of the shopping centers are located within close proximity of each other in and around Orchard Road. They house the major department stores and shops.

One of the best ways to shop these centers is to begin on Tanglin Road at the Singapore Handicraft Centre. Tanglin Road is just off the western end of Orchard Road. From there you can walk north along Tanglin Road visiting the Singapore Handicraft Centre, Tudor Court, and the Tanglin Shopping Centre and then enter Orchard Road. Continue east on Orchard Road covering both sides of this long street and also walk north a few hundred feet along Scotts Road.

Walking north and east along this Tanglin-Orchard-Scotts Roads shopping corridor you will come to the following shopping centers:

SHOPPING CENTERS

- **Singapore Handicraft Centre:** Located on Tanglin Road next to the lovely Pavilion Intercontinental Hotel, this shopping center specializes in handicrafts from 16 countries from South and Southeast Asia. The shops here offer an excellent selection of tourist gifts curios, souvenirs, and knickknacks, especially paintings, Oriental carpets, woodcarvings, batik, and jewelry. A Malay night market (*pasar malam*) is held here every Wednesday night from 6pm to 10pm and every Friday, Saturday, and Sunday evening from 4pm to 10pm.

- **Tudor Court:** One of Singapore's newest and most upscale shopping centers for designer labels. Packed with boutiques offering the latest fashion clothes and accessories from Europe, Japan, and Australia. Includes such shops as **Luciano Soprani, Ermenegildo Zegna, Maxims de Paris, Diane Freis, Ken Done, Vienna Bijou, R. Martegani,**

Roberta De Camerino, Mariella Burani, Louis Azzaro, and Gianfranco Lotti. Local shops include Risis Singapore and Selangor Pewter.

- **Tanglin Shopping Centre:** Located within a five-minute walk and just north of the Singapore Handicraft Centre where Tanglin Road meets Orchard Road. This is an excellent place to shop for antiques, primitive art, furniture, porcelain, Thai and Chinese silk, carpets, curios, and paintings. Be sure to explore the many shops lining all levels of this shopping centre. Our favorite shops here include Tiepolo, Bareo, Tatiana, Mata-Hari, and Funan for Southeast Asian antiques, artifacts and crafts.

- **Forum Galleria:** Located on the south side of Orchard Road, between the Ming Court and Hilton Hotel, this is one of Singapore's newest shopping centers. Filled with good quality boutiques, art, antique, jewelry, footwear, carpet, and clothing stores. Has one of the largest Toys 'R' Us shops in all of Asia. Includes one floor of food outlets -- Rasa Forum.

- **Far East Shopping Centre:** Located next to the Hilton Hotel, the four floors are filled with jewelry, tailor, antique, electronic, and souvenir shops. Look for Asian Jewellery and House of Hung for nice jewelry pieces; Borobudur Arts and Crafts for Balinese, Javanese, and Sumatran carvings and souvenirs; and China Crafts and Kwok Gallery for good quality arts and antiques.

- **Liang Court:** A small shopping center across the street from the Far East Shopping Centre. Includes the Daimaru Department Store and other upscale shops. Popular shopping center for Japanese expatriates.

- **Delfi:** On the north side of Orchard Road, this small shopping center includes Japanese fashions, boutiques, kitchenwares, jewelry stores, and crafts. Includes department stores and a large golf shop. Popular shopping stop for Japanese tourists.

- **Orchard Towers:** Next to Delfi, this large shopping center includes several shops selling antiques, curios, jewelry, fabrics, ready-made clothes, and food. You will find such quality shops as **Larry Jewelry**, one of Singapore's best jewelers.

- **Shaw Centre:** Just off Orchard Road on the west side of Scotts Road. A good place for Chinese rosewood furniture, clothes, jewelry, lamps, and curios.

- **Far East Plaza:** On the east side of Scotts Road, between the Goodwood Park and Hyatt hotels. A very crowded center with over 800 shops selling a wide assortment of average quality goods, especially clothes, footwear, records, cassettes, sound equipment, electronic goods, and computerware. Includes many fast-food restaurants. A favorite place for young people and bargain-seekers.

- **Scotts:** On the east side of Scotts Road between the Hyatt and Dynasty Hotels. A good quality shopping center with nice boutiques, camera shops, sound equipment stores, and a Metro department store which houses the **Studio,** Singapore's showcase for local fashion designers.

- **Lucky Plaza:** On the north side of Orchard Road next to the Dynasty Hotel and Tangs department store. Filled with tourist shops selling cameras, sound equipment, stereos, radios, clothes, jewelry, watches, carpets, and all types of curios. Includes a Metro department store. Once a good place to bargain for goods as well as get a bargain in the process, this shopping center has declined recently and tends to be overrun by touts and *"Hey, you mister"* shops. Be careful in buying cameras and electronic goods here. Very crowded and noisy. Some of the best shops found here are **Larry Jewelry** and **China Silk House.**

- **Wisma Atria:** Across the street from Lucky

Plaza, this is another one of Singapore's newest shopping centers. Anchored by Isetan Department Store, Wisma Atria includes five floors of good quality shops selling clothes, sporting goods, jewelry, leather, souvenirs, toys, cameras, and electronic goods. A pleasant area to both shop and eat. Some of Singapore's best boutiques, jewelry stores, and home decorating shops are found here: **Je T'aime** for jewelry; **Designer Labels, Mayeelok** and **Tin T** for fashion clothes; and **Legaspi, Kashmir Carpet House,** and **Ming House** for arts, crafts, and home decorative items.

- **The Promenade:** Just a two-minute walk east of Lucky Plaza. This is one of Singapore's most elegant shopping centers. Go here if you want top quality. Great place for designer clothes, beautiful home furnishings, Asian arts and crafts, paintings, antiques, and jewelry. Look for **Jessica, Tyan, Man & His Woman, Franc, Ayers Design, Apricot Design, Matsudu, Art Forum,** and **Hiro Jewelry.**

- **Paragon Shopping Centre:** One of Singapore's newest upscale shopping centers located next to The Promenade. Numerous exclusive shops offer jewelry, handicrafts, optical goods, fabrics, sportswear, designer clothes, leather goods, and more. Includes a Metro department store on the top floor.

- **Centrepoint:** A five-minute walk east of The Promenade. Home of **Robinson's** department store as well as numerous shops offering arts and crafts, clothes, carpets, jewelry, silverware, Korean chests, and Filipino bamboo furniture. Includes several trendy fashion boutiques and upscale shops. Look for **China Silk House** for nice fabrics and stylish clothes; **Da-Ching** for Korean chests and home decorative items; **Art Focus** for local paintings and poster art; and **Tabriz** and **Qureshi's** for Oriental carpets. Centrepoint also has branches of Singapore's two largest bookstores -- **Times** and **MPH.**

- **Cuppage Terrace and Centre:** Located directly behind Centrepoint. Filled with food stalls and two good antique shops: **Babazar** and **Petnic's**. Babazar has one of Singapore's finest collections of arts and crafts from South and Southeast Asian countries. If you are looking for home decorative items, antiques, jewelry, and clothes from India, Indonesia, Thailand, and Burma -- especially textiles, furniture, tribal carvings, rugs, pillow covers, carved panels, Burmese orchestra stands, and lacquer containers--Babazar is a wonderful shopping experience. You will also also find a nice art gallery on the top floor of Cuppage Terrace offering good quality oils and watercolors -- **Della Butcher Gallery.**

- **Orchard Point** and **Orchard Plaza:** Across the street from Cuppage Centre and Terrace, on the corner of Orchard and Cuppage roads. This is Singapore's center for art galleries. Go to the fourth level where you will find the paintings of Singapore's best artists in several excellent galleries: **Central Arts Place, Sin Hua Gallery, Kua Fong Gallery, Orchard Gallery,** and **Liufa Gallery.** On the lower level look for **The Thai Room** for silk, arts, and crafts, and the **Malaysia Reptile Shop** for crocodile leather items. The other levels have clothes, tailor, art, craft, electronic, and jewelry shops.

- **Specialists' Shopping Centre:** Across the street from Orchard Point and Orchard Plaza. Includes good quality boutiques, hobby craft shops, and the **John Little** department store.

- **Plaza Singapura:** Located east of the Meridian Hotel at the corner of Orchard Road and Oldham Lane. Contains a Japanese department store and several specialty shops offering clothes, leather goods, electronics, handicrafts, and home furnishings. Popular shopping center for locals.

- **Raffles City Complex:** Located across the street from the historic Raffles Hotel on Bras Basah Road, North Bridge Road, and Beach

Road, this is one of Singapore's largest and most ambitious hotel, office, and shopping complexes. Includes the Westin Plaza Hotel and the 73-story Westin Stamford Hotel -- the tallest hotel in the world. The shopping complex consists of three floors anchored by the Sogo department store. Includes some excellent arts, crafts, jewelry, and clothing stores. Look for **Larry Jewelry** and **Chap Mai Jewelry** for good quality jewelry; **Selangor Pewter, Gifts & Souvenirs, Chinese Embroidery House,** and **Elsee's Place** for souvenirs; **Chinese Cloisonne Ware** and **Centuries Arts & Crafts** for Chinese handcrafted items; and **The Collector's Gallery** for paintings by local artists. **Ed Kwan,** in the adjacent Westin Stamford Hotel shopping area, is one of the best tailors in Singapore.

- **Marina Square:** Located at the end of Stamford Road, one block from the Raffles Hotel and the Raffles City Complex. Consists of three deluxe hotels -- The Oriental, Marina Mandarin, and Pan Pacific -- joined together by a large shopping arcade with over 250 specialty shops. A mixed shopping area of average to excellent shops. Filled with trendy boutiques, footwear, tailor, home furnishing, handicraft, souvenir, antique, music, jewelry, and book stores. Unlike other shopping centers, this one is laid out as an indoor pedestrian mall complete with street signs and benches. Anchored by the **Metro** and **Tokyu** department stores, you will find several nice shops in this shopping center: **China Silk House** for excellent quality silk fabrics; **Minh Anh** for nicely designed jewelry; **B. P. De Silva** for excellent quality jewelry, silver, and pearls; **Guenter Lienau** for batik paintings; and **Bonia** for Italian leather bags and shoes. For one of the most uniquely designed and disorienting bookstores in the world, stop at **Page 1** on the third level. You will find a **Times** bookstore and a McDonalds, Ponderosa, and Kentucky Fried Chicken in this shopping arcade. You will also find some very nice shops in the adjacent Marina Mandarin Hotel Shopping Arcade.

Outside the Tanglin-Orchard-Scotts Roads area, you will find a few other shopping centers, such as the **Golden Landmark** next to Arab Street and **Liang Court** on River Valley Road. Some of the most popular shopping centers are **People's Park Complex** and **People's Park Centre**, both along Eu Tong Sen Street adjacent to New Bridge Road in Chinatown, and the **Holland Road Shopping Centre** in Holland Village.

The **People's Park Complex** and **People's Park Centre** shopping centers in Chinatown are packed with all types of clothes, electronic goods, computerware, footware, luggage, appliances, textiles, and jewelry. Both shopping centers are popular with locals as well as tourists.

At the other end (west) of the city proper -- up Orchard and Tanglin roads and along Holland Road -- are two popular expatriate shopping areas: **Holland Road Shopping Centre** and **Cold Storage Jelita**. While off the normal beaten tourist path, these shopping areas are favorites of many expatriates with good taste. Both areas are well worth visiting, especially if you are looking for furniture or home decorating items. Best of all, there are no tourist crowds in these areas!

Shops in the **Holland Road Shopping Centre** and along adjacent **Lorong Mambong Street** offer a good selection of arts, antiques, and home furnishings. Within Holland Road Shopping Centre, visit **Lim's Arts & Crafts, E&E Antiques, The Pagoda House, Visual Dharma,** and **Jessica.** Along nearby Lorong Mambong Street, we recommend stopping at **Classic Antique House, Avant Garde Design, Excel Caneware,** and **Holland Village Gallery.**

Cold Storage Jelita is the name given to a small neighborhood shopping center just down the road from Holland Road Shopping Centre. It has two very nice shops -- **Renee Hoy Fine Arts** and **Jessica** -- offering excellent quality arts, antiques, and home furnishings. We highly recommend Renee Hoy Fine Arts for arts, antiques, and home decorative items. Renee Hoy offers quality goods and excellent service as well as reliable packing and shipping. Jessica has a good selection of Korean chests and Chinese cabinets.

You will also find several shopping complexes along the **East Coast** which primarily cater to locals. Time permitting, you may want to explore by car the **Geyland** and **Katong** areas. Geyland is primarily a Malay community; Katong is occupied by the Paranakan (Straits Chinese) community. The largest and most popular shopping centers in these areas are the **City Plaza, Lion City Hotel and Shopping Complex, Tanjong Katong Complex,**

Roxy Centre, Katong Shopping Centre, Marine Parade, and Parkway Parade.

Hotel Shopping Arcades

Most major hotels will have a small to medium-sized shopping arcade located on the bottom floor or in a separate attached building. The quality of shops in these arcades is often excellent to outstanding. They offer everything from top European and Japanese designer clothes to local antiques and handicrafts. Singapore's best hotel shopping arcade is the **Me Shopping Gallery** in the Hilton Hotel on Orchard Road. Here, you will find several exquisite fashion and accessory shops: **Daks, Gianfranco Ferre, Fendi, Jaeger, Gottex, Lanvin, Ad Hoc, L'ultimo, Singora, Maud Frizon, Georgio Armani, A. Testoni, Valentino, Alfred Dunhill, Loewe, Davidoff Boutique, Gucci,** and **Louis Vuitton.**

The **Mandarin Hotel Shopping Arcade** at the Mandarin Hotel on Orchard Road also has numerous quality shops. It is filled with designer boutiques and small shops selling a large variety of arts, crafts, carpets, curios, clothes, and footwear. Look for **Pierre Jewellery, Piaget, Borbonese, Miss Ming, Club 21, Sonia Rykiel, Djien Boutique, Moda Italiana, Casa Moda, Shah Abas Carpets & Arts, Sin Kee Arts & Crafts, Irving Mall Jewellery, Leather Trends, Royal Pewter House, Prestige Jewellery, La Donna,** and **A. Testoni.** For unique silver and porcelain work, visit **George Jensen.** For excellent quality Chinese paintings, ceramics, and antique Buddhas, visit the **Mandarin Galleries.**

The **Pavilion Inter-Continental Hotel,** just off Tanglin Road and next to the Singapore Handicraft Centre, also has a few nice shops in its shopping arcade. You will find **Hermes, Dunhill, Pierre Balmain, A. Testoni,** and **Mikimoto** here.

Many of the other hotels, such as the **Hyatt Regency** and the **Dynasty,** have small shopping arcades with nice shops. The **Westin Stamford Hotel** and **Westin Plaza Hotel** -- both located in the new Raffles City convention center -- have small shopping arcades. You should visit **Raffles City** as well as the new hotel-shopping-recreation complex across the street -- **Marina Square.**

Within the **Marina Mandarin Hotel Shopping Arcade,** stop at **Primrose** for beautiful fabrics, rugs, and baskets for interior decorating; their dhurries from India are exquisite, and most items in this shop are color-coordinated for discerning shoppers. Stop at **Palco Antiques** for ceramics, tapestries, Buddhas, and instruments from China,

Tibet, Thailand, and Burma; **New Peking** for arts and souvenirs; **Chen Lee** for semi-precious stones and jewelry; **Crystal Tera** for an interesting collection of European crystal and porcelain; **Le Choix** for the latest in Parisian fashion; and **Avante** for designer-label (Cartier, Charles Jourdan, Yves St. Laurent, Polo Ralph Lauren) bags and purses.

Department Stores

Most of the major department stores are concentrated in and around the Tanglin-Orchard-Scotts roads area. All of these stores are air-conditioned, and most are found within the shopping centers. They offer a wide selection of goods from all over the world: cosmetics, jewelry, clothes, accessories, furniture, appliances, household items, toys, records, cassettes, radios, and televisions. The quality of goods available varies from one department store to another. Some are crowded and congested, offering inexpensive clothes and electronic goods for young people, whereas others offer upscale products for more discerning shoppers.

The department stores have different ownerships which, in turn, have different product orientations. Locally owned department stores, such as **Metro, Metro Grand, Tangs,** and **Klasse,** offer excellent quality products produced in Singapore-- especially locally designed and produced fashion clothes. The Japanese are well represented with their **Isetan, Daimaru, Yaohan, Le Classique, Sogo, Tokyu,** and **Mitsukoski** department stores. These stores are well stocked with Japanese goods. The English have **Robinson's,** and the French have **Galeries Lafayette**--both offering excellent quality products.

The major department stores in the Tanglin-Orchard-Scotts Roads area include the following:

DEPARTMENT STORES

- **Isetan:** Liat Towers and Wisma Atria on Orchard Road. Good selections. Popular with tourists and locals alike.

- **Klasse:** Lucky Plaza and Centrepoint. Good buys on imported Chinese goods. Another Klasse branch, called **Yuyi,** is located across the street from the Mandarin Hotel.

- **John Little's:** Specialists' Shopping Centre on Orchard Road.

- **Le Classique:** Tanglin Road across the street from Tanglin Shopping Centre. Stocks designer-label clothes. Bus loads of Japanese tourists are brought here to shop. Also has a branch shop in the Goodwood Park Hotel on Scotts Road.

- **Meitetsu:** Delfi on Orchard Road.

- **Metro Far East:** Far East Shopping Centre on Scotts Road. Excellent quality locally designed fashions appropriate for Western tastes.

- **Galeries Lafayette:** Next to the Hilton Hotel and the Far East Shopping Centre. An upscale department store offering excellent quality clothes with such designer labels as Christian Dior, Nina Ricci, Hermes, Givenchy, Charles Jourdan, Ungaro, and Porsche Design.

- **Metro Grand:** Lucky Plaza on Orchard Road, Scotts Shopping Centre on Scotts Road, and the Marina Square shopping arcade.

- **Sogo:** Raffles City Shopping Centre at Stamford, North Bridge, Bras Basah, and Beach roads.

- **Tokyu:** Marina Square shopping arcade.

- **Metro Orchard:** Holiday Inn Building on Scotts Road.

- **OG Elite:** Plaza Singapura on Orchard Road

- **OG Orchard:** Orchard Road.

- **Printemps:** Hotel Meridien on Orchard Road.

- **Robinson's:** Centrepoint and Specialists' Shopping Centre on Orchard Road.

- **Tangs:** Orchard Road.

- **Yaohan:** Plaza Singapura on Orchard Road.

You will also find department stores in other areas of the city. Many are branches of stores found along Tanglin-Orchard-Scotts roads. The major ones include:

- **Cortina:** Colombo Court on North Bridge Road.

- **Daimaru:** Liang Court, River Valley Road.

- **Galeries Lafayette:** Goldhill Square on Thomson Road.

- **Isetan:** Apollo Hotel on Havelock Road and Parkway Parade.

- **Klasse:** Peninsula Plaza on Coleman Street.

- **Le Classique:** York Hotel.

- **Metro Supreme:** Supreme House on Penang Road.

- **OG People's Park:** Upper Cross Street.

- **Robinson's:** Clifford Centre at Collyer Quay.

- **Tashing:** People's Park Complex on New Bridge Road.

- **Yaohan:** Bukit Timah Plaza at Jalan Anak Bukit; Yuan Ching Road in Jurong; Parkway Parade; Thomson Plaza on Upper Thomson Road; Amber Close in Katong.

Emporiums

Emporiums in Singapore are structured similarly to department stores. The Chinese emporiums are basically department stores offering imported goods from China, such as inexpensive clothes, silks, and brocades. Other emporiums offer a cross-section of goods from all over Asia.

The **Chinese Emporium** is located in the International Building on Orchard Road. An **Oriental Emporium** is located in People's Park Center and an **Overseas Emporium** is found in the People's Park Complex -- both near each other along New Bridge Road in Chinatown. Other emporiums are found in **Katong** (City Plaza on Tanjong Katong and Joo Chiat Complex on Joo Chiat Road) and **Holland Village** (Holland Road Shopping Centre) as well as on **Balestier Road** (Shaw Plaza), **Mountbatten Road** (Katong Shopping Centre), **Queensway/Alexandra Road** (Queensway Shopping Centre), **Rochor Road** (Rochor Centre), **Bukit Timah Road** (Buket Timah Plaza), **Kitchener Road** (President Emporium in the Hotel Merlin), and **Commonwealth Avenue** (Tah Chung Emporium).

Markets

The traditional open-air markets which sell inexpensive goods have all but faded from Singapore. Most of the remaining markets are the traditional neighborhood "wet" markets primarily selling meats, vegetables, and fruits. Other than the cultural experience, these markets offer little of interest to international shoppers.

Most of the street bazaars have moved indoors or disappeared altogether. However, many of the traditional shops in Chinatown, Little India, and Arab Street have a bazaar-quality about them. Many of these shops spill over onto the sidewalks, and in certain areas you still find street peddlers displaying their goods on the sidewalk. You can still get a glimpse of such markets by visiting the old **Thieves' Market** area on Sungei Road, the **Kreta Ayer** complex in Chinatown, the street peddlers along Temple Street in Chinatown, and the **Singapore Handicraft Centre** on Wednesday, Friday, Saturday, and Sunday evenings.

SHOPPING RIGHT, SHOPPING WELL

Your shopping in Singapore should go well as long as you observe certain basic shopping rules.

SINGAPORE SHOPPING RULES
---

1. **Avoid touts.** You will occasionally encounter individuals on the street who want to show you where to shop, especially around Orchard Towers and the Far East Shopping Centre. While it is illegal for them to solicit in this manner, it still goes on. Avoid these people. They will take you to a shop that gives them a commission which, in turn, is added to your tab!

2. **Bargain where appropriate.** The Singapore

Tourist Promotion Board is campaigning a-
gainst the bargaining culture. In the meantime, bargaining remains alive and well in
Singapore. While you can not bargain in the
fixed-price department stores, you can
bargain in most other places. Expect jewelry
stores, for example, to give substantial discounts off the marked prices. Discounts on
other items should average 20 to 30 percent
with some as much as 40 to 50 percent.
Even stores you may think will not give you
a discount often do if you just ask *"Do you
give a discount?"* This question may result
in a 10 percent discount.

3. **Compare prices.** In addition to doing your
comparative pricing research at home prior to
arriving in Singapore, the many shops in
Singapore also offer numerous opportunities
to compare prices on similar items. Shops
tend to be competitive and are willing to
bargain to get your business. A good starting point is to visit the fixed-price department stores to get an overview of Singapore's
products and prices. Keep in mind that the
shops along Orchard Road pay the highest
rents in all of Singapore and thus they must
add this overhead cost to their prices. You
can often do better on prices in shops elsewhere here in Singapore, but those shops
may not have the same quality of goods as
those found along Orchard Road. Less is not
always better.

4. **Ask for receipts.** All shops are supposed to
give receipts. However, in many cases you
will have to ask for one. Always collect
receipts to deal with both Customs officials
and any potential problems you may have
with your purchase. Consider using your
credit card to purchase big ticket items which
might later pose problems due to misrepresentation.

5. **Get international guarantees.** When buying
electronic goods, check to see if the item
works properly and is covered under an international guarantee. The warranty card should
be included with the item. If it does not

come with such a guarantee, you will be taking a chance.

6. **Report any problems to the Singapore Tourist Promotion Board.** The STPB is committed to promoting Singapore as a reputable place to shop. Should you have a problem with a merchant, register your complaint with the STPB: 131 Tudor Court, Tanglin Road, Singapore, 1024, Tel. 2356611; or Raffles City Tower #37-00, 250 North Bridge Road, Singapore 0617, Tel. 3396622 or Telex STBSIN RS 33375.

SHIPPING

You should have no problem shipping your goods from Singapore as long as you shop in reliable shops. Shops catering to international shoppers are experienced in packing and shipping purchases abroad. Most will use good packing materials -- bubble-wrap is widely used -- and take care of all shipping arrangements. Make sure you have a receipt for your shipment in case you later have a problem in receiving it.

Keep in mind that you only need to make one shipment from Singapore since most shops will consolidate all of your purchases into a single shipment -- but only if you ask them to do so. Most major hotels also can assist you in making contact with reliable local shippers who will consolidate your shipments. Make sure you fully insure the shipment against both loss and breakage as well as get paperwork that indicates the goods to be shipped in case you later have a problem in receiving it.

ENJOYING YOUR STAY

There is much more to Singapore than just shopping. As a totally integrated travel experience, Singapore offers a wonderful array of sightseeing, recreational, entertainment, and gastronomic opportunities. Most of these you can easily do on your own or you can join regularly scheduled tour groups.

As a walking city, you can see most of the interesting sights by taking walks into special areas of the city. The Singapore Tourist Promotion Board publishes a useful booklet which enables you to conduct your own one to three hour walks in different areas of the city -- *Singapore Tour It Yourself*. The maps and accompanying descriptive information will take you to numerous historical sights, peoples, and shops.

SINGAPORE'S ADDED ATTRACTIONS

- **Arab Street District:** Includes the Sultan Mosque along with residences and shops.

- **Botanic Gardens:** A beautiful park with 2,500 plants of 250 different hybrids and species located along Napier and Cluny roads near Orchard Road.

- **Chinatown Streetwalk:** Includes temples, shrines, noted buildings shops, architecture, and special streets.

- **Colonial Heart Streetwalk:** Covers the General Post Office, Empress Place, Victoria Theatre, Victoria Memorial Hall, Sir Stamford Raffles Landing Site, Parliament House, Supreme Court, City Hall, St. Andrew's Cathedral, Armenian Church of St. Gregory the Iluminator, and Fort Canning Park.

- **Little India Streetwalk:** Puts you in Hindu and Buddhist temples, mosques, Parrer Park, and special streets.

- **Sentosa -- Singapore's Resort Island:** Take a ferry or cable car to this pleasant recreational island. Visit the Wax Museum, Fort Siloso, Maritime Museum, Coralarium, World Insectarium, Rare Stone Museum.

- **Singapore Zoological Gardens:** Over 1,600 animals representing 170 species on display in 60 exhibits.

- **Change Alley:** Collyer Quay. Takes you through this world famous alleyway as well as the nearby aerial Change Alley of money-changers and bazaar vendors.

- **Changi:** This East Coast visit includes the famous POW Changi Prison, Changi Village shopping area, Changi Point, Changi Beach, and Somapah Road.

- **Harbor Cruises:** Chinese junks depart from Clifford Pier every afternoon at 3pm and 4pm for 2 1/2 hour cruises. Twilight cruises take 3 hours and depart at 6pm.

Other self-guided walking tours include Mount Faber, National Museum and Art Gallery, Pernankan Place, Raffles Hotel, and Singapore Science Centre. At night you can attend cultural shows at the Hyatt Regency, Mandarin Hotel, and Raffles Hotel; take a 3-hour dinner cruise; visit Merlion Park; poke through the Night Markets (*pasar malam*) at the Singapore Handicraft Center on Wednesday, Friday, Saturday, and Sunday evenings and on Sentosa Island on Friday, Saturday, and Sunday evenings; take a trishaw tour of Little India and Chinatown; or enjoy performances at Victoria Concert Hall and Victoria Theatre (Empress Place). Outside the city proper you will find many additional attractions such as temples, mosques, churches, a crocodile farm, war memorials, gardens, and reservoirs.

Many tour companies offer relatively inexpensive, convenient, and comfortable half-day to three-day **tours** of Singapore and parts of nearby Malaysia. One of the first tours you may want to join is the "City Tour." This three to four hour tour will give you an excellent overview of all the major parts of Singapore. Most tour companies include Orchard Road, Raffles Place, Chinatown, Little India, Arab Street, Change Alley, Shenton Way, Mt. Faber, Botanic Gardens, Raffles Hotel, and several historical sites on their City Tour. Other tours take you to the zoo, harbor, selected night spots, Sentosa Island, and other sights around Singapore Island. The tour companies also regularly schedule one to two-day trips to the historical city of Malacca on Malaysia's East Coast, Kuala Lumpur, plantations in Malaysia, Desaru (Malaysia's beach playground in the southeast), and Kukup (plantations and unique fishing village in southwestern Malaysia). Other tours can be arranged to the many tourist destinations in Malaysia.

One of the great treats in Singapore is the **food**. You can easily spend most of your free shopping time just feasting on the fabulous food you see everywhere. Try some of the many Chinese, Japanese, Indian, Muslim, Malay, Indonesian, Thai, Nonya, Continental, French, Swiss, Italian, Mexican, and American restaurants found in this city. Some of Singapore's best ethnic restaurants include **Azizah's** (36 Emerald Hill Road, Tel. 235-1130) for Malay cuisine; **The Banana Leaf Apolo** (56-58 Race Course Road, Tel. 293-8682) and the **Tandoor Restaurant** in the Holiday Inn Parkview (Cuppage and Cavenagh roads, Tel. 733-8333) for Indian cuisine; the **Jurong Seafood Restaurant** (35 Jurong Pier Road, Tel. 265-3525) for Singapore seafood; **Bibi's Restaurant** (Peranakan Place Complex, Orchard Road, Tel. 732-6966) for Nonya food as well as a cultural show in the evening; and **Newton Circus** and **Satay Club** for hawker food. Many visitors also enjoy the food stalls at the **Singapore Handicraft Centre**.

If you would like a beautiful and romantic view of the city at night, we highly recommend the **Compass Rose** (Tel. 338-8585) on the 70th floor of the Westin Stamford Hotel, Raffles City; make reservations at least a day ahead for this elegant and popular Continental restaurant. The Mandarin Hotel's revolving restaurant -- **Top of the M** -- also affords a good view of the city. The **Harbour Grill** in the Hilton International Hotel serves excellent Continental cuisine, and **Hugo's** in the Hyatt Regency serves dinner only in an elegant setting. The colonial Tiffin curry lunch at the **Tiffin Room** in the Raffles Hotel will give you a sense of what the old days were like in this famous colonial hotel. The many breakfast and luncheon buffets served in hotel restaurants are a real treat. The **Belvedere** in the Mandarin Hotel still gets high marks for serving one of the best luncheon buffets in Singapore.

If you are into **sports**, Singapore can keep you happily occupied. You can relax on the beaches, attend cricket and soccer matches, observe horse races and rugby, play golf and tennis, swim, bicycle, jog, horseback ride, snorkel, waterski, windsurf, fly, or play squash.

Singapore's entertaining **nightlife** includes discos, music clubs, pubs and beer gardens, bars, cocktail lounges, Chinese opera, cultural shows, music, dance, drama, and theater. However, after a full day of intense shopping and sightseeing, you may just want to go to bed!

Singapore offers wonderful shopping opportunities, but it is also a place to relax, pamper yourself, gain a few pounds, and enjoy a bit of Southeast Asian society and culture. A truly international city, Singapore puts you in touch with the rest of the world without having to go through the pain of exploring so many different countries. In Singapore, shopping is one big smorgasboard of learning and buying opportunities. Spend four days here, and you will not be disappointed. Spend a week in Singapore, and you may be ready to move on to even more exotic shopping places, where you will undoubtedly reminisce fondly about Singapore's shopping convenience and comfort -- and its remarkable cleanliness and orderliness!

PART III

SECRETS OF EXOTIC MALAYSIA

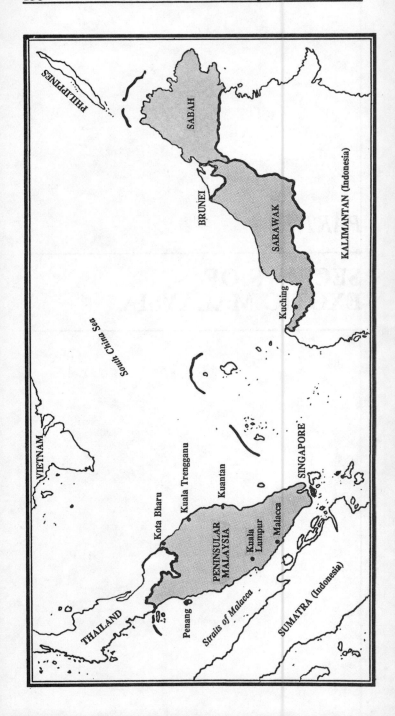

Chapter Seven

WELCOME TO MALAYSIA

Malaysia is another one of Asia's delightful surprises. A lush tropical country with beautiful beaches, idyllic islands, cool mountains, challenging jungles, and an interesting and diverse population, Malaysia is a relatively modern country offering numerous shopping opportunities for those primarily interested in handicrafts, textiles, artifacts, and art.

SURPRISING MALAYSIA

Malaysia is one of the least known Asian countries for travel and shopping. But first-time visitors are often surprised with what they find: the beautiful architecture of Kuala Lumpur; modern cities offering first-class amenities for travelers; cleanliness and orderliness; colorful and friendly peoples; excellent food, accommodations, transportation, and communication; and plenty of sightseeing and recreational activities. Best of all, it offers many good shopping opportunities.

Unlike urban Singapore, Malaysia is a much more diverse travel and shopping experience. Singapore has its fabulous shopping centers, restaurants, parks, and recreational activities, but Malaysia also has beaches, mountains, and jungles. In Malaysia you can "shop 'til you drop" on one day and be on a jungle or river safari the next. Our advice: go to Singapore to enjoy an urban travel and shopping experience, but go to Malaysia to experience a broader and more adventuresome range of travel and shopping experiences. While you should enjoy visiting Singapore, you will probably love traveling and shopping in **both** Singapore and Malaysia. To visit Singapore without going on to Kuala Lumpur, Malacca, Penang, or Kuching would be to miss out on some of the most interesting and surprising travel and shopping in Asia.

GETTING TO KNOW YOU

Malaysia is not another Singapore, although in many respects its cities have the feel and look of Singapore. Kuala Lumpur is a surprisingly modern and cosmopolitan city which has retained much of its old architecture as well as introduced new architectural forms reflecting its Islamic heritage. Singapore's architecture may be impressively modern and Western, but it reflects few ties with its past. The predominately Chinese cities of Penang and Malacca remind one of Singapore's ethnic enclaves of Chinatown, Arab Street, and Little India.

But the comparisons with Singapore end with the architecture and character of only a few Malaysian cities that are predominately Chinese. The majority of Malaysia's population is Malay and Muslim, and most of the country is rural in character. Here you will discover very different cultures from what you observed in highly westernized Singapore. Leave the big cities where the Chinese dominate local economic activity and you will discover another Malaysia that is both traditional and modern. Malay Muslims tend to be very religious and conservative in their dress and behaviors, especially as one travels to the more traditional communities along the East Coast.

We highly recommend Malaysia for several reasons. First, this is a relatively **easy country** to visit. In most areas you will be visiting -- cities and towns -- the people speak English, communities are clean and orderly, and you will find excellent hotels, restaurants, transportation, travel services, and shopping centers to make this a very convenient and comfortable place to visit.

Second, Malaysia is both an **exotic and interesting** place to visit. In Malaysia you observe a kaleidiscope of colorful cultures which are practiced side by side. Discover a beautiful Muslim mosque and it is likely to be just

down the street from an ornate Hindu temple, awe-inspir-
ing Buddhist and Taoist temples, and Catholic and Protes-
tant churches. Colorful festivals and celebrations are
continuously going on amongst the Malay, Chinese, and
Indian communities -- festivals related to each community's
religious practices as well as national celebrations that tie
all three communities together into a nation of diverse
peoples. At the same time, the Malaysian landscape includes gorgeous beaches, islands, mountains, and jungles.

Third, Malaysia is a country of **varied landscape and
travel opportunities.** Here you will discover gorgeous
beaches, islands, mountains, and jungles. You can spend
much of your time soaking up the sun on the East Coast's
numerous beaches, scuba diving in some of the world's
best waters, exploring mountain resorts, or venturing into
the wilds of Peninsula Malaysia's as well as Borneo's
interior where you will discover interesting flora, fauna,
and tribesmen.

Fourth, Malaysia is a **country of talented craftspeople**
who produce a dazzling array of handcrafted items, from
textiles and woodcarvings to jewelry and brassware. When
you visit Malaysia you will also have an opportunity to see
new and unusual products of importance to the local culture, visit factories where you can observe craftspeople at
work, and see products being used in ceremonies and
festivals. You may learn to appreciate both the production
and use of items you are likely to purchase. As such,
shopping in this manner in Malaysia has much more meaning than shopping in stores that display products that have
already passed through the hands of two or three middlemen. In Malaysia you will learn about your purchases.
Indeed, they may well become some of your most prized
possessions because each will have a unique story relating
to your broader travel and learning experiences in Malaysia.

Fifth, Malaysia is an **inexpensive** country to visit, moreso than Singapore. Food, hotels, and transportation are
some of the least expensive in the world. Indeed, Kuala
Lumpur ranks as one of the world's 10 cheapest cities.
Even first-class and deluxe hotels are inexpensive by world
standards. If you want to go first-class and pamper yourself without spending a fortune, Malaysia is a great place
to splurge. You will get top value for your dollar.

Sixth, Malaysia is a country of **surprising and fun
shopping.** Discover its shopping centers, department
stores, shophouses, markets, and factories and you will
come alway with many interesting shopping stories and
products to enhance your wardrobe and home decor. And
just when you think you have covered most of Malaysia's

shopping delights from a journey through the cities and towns of Peninsular Malaysia, you go to East Malaysia where you uncover a whole new world of shopping in Kuching, Sarawak.

LOCATION AND GEOGRAPHY

Joined to Singapore by a causeway and to Thailand by a jungle border, Malaysia is Singapore's closest northern and Thailand's closest southern neighbor. Consisting of Peninsula Malaysia with 11 states and East Malaysia on the island of Borneo with two states, Malaysia is both a highly urbanized and rural country. The West Coast of Peninsula Malaysia is the country's industrial center. Here such cities as Penang, Butterworth, Ipoh, and Kuala Lumpur set the development pace for the country. The East Coast is a relatively underdeveloped area of jungles, Malay villages, small towns, tourist resorts, and oil fields. East Malaysia, consisting of the states of Sabah and Sarawak, is Malaysia's frontier of small river towns, inpenetrable jungle, and fascinating tribal peoples who primarily live in the interior of this vast country.

POPULATION

Malaysia is a multi-racial country with a population of nearly 18 million. The three major communities -- Malays (54%), Chinese (34%), and Indian (10%) -- coexist in relative, although sometimes strained, harmony along with such minorities as Arabs, Eurasians, Singhalese, and Europeans as well as Aboriginals (*orang asli*) in the jungles of Peninsular Malaysia and the tribal Iban, Bidayuh, Melanau, Kenyah, Kayan, Bisayah, Kadazan, Murut, Kelabit, and Kedayan in Sarawak and Sabah.

CLIMATE, SEASONS AND WHEN TO GO

The climate in Malaysia is decidedly tropical. The weather is generally hot and humid in the lowlands and along the coast areas, and relatively mild and often cool in the highlands. The weather will vary considerably from one part of the country to another. For example, the East Coast, Sabah, and Sarawak experience a monsoon season from November to January when it sometimes constantly rains day and night. Other parts of the country experience a rainy season during these months, but the rains tend to be intermittent. The overall best time to visit Malaysia is during the months of February to October. However, other months can also be pleasant depending on where you plan to travel.

GETTING THERE

You can get to Malaysia by air, train, car, or boat. Most visitors, however, arrive by plane. Several major airlines service Malaysia. However, most direct flights from North America and Europe first stop in Bangkok or Singapore before proceeding on to Penang or Kuala Lumpur. The national carrier -- Malaysian Air System -- does have direct flights from North America and Europe to Kuala Lumpur.

You can take a train or drive from Singapore and Thailand into Malaysia. Several shipping companies also stop in Malaysia's major ports.

DOCUMENTS

Most visitors to Malaysia only need to arrive with their passport. Citizens from Commonwealth countries, Ireland, Switzerland, the Netherlands, and Liechtenstein do not need visas. Citizens from the U.S., West Germany, Italy, France, Norway, Sweden, Denmark, Belgium, Finland, Luxembourg, and Iceland do not need visas for stays of up to three months. Citizens from other countries will need visas. When you arrive in Malaysia, Immigration will give you permission to stay for 30 days. If you are arriving from an area infected with yellow fever, you will need a health certificate indicating that you have the appropriate vaccination.

There is one exception to these visa rules. Visitors entering Sarawak from Peninsular Malaysia must pass through Immigration a second time. Upon arrival in Sarawak you are granted a special 14-day visa which is also valid in Peninsular Malaysia and Sabah. However, visas issued in Peninsular Malaysia and Sabah are not valid in Sarawak.

ARRIVAL AND DEPARTURE

Given Malaysia's multiple arrival points, each city or border crossing will be a different arrival experience. If you arrive and depart by air, you will find relatively modern airports which also tend to be very crowded and confusing at times. Most major airports offer a full range of services, from duty-free shops to hotel, transportation, and tour service desks to assist you with local arrangements upon arrival.

CUSTOMS, IMMIGRATION, AND EXPORTING ANTIQUES

Malaysian Customs and Immigration are relatively efficient -- they dispense with lines very quickly. Unless you look like a suspicious drug user or dealer, you should be able to complete Customs and Immigration within minutes. Like Singapore, Malaysia has stiff penalities for those found with drugs. Most drug dealers are executed regardless of their nationality.

You can bring into Malaysia the usual international allotment of duty-free liquor and tobacco -- one quart of liquor and 250 grams of tobacco or cigars, or 200 cigarettes.

You will see signs in many airport arrival halls telling you to register with Customs any antiques you may be bringing into the country -- so that you won't risk running into trouble when you try to leave Malaysia with them. If you buy antiques in Malaysia, you will need an export licence for all antiques dating prior to 1850.

CURRENCY AND CREDIT CARDS

The Malaysian dollar, the ringgit, is equal to US$.39 or M$2.60 is equal to US$1. Recent devaluations of the Malaysian dollar mean you will have more purchasing power in Malaysia than in Singapore. Travelers checks and credit cards are widely accepted in the major cities throughout Malaysia. The best places to exchange money are with banks and licensed money-changers.

SECURITY

Malaysia is a relatively safe country in which to travel as long as you take the normal precautions for your safety and your valuables. Law and order is well managed in most parts of Malaysia. However, we do not recommend wandering off on the high seas or into the highlands and jungles on your own.

TIPPING

Malaysia follows the same practice as Singapore on tipping -- it is not expected nor is it a normal practice. Hotels and major restaurants will add a 10% service charge to your bill as well as local taxes. Taxis and tour guides do not expect to receive tips. However, tips are accepted and money does talk if you need some special assistance.

DRESS

While you should plan to wear light weight natural fibre garments and comfortable walking shoes, you should also dress in an acceptable fashion. Casual clothes are very acceptable, but anything that shows too much skin, such as low-cut blouses, T-shirts, and shorts, can be offensive to the more conservative elements in Malaysia's Muslim society. Especially when traveling on the East Coast, be very modest in how you dress.

LANGUAGE

Several different Chinese and Indian dialects are spoken in Malaysia. While Bahasa Malay is the official language, English is widely spoken and is the major language for communicating between ethnic groups. You will have no problem getting around in Malaysia with English. All shopkeepers will speak English.

BUSINESS HOURS

Business hours in Malaysia vary depending on which part of the country you visit. West Malaysia observes a half day on Saturday and all day Sunday as holidays. Offices will be closed at these times, but shops will be open since these are major shopping periods for local residents. East Malaysia has a different pattern: half day Thursday and all day Friday are the holidays in deference to Islam. In some areas few shops will be open during these times.

Most shops are open from 9am to 6pm, although many shopping centers stay open until 10pm and some shops may open and close earlier or later. Most night markets are open from 6pm to 11pm. Most fresh markets open at 6am and close in late morning or early afternoon.

TRANSPORTATION

Malaysia has an excellent transportation system with good roads, regularly scheduled flights to major cities and towns, and a railway system linking Penang (Butterworth) with Kuala Lumpur and Singapore. Flights, however, are often fully booked given the limited capacity of the national carrier, MAS. Be sure to book your domestic flights well ahead of time, and confirm your flights at least 72 hours before departure. If you fail to confirm in sufficient time, you will most likely loose your flight and thus have difficulty connecting to your destination.

Transportation within cities is also relatively convenient. Taxis, buses, and trishaws are inexpensive. We prefer using taxis for shopping convenience and comfort. However, taxis in some cities and towns may be difficult to find. You may have to call for a taxi or go to a hotel which has a taxi stand. Shopkeepers will help you get a taxi if you just ask them for assistance. Most major shopping centers will have a taxi queue.

TOURS, TRAVEL AGENTS, AND INFORMATION

Most major cities have several reputable tour companies that offer everything from the three-hour city tour to a three-day river or jungle safari. In most major cities you will find a branch of the national Tourist Development Corporation (TDC) which provides maps, brochures, and information on the local area as well as cities and states throughout the country. Most cities will also have a state tourist office which provides even more information than the TDC office. Both offices also cooperate in dispensing each other's literature. We recommend visiting both offices. Be sure to ask questions since the personnel in these offices are usually very helpful. Most airports and hotels will have an information section where you can pick up maps and brochures on tours, sights, and local points of interest.

FOOD AND DRINK

In addition to offering excellent and inexpensive cuisines from all over the world, the food in Malaysia is safe to eat. Malaysian health and sanitation standards are very good. Even the tempting hawker food stalls should be safe eating establishments. You will find the usual assortment of soft drinks, teas, and coffees as well as excellent local beers and canned fruit juices. While the tap water is safe to drink in most Malaysian cities, we still prefer bottled water.

ACCOMMODATIONS

Most Malaysian cities offer a good range of inexpensive to moderate and expensive accommodations for travelers. The East Coast in particular has inexpensive accommodations and is one of the favorite areas for budget travelers. Expensive deluxe and first-class accommodations in Malaysia are generally reasonable and service and amenities are some of the best in the world.

ELECTRICITY

Electricity in Malaysia is 220-240 volts, 50 cycle AC power. Some hotels have 110-volt outlets. Be sure to take a converter with you for your 110-volt appliances or ask hotel housekeeping for assistance. Many electrical outlets use a three-prong plug which you will need to purchase or borrow from housekeeping should your appliances use a different configuration. Better still, purchase a small converter kit that includes a set of universal plugs that you can use anywhere in the world.

RESOURCES

Once you arrive in Malaysia, the Tourist Development Corporation as well as the local tourist offices will have a great deal of informative tourist information -- maps, brochures, and booklets. We recommend stopping at these offices as soon as you arrive in a city. These offices also maintain information booths at the airports. *A Visitor's Guide to Melaka* is the best overall state visitor's guide published in Malaysia; you can get a copy at the state tourist office once you arrive in Malacca or through the TDC office in Kuala Lumpur. Other states, such as Penang, are modeling their tourist guides after the Malacca example.

Prior to arriving in Malaysia, you may want to look at a few books on Malaysia. An APA Insight Guide entitled *Malaysia* provides a good overview of the history, society, and culture of Malaysia as well as a few travel tips. Like other books in this series, read this book before you arrive in Malaysia; it's not a good travel companion given its size. The Lonely Planet publishes an informative *Malaysia, Singapore, and Brunei: A Travel Survival Kit* which primarily emphasizes hotels and restaurants for budget travelers and backpackers. It's also filled with useful local travel and sightseeing information which you may find useful. Fodor's also publishes a volume entitled *Southeast Asia* which has a brief section on Malaysia. The Times Travel Library (Singapore) publishes three nice volumes heavy on pictures but light on text: *Kuala Lumpur*, *Penang*, and *Borneo*.

If you are interested in learning about the arts and handicrafts in Malaysia, we recommend reading Mubin Sheppard's *Living Crafts of Malaysia*, Lucas Chin's *Cultural Heritage of Sarawak*, and Edric Ong's *Pua: Iban Weavings of Sarawak*. However, most of these books are mainly available in bookstores, museums, and shops of Singapore and Malaysia. When in Kuching, visit the bookstore in the Holiday Inn for an excellent collection of hard-to-find books on Borneo.

For history, adventure, and short stories, you might enjoy R. Winstead's *A History of Malaya*, N. J. Ryan's *A History of Malaysia and Singapore*, F. Spencer Chapman's *The Jungle is Neutral*, Eric Hansen's *Stranger in the Forest: On Foot Across Borneo*, Redmond O'Hanlon's *Into the Heart of Borneo*, and W. Somerset Maugham's *Borneo Stories*.

Chapter Eight
PENANG

Penang is a colorful island of many discoveries and pleasures. Step into the narrow, congested streets of Georgetown, cruise through the city in a creaking trishaw, stand at the top of Penang Hill, explore the night markets and noisy restaurants, ride a ferry, or walk along the waterfront and you soon discover the lure of tropical, colonial, and Chinese Southeast Asia. This is the Asia that so captivated the likes of W. Somerset Maugham, Joseph Conrad, Noel Coward, and many travelers today who still find Penang Island to be a comforting crossroad to the rigors of a more challenging Southeast Asia.

PLEASURES ON ITS SHORES

Penang is an anomaly of sorts -- it's not the "real" Malaysia nor is it another Singapore or Hong Kong. Enter Penang and you seem to step back into an arousing Singapore of the early 1960s. For you are about to discover a seemingly modern city and island with a unique historical and cultural character reflecting its strategic location and diverse population. You may not "shop 'til you drop" here

-- shopping is interesting rather than fantastic -- but you will stop to shop at a more leisurely pace on this extremely interesting island.

Penang is a favorite destination for many people who enjoy truly diverse travel and shopping experiences. The island offers a variety of beach resorts, shopping opportunities, and tourist sites to please most any visitor. It's an easy place to get around in since English is widely spoken and understood, and most signs are written in English. Penang is a lovely island with beautiful beaches, hills, mountains, and jungles as well as a charming harbor. Penang, one of the most colorful and culturally diverse areas in Asia, exhibits an interesting mix of Chinese, Malays, Indians, Thais, Indonesians, Singaporians, Japanese, Taiwanese, Europeans, and North Americans. The people are generally friendly and willing to assist you with your travel and shopping needs. Penang's food is reputed to be the best in all of Malaysia -- and possibly Southeast Asia -- with many people traveling from Kuala Lumpur, Singapore, and Taiwan just to sample Penang's unique and varied cuisine. Overall, Penang has a great deal to offer any visitor.

ARRIVAL

You can reach Penang by air, sea, rail, or road. An island situated less than 10 kilometers from the mainland, Penang is regularly serviced by four international airlines (MAS, Thai Airways, Singapore Airline, and Cathay Pacific) as well as connected to the mainland by a 13.4 kilometer toll bridge - the longest in Asia - and a ferry service. If you are arriving from Thailand, Singapore, or other locations in Malaysia, you can reach Penang by train via Butterworth, the port city directly opposite Penang Island, or by any of several roads to Butterworth. From here you can take the ferry or bridge to reach the island. If you are flying into Penang, you will land at the Penang International Airport at Beyan Lepas, 16 kilometers south of Georgetown.

If you are first entering Malaysia by air, you will find the Penang International Airport to be both convenient and efficient. Immigration is fast and courteous. The baggage retrieval area is next to the duty-free shop, a currency exchange desk, a tourist information desk, and Customs. Free baggage carts are located next to the baggage section. The tourist information desk has brochures on Penang as well as other other Malaysian states. At Customs you can proceed directly to a green exit on your right if you have nothing to declare or move directly into the Customs inspection lines if you have declared items. After Customs, proceed directly through the doors. Car rental (Avis, Hertz, Thrifty, and Budget), taxi, limosine, and currency exchange service desks are located immediately to your left and right. The Shangri-la International Hotel has a desk to the right where you can get information and make reservations for one of its four deluxe hotels: Rasa Sayang, Shangri-la, Golden Sands, and Palm Beach.

The trip from the airport to Georgetown takes about 25 minutes depending on traffic conditions. The taxi fare from the airport to downtown Georgetown is M$15.

GETTING TO KNOW YOU

Penang, one of 13 States in the Federation of Malaysia, consists of both an island and a coastal strip. Located on the northwestern coast of Peninsular Malaysia, directly west of the Indonesian island of Sumatra and the Straits of Malacca, peninsular Penang is best noted for the bustling industrial and port city of Butterworth. This city is of little interest to tourists other than as a transit point if traveling by rail, road, or sea to the island of Penang.

Penang Island, known as the "Pearl of the Orient" and at times referred to as the "Betel Nut Island", "Isle of Temples", and "Gateway to the East", is 285 square kilometers in area and houses a population of over 500,000. A tropical and mountaineous island boasting a quaint harbor and lovely sunsets, it runs approximately 24 kilometers from north to south and 14.5 kilometers from east to west. Consisting of both rural and urban areas, it's major city and tourist destination is the historical Georgetown.

Penang is best approached as three related travel and shopping destinations: Georgetown, Batu Ferringhi, and the remainder of the island. Each area offers a different type of travel and shopping adventure. If, for example, you enjoy lying on the beach and staying in resort type accommodations, then the northern beach area called **Batu Ferringhi** offers an oasis of sun, beach, and luxurious hotels to cater to your every need. Here you will find numerous shops offering a large variety of items normally associated with beach resorts--beachwear, souvenirs, and handicrafts.

If your interests include experiencing the local history and culture in a predominately Chinese setting, then downtown **Georgetown** may well become your favorite Penang destination. This is a bustling city distinctive for its thousands of aging two-story red-tiled Chinese shophouses, narrow sidewalks and one-way streets, modern high-rise

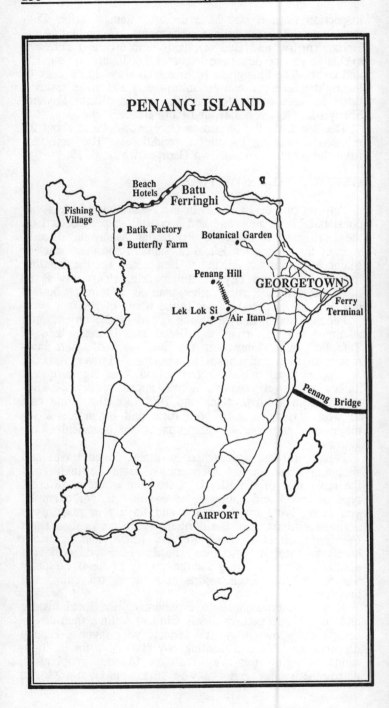

PENANG ISLAND

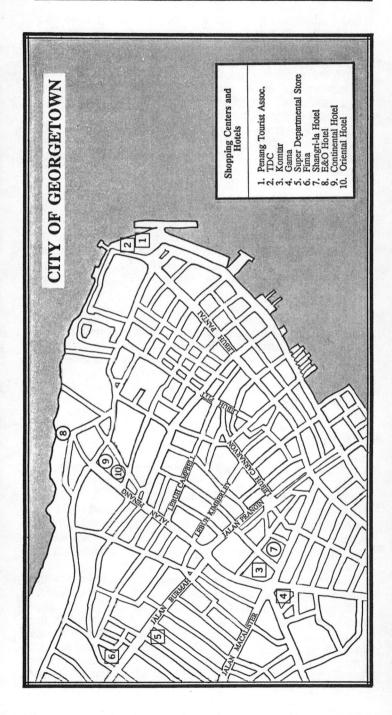

CITY OF GEORGETOWN

Shopping Centers and Hotels

1. Penang Tourist Assoc.
2. TDC
3. Komtar
4. Gama
5. Super Departmental Store
6. Fima
7. Shangri-la Hotel
8. E&O Hotel
9. Continental Hotel
10. Oriental Hotel

office buildings and hotels, and trishaws plying busy thoroughfares. This is Penang's shopping center where you
will find traditional night markets offering cheap clothes,
footwear, and foods; Chinese shophouses selling everything
from local consumer goods to famous duty-free cameras;
and modern air-conditioned shopping centers, hotel shopping arcades, and department stores offering the latest in
trendy clothes and electronic goods.

Georgetown is alive from early morning to late at night
with people engaging in their two favorite pastimes --
eating and shopping. It's a city that still retains much of
its colonial character. It's the only city in Asia that feels
like a combination of Rangoon and Singapore. It's as if
Georgetown were transplanted right out of the history
books and novels of such illustrious former residents as W.
Somerset Maugham and Noel Coward. Stop, for example,
at the historical E&O Hotel and you will step back into the
history of other grand but decaying Southeast Asian hotels
such as the Strand in Rangoon and the Raffles in Singapore. But put yourself in the Shangri-la Hotel or the Rasa
Sayang Hotel and you will think you are in modern, upscale Singapore!

Beyond Batu Ferringhi and Georgetown you will discover a beautiful tropical island of narrow winding roads,
scenic views, fishing villages, temples, waterfalls, botanic
gardens, and groves of nutmeg, cloves, and banana trees.
Along the way you can purchase souvenirs, clothes, and
food from vendor stalls as well as visit a butterfly farm
and batik factory where you can also purchase unique
items.

THE STREETS OF PENANG

Like many Asian cities, Georgetown can be disorienting
for first time visitors. In general this is a clean, well
maintained, and orderly city, although it has a decidedly
worn, aging look about it. While the layout of some
streets follows the logic of a grid plan, the organization of
other streets appears to be a product of helter-skelter urban
growth paying homage to an occasional traffic circle to
give the streets some sense of logic.

Similar to other cities in Malaysia, Georgetown has the
maddening habit of changing street names in the middle of
a street. But it does have a sufficient number of landmarks and good maps to assist you in overcoming the
general lack of coherent street organization. By all means
do pick up a map of the city to help you navigate its
streets. The best maps are provided by the Penang Tourist
Association (*Island Penang and City Map*) and the Shan-

gri-La Hotel (*Within Walking Distance*).

The streets of Georgetown are visually chaotic. Worn two-story shophouses with narrow streets and covered sidewalks outlined with steep open drainage ditches (Watch your step!) provide access for a bewildering combination of cars, buses, trucks, motorcycles, trishaws, bicycles, and pedestrians in the pursuit of limited street and sidewalk space. Motorcycles and bicycles, along with truck deliveries, often park in the middle of sidewalks forcing pedestrians into the streets where they must dodge the many vehicles plying the narrow, crowded roads.

Georgetown's major shopping area is centered around **Jalan Penang**. Stretching from the Gama Department Store and Komtar shopping and office complex in the south to the famous waterfront E&O Hotel in the north, Jalan Penang is less than two kilometers in length. Except for the Komtar shopping and office complex, this is a road of small shophouses offering a large variety of consumer and luxury goods. Several streets adjacent to Jalan Penang -- Burmah, Campbell, Chulia, Pitt, Kimberley, Carnarvon -- also offer a variety of shopping opportunities, from department stores to shophouses and vendor stalls.

The best ways to navigate the streets of Penang and Georgetown are to:

- Purchase a good map of both Penang Island and the streets of Georgetown available at bookstores, sundry shops, or through the Penang Tourist Association.

- Visit the Penang Tourist Association and the Tourist Development Corporation offices on Tun Syed Sheh Barakbah Road and the Tourist Development Commission booth on the third floor of the Komtar Building for information and literature on Penang.

- Take a tour, rent a car, or hire a car and driver to visit all of Penang Island.

- If you are staying in downtown Georgetown, include a visit to the Batu Ferringhi area during your around the island trip or take a bus or taxi to Batu Ferringhi.

- If you are staying in Batu Ferringhi, take a bus or taxi to downtown Georgetown. Start your shopping adventure at the E&O Hotel or at the Shangri-La Hotel or the adjacent Komtar office and shopping complex.

- Given the close proximity of Georgetown's major shopping streets to one another, you can easily cover these areas on foot or by trishaw within a day or two.

- When the weather is hot and humid, hire a trishaw by the hour to take you from one shop to another along Georgetown's major shopping streets.

- Watch where you walk when entering streets or sidewalks. You can easily fall into the steep open drainage ditches and break a leg.

Don't forget that Penang's streets are especially colorful at night. This is a non-stop shopping and eating city. Plan to go shopping in the evenings and combine shopping with sampling Penang's many excellent restaurants and famous street hawker food stalls. If you are lucky to be in Penang when the Night Market is held in the Gurney Street area, you will be in for a wonderful shopping and gastronomic treat as the famous food hawkers of Gurney Street meet with the colorful Night Market.

WHAT TO BUY

The streets and shops of Penang abound with everything from the latest in electronic goods to antiques from China and Indonesia. You can buy the usual duty-free items at the airport or in a few Georgetown shops or browse for inexpensive clothes in crowded market stalls. While Penang is by no means a shopper's paradise on the scale of Hong Kong, Bangkok, or Singapore, it does offer a substantial number of shopping opportunities to keep you busy shopping for at least two full days.

You will find the best shopping buys on locally produced products: batik, pewter, nutmeg, display butterflies, jewelry, and rattan and cane items. Penang has a few antique shops offering a mix of local and imported antiques. Handicrafts from other Malaysian states, such as silver from Kelantan, are found in many shops in Penang. You will also find the usual assortment of imported duty-free items, such as cameras, radios, perfumes, liquor, and cigarettes, at some of the most competitive prices in all of Asia. Given Penang's close proximity to Thailand, you will find numerous Thai handicrafts, clothes, and footwear in the shops and stalls of Penang.

Antiques and Curios

Penang's antique shops are by no means as numerous as those in Malacca, nor do they offer the range and depth of antiques one might expect in serious antique shops. Most local antique shops carry a diverse range of old and new items, from Chinese collectibles to contemporary Thai and Burmese handicrafts. Most offer small collectibles that can be easily packed in a suitcase. Don't expect to find many large antique furniture pieces as you will find in Malacca.

The typical Penang antique shop carries a diverse mix of art, antiques, and handicraft items reflecting their local Chinese and Malay roots as well as their close proximity to both Indonesia and Thailand. Most are small shophouses cluttered with small items in display cases and on the floor and walls. Given the traditional nature of displaying goods in these shops, you will probably be visually disoriented by this browsing experience. Therefore, take your time; look up, down, and around as you stroll up and down the aisles at least twice. Don't forget that most shops also have a back room with additional items. Many items in this room are too large to be displayed, are in the process of being restored, or are being stored because of the lack of display space in the front room. Be sure to examine these back rooms since you may very well find your favorite treasure there.

Many antique shops in Penang are filled with Chinese porcelain, celadon, decorative woodcarvings, ivory, jewelry, and cloisonne; Selangor and Penang pewterware, Malay batik, and kris; Thai and Burmese woodcarvings, lacquerware, Buddha figures, and dolls; and Indonesian wayang puppets, Balinese masks, and Batak primitive woodcarvings; and antique furniture, cameras, and bric-a-brac.

Penang's antique shops tend to be concentrated in a one block section of **Penang Road**, just south of the E&O Hotel, as well as in a few shops in the **Batu Ferringhi** area. Along Penang Road look for **Syarikat Peking Arts and Crafts, Federation Arts and Crafts, China Handicraft Company, Oriental Arts Company, Kamsis**, and **Asia Handicrafts**. All of these shops are located next to one another and offer similar types of antiques and curios. Further south along Penang Road you will find a few additional shops selling handicrafts, curios, and an occasional antique.

Along Batu Ferringhi look for **Asia Handicrafts**, which is a branch shop of Asia Handicrafts on Penang Road. This shop has a good selection of antiques and handicrafts, including Buddhas, porcelain, wayang puppets, opium weights, Balinese and Batak masks, jewelry, cloisonne, and pewter. They even do tailoring work at the back of the shop! Just down the street on the second floor of the Rasa Sayang Hotel shopping arcade you will find one shop with a small selection of good quality antiques: **Tai Pan.**

Handicrafts

Shops in Penang abound with handicrafts from Malaysia, Thailand, Burma, Indonesia, China, and India. As a port city in close proximity to other Asian countries, Penang offers a wider selection of handicrafts from Thailand, Burma, Indonesia, and China than other cities in Malaysia. If you are looking for Malay handicrafts, expect to find pewterware -- both Selangor and Penang name brands -- batik, silverware, kites, shells, baskets, and pottery. Many of the Malaysian handicrafts are actually imported from the East Coast rather than made in Penang. Thai handicrafts include small dolls, lacquerware, and woodcarvings. Burmese handicrafts include tapestries (*kalagas*) and puppets. Indonesian handicrafts include wayang puppets, batik, masks, and woodcarvings, many of which are made in Bali. Chinese handicrafts include jade and ivory figures, cloisonne, chops, and embroidiery.

Look for handicrafts in shops along Penang Street, Bishop Street, and Batu Ferringhi as well as in antique shops, hotel shopping arcades, department stores, and markets. The antique shops on upper Penang Road near the E&O Hotel have a large selection of handicrafts from Thailand and Indonesia. **Hong Giap** (308-310 Penang Road) has one of the largest selections of handicrafts and leather in Penang, including jewelry, jade carvings, woodcarvings, Thai dolls, ivory, Balinese masks, cloisonne, pewter, batik, perfumes, silverware, and watches. While the selections here are good, beware of Hong Giap's tourist prices. Be sure to bargain for big discounts -- at least 50% -- in this shop since the asking prices tend to be high. In the **Komtar** shopping complex you will find a few gift shops offering handicrafts as well as the **Super Departmental Store** which has a handicraft section on the fourth level. For local pottery, visit **Asia Pottery** at 547 Tanjung Bungah.

If you are in the Batu Ferringhi area, look for handicrafts at two art shops. **Art's Village** primarily sells batik paintings and T-shirts. However, it also offers handcrafted silver and pewter as well as pillow covers and blankets from the hilltribes in Northern Thailand! **Yahong Art Gallery** (58-D Batu Ferringhi) also primarily sells batik paintings, but it offers one of the largest selections of handicrafts in Penang, including jewelry, jade, ivory, Thai hilltribe pillow covers, pewter, ceramics, Balinese carvings, leather purses, silver, Chinese embroidery, Burmese tapestries, puppets, chops, cloisonne, and Thai woodcarvings. **Asia Handicrafts** also offers a good range of Malaysian, Thai, and Indonesian handicrafts.

Pewter

Shops in Penang offer two brands of pewterware, Selangor Pewter and Penang Pewter. The more popular Selangor Pewter is available in most hotel shops and stores offering handicrafts and gift items. To see the latest range of Selangor Pewter designs, visit the **Selangor Pewter** showroom and demonstration center on Farquhar Street, just adjacent to the E&O Hotel. For Penang Pewter, visit **Penang Pewter and Metal Arts** at 60 Weld Quay.

Art

While Penang is not a noted center for Asian art, it does contribute to the Malaysian art scene. You will find some oils, watercolors, and batik paintings done by local artists depicting both rural and urban scenes.

Malaysia's most famous batik painter, Chuah Thean Teng, owns the **Yahong Art Gallery** at 58-D Batu Ferringhi Road. A frequent exhibitor in Malaysia and abroad, Teng's paintings have been well received by international galleries and art connoisseurs. When you enter this shop, you will primarily see handicrafts for sale. Be sure to go to the second floor gallery where you will see Teng's and his son's batik paintings on display. Teng's paintings have been strongly influenced by Picasso, Gauguin, and Matisse. The quality is very good, and accordingly the prices are expensive. Expect to pay anywhere from M$1,000 to M$10,000 for a good quality batik painting by this master batik painter. These prices clearly reflect high quality work as well as the international reputation of this unique artist.

The nearby **Craft's Art Gallery** offers an extensive collection of batik paintings by Tan Thean Song and a few other local artists at relatively inexpensive prices. Primarily depicting village scenes and using a traditional batik painting style, Tan Thean Song's works sell from between M$200 and M$800. You will often find the artist working in his studio at the back of the gallery where you can see the batik painting process, meet the artist, and ask questions. Tan Thean Song's batik paintings are also on display and for sale at the nearby batik factory, **Craft Batik** (651, Mk. 2, Telok Bahang).

You will find a few art galleries in Georgetown. For oils, watercolors, and batik paintings, a small shop facing Penang Road on the ground floor of the Komtar shopping complex has a limited selection.

Batik

You will find several shops selling batik by the meter or as ready-made garments or in the form of paintings, stuffed animals, placemats, and umbrellas. While we have not been taken by the colors, designs, and styling of the local batik fabrics and garments, you may find just the fabric or garment you desire. Our only recommendation is that you first visit a batik factory and showroom and then browse through various shops and market stalls offering batik fabrics and garments. If you find something you like, buy it.

Most of the batik made in Penang is stamped using copper hand block presses or "chops" rather than hand drawn (*batik tulis*). Penang is a good place to visit a batik factory to observe the batik process as well as shop at a factory store. The largest batik factory, and one that is on most island tours, is **Craft Batik** (651, Mk. 2, Telok Bahang). Here you can tour the factory to learn about each step in the batik printing process, from preparing the wax to dyeing the cloth. The factory shop is well stocked with batik fabric, ready-made garments, batik paintings, stuffed animals, handicrafts, and curios. Other batik factories in Penang include **Pulau Pinang Batik Factory** (2325-A Sungei Nibong Besar) and **Permai Batik** (729-A, Sungei Nibong).

You will find plenty of batik fabrics and ready-made garments in the shops, department stores, and markets of Georgetown. Look for shops selling batik along Penang, Campbell, and Bishop streets. Most department stores have a section selling batik fabrics and garments. **Penang Bazaar** (Penang Road) and **Picadilly Bazaar** (Kuala Kangsar Street) -- two of Penang's major dry markets -- have a large selection of batik fabrics.

Jewelry

While by no means a serious competitor to Hong Kong, Bangkok, or Singapore for jewelry, Penang does offer basic selections of jewelry at duty-free prices. Here you can buy traditional gold and silver jewelry, unset gemstones, and precious and semi-precious jewelry in contemporary and classic designs. The workmanship is good and prices are reasonable. Shops will do special made-to-order work using your designs or pictures from jewelry catalogs. Most of the shops are found in downtown Georgetown and in hotel shopping arcades.

One of the largest shops in Malaysia is **Yew Klien Jewellery Centre** at 17 Gottlieb Road. This store also has branches in Kuala Lumpur, Singapore, and Hong Kong. The two floors of this shop offer a wide range of jewelry and accessories such as leather purses and scarfs. You will find both set and unset Australian opals, Burmese and Thai rubies, Sri Lankan sapphires, Nepalese turquoise, Australian coral and rose quartz, Malaysian hematite, Burmese ivory, and Chinese pearls. The shop will also make to order jewelry using your own designs. Expect to receive at least a 10% discount on gold items and a 10-20% discount on all other items with little or no bargaining effort. With a little more effort, you should be able to do better.

Another famous jewelry shop, **De Silva Jewellers**, offers good quality silver and gold jewelry with designs appropriate for most international travelers. They have two shops, one in downtown Georgtown at 1 Bishop Street and another in the shopping arcade of the Rasa Sayang Hotel at Batu Ferringhi. You will also find other De Silva family shops in Kuala Lumpur, Kota Bharu, and Kuching.

Campbell Street and **Pitt Street** in downtown Georgetown are famous for their gold and jewelry shops. Here you will find several small shops selling 22 and 24 karat gold bracelets, rings, and necklaces using local designs. For more contemporary designs, visit **Kim How Jewellers'** two shops at 9-11 Campbell Street and 86-88 Pitt Street. For inexpensive costume jewelry, browze through the shops along **Lorong Pasar**.

You will also find several jewelry shops on the ground floor of the **Komtar** shopping complex as well as in the **Penang Plaza** shopping center. Several shops in the Komtar shopping complex front on to Penang Road: **Jade House, Poly Jewellery, Bright,** and **Kim How Gems**. They offer a combination of traditional gold jewelry, gemstones, and a variety of jewelry in contemporary and classic designs.

Clothes and Accessories

Penang is not a clothes and fashion center in Malaysia. Nonetheless, you will find plenty of locally produced batik clothes and T-shirts as well as inexpensive garments imported from Thailand in the shops and markets of Penang. However, we have not been enthusiatic about the colors and styling of garments found in the shops of Penang.

For batik clothes, visit the **Craft Batik** factory at 651, Mk. 2, Telok Bahang. They have a large selection of clothes for men and women. Although the tailoring leaves much to be desired, you may find some nice batik patterns not available in other shops. Other batik shops selling the usual assortment of shirts, dresses, and accessories are found in downtown Georgetown along **Penang Road** as well as in the shops and department stores of the **Komtar** shopping complex.

Penang's markets and stalls sell a large assortment of inexpensive clothes and accessories from Thailand, Hong Kong, and Taiwan. During the day visit the **Penang Bazaar** at the corner of Penang Road and Campbell Street. This large cloth market includes inexpensive clothes as well as shoes, handbags, and other accessories. The **Night Market**, which changes locations every two weeks, is filled with small stalls selling inexpensive jeans, T-shirts, jackets, shirts, blouses, and dresses. Many of the items are fakes imported from nearby Thailand. So don't expect that your M$8 "Benetton" shirt is the real thing or will last very long given the questionable workmanship of such items! Also look for similar night stalls in front of the **Super Komtar** shopping complex on Tek Soon Road (Lebuh Teck Soon), adjacent to **Komtar** and just behind the Shangri-La Hotel. Here you will find racks and racks of inexpensive clothes lining the sidewalk in front of the shopping complex.

Duty-Free

Penang advertises itself as a duty-free port comparable to Hong Kong and Singapore. As a result, many shops offer imported cameras, electronic items, and sporting goods from Japan, Korea, Hong Kong, Taiwan, and Singapore as well as such usual airport duty-free items as liquor, cigarettes, perfumes, watches, and candies.

However, Penang's duty-free items are bargains only for individuals who come from countries where duties are extremely high, such as India, Thailand, Indonesia, Japan, Australia, and New Zealand. They are not bargains for Americans and Canadians who have the price advantages of large discount and mail-order houses. Cameras and electronic items are still cheaper through major discount houses in the United States than anywhere in Asia, including the countries of origin. The same Canon EOS650 camera, for example, that sells for US$510 in Penang's duty-free shops, can be purchased at New York discount houses for US$425.

Stores selling duty-free cameras, electronic goods, and

appliances are found on the ground floor of the **Komtar** shopping complex near the jewelry stores as well as along Penang Road. Small duty-free shops are also found in the airport's international departure lounge.

The More You Look

Penang has many other shopping attractions you may discover during your stay. If you are interested, for example, in exploring junk shops, head for **Rope Walk** which is located on Pintai Tali Road between Kimberley Street and Prangin Road in downtown Georgetown. Here you can browse through several junk shops for that hidden treasure you've been looking for.

Penang is also renowned for its butterflies. If you visit the **Butterfly Farm** at Teluk Bahang, you can buy a large assortment of mounted butterflies along with bugs and spiders. Dead butterflies, bugs, and spiders are not our idea of a great shopping find, but these are unique additions to some travelers' shopping adventure, especially if you are into collecting examples of the local fauna. Expect to find similar items in several handicraft shops in Penang as well as in other cities in Malaysia, including Kuala Lumpur, Malacca, and Kuching, and in Singapore.

Computer shops also sell pirated software programs at the fraction of the original costs. Since pirated software in both Malaysia and Singapore is ostensibly illegal, you will be shopping on the black market. But no one, other than U.S. computer software companies and U.S. Customs, will give you any trouble buying in this manner, and the likelihood you will run into a problem with them is slight. Because of the legal problems, we are reluctant to name shops that offer such items. All you need to know is how to approach a shop, ask the right questions, and receive your goods. You can buy such software in several computer shops by merely asking for it. The shops do not display the software in the open since it would be illegal to do so. You must ask if the shop can get you a particular program. For example, walk into a shop and ask the salesperson: *"Do you have WordPerfect 5.0 and D-base IV."* The shopkeeper will most likely respond: *"Yes, we can get it for you. When do you need it?"* The shopkeeper, in effect, has the software duplicated for you and delivers it to you at a set time. Expect to pay about US-$70 in Penang for a US$500 piece of software, including the manuals and diskettes. Chances are your software packages will be ready for delivery within a few hours -- usually one-day service. If you don't have room to carry the programs with you or if you are an American worried about U.S. Customs confiscating the purchases, have the shop mail the software by parcel post to your home address.

WHERE TO SHOP

Shopping in Penang is concentrated in small street front shophouses, shopping centers, department stores, hotel shopping arcades, factories, markets, and street stalls. If you plan to shop Penang well, you should concentrate your shopping efforts in downtown Georgetown, along the beach front Batu Ferringhi area, and in a few areas around the island.

Street Front Shophouses

The major shopping streets in downtown Georgetown are lined with rows of small, worn two-story red-tiled shophouses selling everything from clothes to household appliances. Most shopping is centered in and around **Penang Road**. We recommend you begin shopping this street at the E&O Hotel at the northeast end of Penang Road; walk southwest along this road until you reach the Komtar shopping complex. You will find numerous shops lining both sides of Penang Road. Initially you will see several antique shops on the east side of the road. These are Penang's major antique shops: **Syarikat Peking Arts and Crafts, Federation Arts and Crafts, China Handicraft Company, Oriental Arts Company, Kamsis,** and **Asia Handicrafts.**

The remainder of Penang Street has a mixed assortment of shops selling clothes, appliances, batik, T-shirts, handicrafts, ceramics, cameras, handbags, baskets, watches, and pens. There are no shops here that we can strongly recommend since the range and quality of goods is not particularly noteworthy, and most shops have a bland, average look about them. **Oriental Curios** (84 Penang Road) offers porcelain, ceramics, and pewter. Look for **Hong Giap** (308-310 Penang Road) for a good range of Malaysian and imported handicrafts, but don't pay their high quoted prices; offer them 50 percent or less. The **Penang Bazaar, Chowrasta Market, and Picadilly Bazaar,** which sell cloth, clothes, footwear, and household goods, are located near the intersection of Penang Road and Campbell Street. **Eng Aun and Company** near the corner of Tek Soon Street has a good selection of batik clothes and yard goods. Their men's batik shirts are reasonably priced. As you cross Tek Soon Street you will come to several shops on the ground floor of the Komtar shopping complex facing Penang Road. You will find several jewelry shops here as well as an art shop selling local batik and oil paintings.

Other major shopping streets in downtown Georgetown either adjoin Penang Road or are within 5 or 10 minutes walking or trishaw distance. Streets with rows of shophouses include Campbell Street, Burmah Road, Pitt Street, Dota Keramat Road, Chulia Street, Carnarvon Street, Pintal Tali Road, Pasar Street, Pantai Street, Bishop Street, Prangin Road, and Macalister Road. **Campbell Street**, for example, is a popular street for jewelry, textiles, shoes, luggage, and pottery. **Burmah Road** includes department stores, emporiums, and shops selling clothes. For rattan and cane products, visit **Chulia Street**. **Carnarvon Street** is noted for its earthernware pots. **Pintal Tali Road** is Penang's junk street with shops offering old pots, antiques, porcelain, and brass products. **Pasar Street** is Penang's Indian street with shops selling a large variety of silk, satin, sarees, bracelets, and clay pots. **Bishop Street** has an assortment of shops selling textiles, antiques, curios, and jewelry.

The downtown Georgetown area is a good place to explore by trishaw. If you rent a trishaw for three or four hours, the driver should be able to take you to all of these major shopping streets as well as permit some time to browse through a few shops that catch your interest. **Batu Ferringhi Road** also has a few shophouses worth visiting, especially if you are interested in arts, antiques, and handicrafts. Interspersed among the numerous hotels and restaurants are three shops offering good quality products: Asia Handicrafts, Yahong Art Gallery, and Craft's Art Galley. **Asia Handicrafts**, a branch of the main shop on Penang Road, carries a wide assortment of Malaysian, Thai, and Indonesian handicrafts. **Yahong Art Gallery** has an excellent collection of handicrafts as well as a gallery of outstanding batik paintings by the famous painter Chuah Thean Teng. **Craft's Art Gallery** primarily offers batik paintings by Tan Thean Song but also includes some handicraft items.

Shopping Centers

Penang has three major shopping centers concentrated in downtown Georgetown. The largest shopping complex is **Komtar** (Kompleks Tun Abdul Razak) located on the corner of Penang Road and Magazine Road, just adjacent to the Shangri-la Hotel. This is actually two shopping complexes joined together: **Komtar** and **Super Komtar**. **Komtar** occupies the first four levels of the 57-floor

Komtar Building that faces both Penang Road and Magazine Road. **Super Komtar** occupies the first six levels of
the same building that faces Prangin Road and Ria Road.
Both shopping complexes have a similar mix of shops
selling fast foods, electronic goods, handicrafts, clothes,
shoes, leather, music, books, jewelry, cameras, toys, and
optical goods.

You will also find three department stores attached to
these two shopping centers: Yaohan Department Store,
Super Departmental Store, Pulau Penang Department Store.
Like many Malaysia shopping complexes, these two tend
to be extremely noisy with blaring rock music and crowds
of young people. The clothes and shoe stores tend to cater
to young people with trendy styles.

The sixth floor of the Super Komtar shopping complex
is a hawker food center, and you will find several Western
fast food restaurants -- McDonalds, A&W Root Beer, Pizza
Hut, Kentucky Fried Chicken -- on different floors of these
shopping centers.

You can find a Tourist Information Centre on the third
level of the Komtar shopping complex. The Centre provides literature on Penang as well as answers questions
you might have concerning your stay in Penang. You can
also purchase tickets here for the 45-minute guided tour of
the 57th floor tower where you will see a cultural gallery
and get a panaromic view of Penang Island. The elevators
are just to the left of the Tourist Information Centre desk.

Other shopping complexes in Penang are small compared to Komtar and Super Komtar. Look for **Penang
Plaza** (also known as **Fima**) on Burmah Road. This three-
level shopping center has shops selling clothing, jewelry,
furniture, electronics, and sporting goods. It also houses
one of the better bookstores in town, Times Books, as well
as a Christian bookstore.

Department Stores

Penang's major department stores are centered in and
around the Komtar shopping complex and along Burmah
Road. The most elegant department store in Penang is
Yaohan, which is located adjacent to Super Komtar. This
multi-level department store offers some of the best quality
products in all of Penang. Within the Komtar shopping
complex, look for **Super Departmental Stores** and **Pulau
Penang Department Store**. Both stores offer a wide
range of medium quality goods primarily catering to local
residents. If you are interested in Malaysian handicrafts,
Super Departmental Stores do have a handicraft section on
the fourth level.

Just across the street from Komtar shopping complex, at the corner of Dato Keramat Road and Brick Kiln Road, is Penang's second largest department store, **Gama Supermarket and Department Store**. Surrounded by food vendors, popular with locals, and crowded, this four-level department store offers everything from clothes to household appliances. The third floor, with its jewelry, gifts, books, and luggage, may interest you the most.

Along Burmah Road you will find another **Super Departmental Store** (on the corner of Rangoon Road) and two emporiums: **Hanjo Emporium** and **Island Emporium.**

Hotel Shopping Arcades

Few hotels in Penang have shopping arcades worth making a trip across town to visit. Most hotels have one or two small shops selling the usual assortment of gifts and sundry goods primarily to their hotel guests. A few hotels have one or two shops that may be of interest to shoppers in general. Exceptions include the old **E & O Hotel** which houses Penang's largest **Selangor Pewter** showroom and demonstration center. Penang's best hotel shopping arcade is found at the **Rasa Sayang Hotel** at Batu Ferringhi. This is a small but good quality shopping arcade. Look for **Flair**, a batik boutique; **Everon** for jewelry; **Designers' Collection** for clothes; **DeSilva** for gold, silver, pewter, and crystal; and **Tai Pan** for arts, antiques, and jewelry.

Factories

Penang has a few factories you can visit to observe local craftsmen at work. These factories also have showrooms where you can examine finished products and make purchases. One of the largest and most interesting factories is the **Pulau Pinang Batik Factory** which is located at 2325-A Sungei Nibong Besar, near the Batu Ferringhi area. This factory offers visitors free tours of their complex. If you have not observed the batik production process, this is a good place to get an introduction. In fact, even though we have observed batik production in Indonesia, we found this demonstration very informative. A guide will take you through each step, from printing designs using copper hand presses and hand drawn batik to the dyeing and drying processes. After completing the tour, you will enter a large factory showroom where you can purchase batik yardage, clothes, paintings, and toys as well as pewter and silver. While the batik clothes may lack appealing designs and styles and are expensive compared to similar garments found in Georgetown shops, the batik paintings are quite nice. Most of the paintings are done by Tan Thean Song who also has a gallery just down the road at **Craft Batik** (651, Mk. 2, Telok Bahang). The prices here are the same, but you will find a larger selection of batik paintings by visiting both shops.

The nearby **Penang Butterfly Farm** (Telok Bahang Road), which is on most island tour itineraries, has a large showroom selling several varieties of colorful butterflies in framed display cases along with different varieties of bugs, tarantulas, jungle grasshoppers, and scorpions -- all of which are deceased! After taking a tour (M$2 for adults, M$1 for children, M$1 for cameras, and M$3 for videos) of the butterfly farm, these criters may have more meaning to you. Kids and collectors love this place, but we have not acquired a taste for integrating these creatures into our home! The showroom also caters to the varied tastes of tourists -- assuming all are not in the market for butterflies and bugs -- by offering the typical assortment of tourist T-shirts, hats, books, purses, belts, Penang pewter, shells, and coasters.

If you are interested in pewterware, be sure to visit the **Selangor Pewter** showroom and demonstration center located next to the E&O Hotel Arcade on Farquhar street. They have an excellent selection of traditional and modern pewter designs that appeal to most any taste. Here you will find nice handcrafted pewter cups, boxes, bowls, tea sets, tableware, picture frames, bracelets, and small gift items.

Asian Pottery at 547 Tanjong Bungah offers a good selection of local made pottery. If you want to visit their nearby factory to observe the pottery making process, ask to do so at their main shop.

Markets and Stalls

Penang has several markets worth visiting as well as numerous vendor stalls located throughout the city. All offer a variety of shopping opportunities for everything from clothes and household goods to food. The most interesting markets and stalls are open late into the evening.

Penang's **Night Market** (*Pasar Malam*) is a curious and fun phenomenon. Unlike markets in other cities, this one rotates from one location to another every two weeks. If you want to know where it is located during your visit, call the Penang Tourist Association (Tel. 366665) for information, ask at your hotel, or read the "Penang Diary" section of the *New Straights Times and Star*. If the market is located along Gurney Drive, you are very lucky. This is the best place to visit this market because it links into the famous Gurney Drive food stall market -- one of Asia's great outdoor food bazaars!

Penang's **Night Market** consists of numerous vendors or hawkers who display their goods on makeshift tables and on the ground. Here you can get good bargains on imported clothes, footwear, and household goods -- inexpensive items that you can also purchase in department stores but without the high overhead costs. Be sure to bargain for everything you buy at the night market. The Night Market is open every night, from 7pm to 11pm, except on days it rains. If it rains during the day, the Night Market may or may not be open, depending on the ground conditions. You will have to visit the current site to discover if enough vendors will show up to make it a viable Night Market.

Gurney Drive is another famous night market and one of Asia's great gastonomic delights. Located on the north shore of the island just three kilometers from downtown Georgetown, Gurney Drive at night becomes an outdoor dining market for hawker foods and restaurants. At night this ocean front road is lined for approximately two kilometers with stalls selling some of the best foods in all of Southeast Asia -- satays, noodle dishes, seafood, and curries. Indeed, many foreign visitors -- especially from Singapore and Taiwan -- come to Penang primarily to spend their time eating along Gurney Drive! It's a fun place to visit. You should not have problems eating at these establishments since the local health authorities supposedly maintain adequate sanitation standards. When the Night Market is held in this area, you can expect to have a wonderful time shopping and eating at the same time!

During the day you will find several wet and dry markets in and around Penang Road in downtown Georgetown. The wet markets sell fruits, vegetables, and meats and are most active in the morning between 7am and 10am. One of the largest such markets is the **Chowrasta Market** on Penang Road. Look for other fresh produce markets at the corner of Campbell and Carnarvon Streets, between Prangin and Maxwell Roads, and at the corner of Burma and Cantonment roads.

The day-time dry markets primarily sell cloth, clothes, footwear, and household goods -- items you are likely to find in small shops, department stores, and supermarkets. **Penang Bazaar**, near Chowrasta Market on Penang Road and between Campbell and Kimberly Streets, is a popular cloth market which also sells a variety of other consumer goods. The adjacent **Picadilly Bazaar** sells similar items. Also look for vendor stalls along Penang Road, at the intersection of Campbell Street and near Chowrasta Market selling a large assortment of clothes and footwear. You will encounter vendor stalls throughout Penang, in Georgetown and Batu Ferringhi, at most tourist sights but especially at temples, and along roads outside these areas. In addition to the Night Market, look for vendor stalls both during the day and night near the Komtar and Super Komtar. The largest number of stalls operate in these areas from 7pm to 11pm every night. While visiting temples such as the famous Kek Lok Si and the Snake Temple, you will discover numerous vendor stalls selling everything from T-shirts and imported handicrafts from Thailand to local medicinal foods.

Kek Lok Si Temple, at the end of Ayer Item Road, has the largest concentration of such vendor stalls located at the foot of the hill that leads up to this interesting Buddhist and Taoist temple complex. As you walk through a long narrow enclosed walkway lined with more than 50 crowded stalls, you will be approached by very aggressive merchants selling clothing, tablecloths, cork carvings, Balinese masks, fake leather purses, bracelets, carved Thai elephants, perfumes, sandalwood fans, Burmese puppets, Thai dolls, swimwear, ceramic Chinese figurines, wind chimes, chopsticks, back packs, briefcases, hats, T-shirts, toys, shoes, belts, sunglasses, post cards, collectors stamps, luggage, kites, and foods. While most of the items are typical tourist kitsch one would expect to find at such highly touristed spots, you may find a treasure or two here or that special T-shirt and postcard. The **Snake Temple** is surrounded by eight vendor stalls primarily selling T-shirts, hats, and postcards.

While driving around Penang Island, you will encounter a few roadside vendors selling locally produced cloves, nutmeg, and coconut snacks as well as souvenirs. The fresh Penang cloves and nutmeg may be of special interest to you if you enjoy using such spices. Various unique snacks made from fresh cloves, nutmeg, and coconut make for some interesting and surprisingly delightful purchases.

ENJOYING YOUR STAY

Penang has much to offer visitors in addition to shopping. It has extremely varied tourist attractions that appeal to all types of tourists. Above all, Penang is rich in history, architecture, beaches, and food.

If you enjoy history and architecture, Penang will keep you occupied for at least two days of intense touring for discovering the unique old and new of this city and island. If you are walking through downtown Georgetown you will get a good sense of the history and culture of Penang's by-gone era. Architecturally unexciting two-story brick and stucco white-washed, red-tiled Chinese commercial row houses, worn by an intense tropical climate, line the streets of Penang's major thoroughfares. In the midst of these aging buildings you will find old colonial buildings as well as such modern office, hotel, and shopping complexes as the **Komtar Building** and **Shangri-la Hotel**.

The **E&O Hotel** of W. Somerset Maugham fame is well worth visiting if you enjoy reviewing what remains of one of Southeast Asia's classic colonial hotels. While not in the class of Bangkok's Oriental, Hong Kong's Peninsula, or even Singapore's Raffles, the E&O Hotel has not reached the seedy depths of Rangoon's Strand. Having a drink or lunch at the ocean front cafe can be a pleasant experience as you contemplate what this place might have been like 50 to 100 years ago.

The nearby **Penang Museum and Art Gallery** houses a modest collection of Penang memorabilia. Other historical buildings worth visiting are Fort Cornwallis on the Esplanade, the High Court, the Municipal Council Building, Saint George's Church, and the Cathedral of the Assumption.

For one of the most interesting adaptations of a Western fast food restaurant to the preservation of a local historical building, we recommend seeing the unique **Kentucky Fried Chicken** building near the Penang Plaza shopping center.

For panoramic views of Penang, be sure to take the funicular railway to **Penang Hill** where you will be able to see most of the island as well as the bustling port of Butterworth on the mainland. This 2722 foot hill is one of the few cool places to escape from Penang's often hot and humid climate. The view from the hill at night is especially romantic, but do be prepared for the mosquitos! You can get another excellent view of Penang by taking the elevator to the permanent cultural gallery on the 57th floor of the **Komtar Building**. Here a 45-minute guided tour will put you in touch with the history and culture of Malaysia as you view historical pictures and examine handicrafts and arts.

Penang abounds with interesting Buddhist, Taoist, and Hindu temples that reflect the cultural diversity of it's island population. One of the most interesting temples is **Kek Lok Si** (Temple of Paradise). The largest Buddhist temple in Malaysia, Kek Lok Si is a mixture of Buddhism and Taoism as well as Burmese, Thai, and Chinese architecture. Beautifully located on a hill side overlooking Georgetown, this temple complex is well worth visiting. You can walk down to the foot of the hill where you can browse through numerous vendor stalls.

The **Snake Temple** is a unique temple occupied by numerous pit vipers drugged by the heavy fog of burning incense as they lazily hang from branches. You can even have your picture taken with one of these snakes curled around your body in case you are looking for a cheap thrill and momento of this unique sightseeing moment.

Wat Chayamangkalaram, or the Reclining Buddha, on Burmah Street houses one of the world's largest reclining Buddhas and hundreds of niches with the ashes of local devotees. Essentially a Thai temple, it has a unique blend of Thai and Chinese architecture. Directly across the street is a Burmese Buddhist temple. It's interesting to compare and contrast the architectural styles of these two temples.

We also enjoy visiting **Leong San Tong Khoo Kongsi**, a Chinese clan house, temple, and theater complex belonging to the Khoo clan. Somewhat difficult to find at Cannon Square just off Pantai Street, this clan temple exhibits one of the best collections of ornate architecture of fine detailed wood, stone, and porcelain carvings.

The **Kapitan Kling Mosque** at the corner of Chulia and Pitt Streets and the **State Mosque** at the corner of Air Itam and Mesjid Negeri Roads are also interesting architectural monuments and cultural sites worth visiting.

If you enjoy gardens and animals, be sure to visit the **Botanical Gardens**. This is a lovely park where you can also observe and feed the sometimes friendly monkeys. Take plenty of peanuts with you or buy them from the boys hawking small bags of peanuts at the front gate. However, offer them no more than 50 percent of their asking price since they are accustomed to gouging tourists with exhorbitant prices.

You won't go hungry in Penang. For one of Penang's great strengths is its **local foods**. You will be delighted to discover some the best curries, noodle dishes, satay, and seafood in Asia at Penang's many restaurants and hawker food stalls. Reflecting Penang's diverse population and cultures, the foods vary from Nonya (combination of Southeast Asian and Chinese), Chinese, Indian, Malay, Thai, Indonesian, and Western. For some of the best hawker food in all of Asia, be sure to visit **Gurney Drive** at night. You can feast cheaply here on all types of local dishes. For a good open air seafood restaurant with cultural entertainment, visit the ocean front **Eden Seafood Village** at 69-A Batu Ferringhi. Some of the best hotel restaurants are found in the **Golden Sands Hotel** (Batu Ferringhi) and

Shangri-la Hotel (Georgetown). For excellent Penang Nonya food, try the **Dragon King Restaurant** at 66 Bishop Street in downtown Georgetown. Penang is also the home for several Western fast-food restaurants, such as Pizza Hut, A&W Root Beer, McDonald's, and Kentucky Fried Chicken, should you have the urge to visit such popular places.

Penang offers excellent accommodations at reasonable prices. If you plan to stay in the downtown Georgetown area, the **Shangri-la Hotel** on Jalan Magazine (Tel. 622-622), adjacent to the Komtar complex, is the best hotel and it is conveniently located in relation to the major downtown shopping areas. The historic **E&O Hotel** at 10/12 Farquhar Street (Tel: 385322) retains much of its old world charm. The **Hotel Continental** at 5 Penang Road (Tel. 26381), **Ambassador Hotel** at 55 Penang Road (Tel.24-101), **Ming Court Hotel** at 202A Macalister Road (Tel. 26131), and **Merlin Inn** 126 Jalan Burmah (Tel. 376166) are also good choices for downtown accommodations.

Downtown Georgetown hotels are primarily used by business travelers rather than tourists. However, more and more tourists find Georgetown to be a convenient location from which to enjoy Penang. The Shangri-la International Hotels provide a shuttle service between their downtown and Batu Ferringhi beachfront hotels -- Rasa Sayang, Golden Sands, and Palm Beach. Consequently, if you have little interest in surf and sand, you may want to stay at their downtown hotel and use their shuttle for visiting the beach.

If you enjoy beaches and beach resort accommodations, stay at one of Penang's fine beachfront resort hotels in Batu Ferringhi. You will find several excellent hotels on this northern section of Penang Island: **Rasa Sayang** (Tel. 811811), **Palm Beach** (Tel. 811621), **Lone Pine** (Tel. 811511), **Golden Sands** (Tel. 811911), **Holiday Inn** (Tel. 811601), **Casuarina Beach** (Tel. 811711), and **Bayview Beach** (Tel. 811311).

Whatever you do, experience Penang's many and varied travel and shopping pleasures. This friendly city may lack the glitz of more cosmopolitan urban centers, but it has a certain charm of a by-gone era touched by a long and illustrious colonial history. Be sure to explore its streets on foot and by trishaw. Stroll along its beaches, gardens, and hills. Above all, shop its many noisy and crowded streets, shopping complexes, department stores, factories, markets, and hawker stalls. But don't forget to sample it's wonderful restaurant and hawker foods. Experience its history, architecture, and diverse culture by touring Penang's many historical sites, buildings, and temple complexes. As you leave Penang, you will be departing from one of Asia's truly delightful travel and shopping destinations.

Chapter Nine

THE EAST COAST

If your travel and shopping interests include arts and crafts, traditional rural cultures, interesting people, festivals, jungles, lakes, rivers, beaches, and resorts, you should definitely include East Coast Malaysia on your travel itinerary. While Penang, Kuala Lumpur, and Malacca are decidedly urban and Chinese in character, the East Coast is the center of rural Malay culture. Here you will quickly slip into the traditional world of the Malays, the *bumi-putra*, or "sons of the soil" as they like to call themselves when specifying their distinct identity in contrast to other groups in pluralistic Malaysia.

The East Coast has long been the travel and tourism backwaters of Malaysia. Lacking a good infrastructure supportive of agricultural development and saddled with a road system subject to frequent flooding, the East Coast has remained outside the mainstream of Malaysia's booming development. While a relatively poor region in Malaysia, the East Coast does offer a great deal to independent travelers who prefer to explore off the beaten path and learn about local people, cultures, and crafts. With beautiful palm tree-lined sandy beaches facing the South China

Sea, quiet villages and towns occasionally punctuated by booming oil complexes and beachside resorts, dense jungles, rugged mountains, sleepy rivers, and formidable swamps, the East Coast has primarily been the travel domain of budget travelers, businessmen, and resort goers. Today it is awakening itself to the influx of more and more export industries and tourists.

GETTING TO KNOW YOU

Budget travelers long ago discovered East Coast Malaysia and passed the word on to fellow travelers that this was a mecca for discovering unique cultures, peoples, lifestyles, lovely beaches, and cheap eats and sleeps. As a result, the East Coast -- especially around the city of Kota Bharu, the State capital of Kelantan -- has a tourist infrastructure skewed toward budget travelers and backpackers.

If you are looking for deluxe accommodations, gourmet restaurants, and well organized tours, they do exist but you will have to look very hard to find such travel amenities here. For the most part, you will discover adequate and inexpensive accommodations, good but basic restaurants, and tourist assistance in the forms of tourist police, tourist offices, and tour companies offering several individualized tours. This is an area that individual travelers have long ago learned to do on their own and with relative ease minus an abundance of first-class and deluxe tourist amenities. So take a car, get some good maps, explore the area on your own, and let serendipity guide you to some wonderful East Coast travel and shopping discoveries!

Today many more tourists are discovering the charms of East Coast Malaysia. Accordingly, a new tourist infrastructure -- first-class hotels, restaurants, tours, and shops - more appropriate for first-class travelers is beginning to develop along the East Coast, primarily in the more resort-minded Kuantan and stretching north to Kota Bharu in the State of Kelantan. Since the East Coast very soon may become a major travel destination in Southeast Asia, get there soon before the crowds arrive!

East Coast Malaysia has much to offer travelers and shoppers. Beginning with the State of Kelantan and the city of Kota Bharu on the northeast coast, here is Malaysia in its most traditional form. Picturesque villages, small towns, and cities are primarily Malay and orthodox Muslim in character. This is an area of fishermen, farmers, and skilled craftsmen. Both men and women dress traditionally, observe traditional customs, and perform traditional ceremonies.

But best of all, shopping opportunities along the East Coast are closely tied to the ongoing Malay culture of highly skilled craftsmen and small cottage industries. Rather than just buying imported products in shops and department stores, on the East Coast you see products being made at their point of origin and used in traditional ceremonies and festivals. You visit craftsmen and artists in factories and in their homes who make the very products you will buy. This becomes the ultimate shopping and travel experience -- learning about the setting, culture, and people relevant to the making of items you acquire and cherish for years to come. Here, you will visit master craftsmen and observe them making the famous textiles (batik and songket), kites, brassware, pottery, silver, mats, and baskets found in abundance in the shops and stalls of Penang, Kuala Lumpur, and Malacca. In so doing, shopping along the East Coast becomes a very meaningful travel experience -- moreso than in many other areas of Malaysia.

NOT ALL IS APPEALING

However, not everything you find along the East Coast may appeal to your sense of taste and style. You may find, for example, the designs of traditional East Coast products to be too traditional and exotic for your home. The making of kites, brassware, batik, songket, pottery, silver, mats, and baskets is interesting to observe and understand in the East Coast setting, but few East Coast craftsmen are sensitive to the design preferences of foreign tourists. Craftsmen tend to produce the same designs over and over to the point where many products are best left in their place of origin rather than transported to the homes of travelers who may later become disappointed with their purchases.

You can clearly see the differences in product designs as you travel from Kota Bharu in the North to Kuantan further South, and especially when you arrive in Kuala Lumpur. Malaysia has made major strides to make the arts and crafts more appealing to the design preferences of foreigners. The government now employs young creative artists and designers who go into the villages and towns to teach local craftsmen new designs more appropriate for the export market. Exporters and shopkeepers who work directly with village craftsmen also commission their own designs.

As a result, you will clearly see major differences in designs if you compare, for example, the batik, songket, silver, and mats offered for sale in the shophouses of Kota Bharu with those offered in the handicraft centers of Infokraf and Karyaneka in Kuala Lumpur or at Mini Malaysia just outside Malacca. The differences are very striking. Unless you are a collector of traditional handicrafts, you will most likely enjoy seeing the products made in their traditional setting in Kota Bharu, but you may not buy much because for some reasons these items have a decidely drab and amateurish look about them. They are interesting, but what can you do with them once you return home? On the other hand, you will most likely get excited about buying the same products in Kuala Lumpur because you find one important difference: the designs and colors have been changed to appeal to your sense of style and taste. This is not by accident; it is by design as Malaysia begins to transform its traditional arts and crafts to appeal to the tastes of Western tourists and commercial houses abroad.

We do not mean to denigrate traditional designs, but neither are we enthusiastic buyers and promoters of what we see being produced along the East Coast. We see a certain naivete among many Malaysians who feel the world is clamouring for more Malay handicrafts -- if only the Malays could produce more for the market. This simply is not true. Design and quality are major problems that need to be addressed by talented artists who can communicate combining traditional processes with more Western-oriented designs.

All arts and crafts dynamically evolve in response to their cultural, social, economic, and political environments. We suggest a great deal more must be done to make Malay arts and crafts more appealing to the larger world. It's true that some people love the traditional designs and will go directly to the East Coast where they can still get the "real thing". But many tourists need greater diversity of selections.

Here we are merely observing a basic fact of commercial life that has existed for centuries in Malaysia: Malay craftsmen produce some of the finest hand work found anywhere in the world, but they do so by copying traditional designs. Few are creative in the sense of developing new designs outside the traditional patterns. It's only when forces outside the culture -- be it the royal courts centuries ago or the government, art and craft associations, or commercial houses today -- begin introducing new design ideas and then link those ideas to an export market that fuels the sale and reproduction of such goods that one begins to see dramatic changes in designs and colors. While arts and crafts have traditional use and can be collected and admired for their historical and intrinsic values, they also are for sale in Malaysia, because they generate employment and economic development in rural areas throughout the country. When you buy these arts and crafts, you help develop artist skills, employ people, and develop the country.

SHOPPING AND TRAVELING THE EAST COAST

The East Coast is perhaps best approached at the very north in the state of Kelantan which borders with Thailand. The state is famous for its unspoilt beaches, picturesque countryside, and Malay culture and lifestyle. The major city is the State capital of Kota Bharu, famous for its culture, crafts, and ceremonies.

We suggest that you either fly into Kota Bharu from where you can rent a car to drive south along the coast or drive from Penang or Kuala Lumpur to Kota Bharu and then proceed south. However, be careful driving this area during the rainy season. We did get caught in some very serious floods during November 1988 -- the worst in over 30 years. All roads from Kota Bharu were completely cut off by flood waters; over 30 people died; and we experienced some frightening moments when we feared we might be swept away as two feet of rushing flood waters surrounded and partially filled our car. This was not our idea of a good time!

We suggest this north-south East Coast driving strategy, because this area is convenient to drive on your own, public transportation and tours are limited, and you will have the advantage of being in Malaysia's most traditional and artistically expressive area first. Here, you will get to see the "real Malays" who produce the largest variety of arts and crafts along the East Coast. As you drive south to the next major shopping areas of Kuala Trengganu in the state of Trengganu and Kuantan in the State of Pahang, you will see fewer locally produced arts and crafts as the East Coast becomes more beach and resort-oriented. Indeed, many of the items available in Kuala Trengganu and Kuantan are imported from Kota Bharu or Kuala Lumpur. Accordingly, you will see changes in styles, designs, and colors as you get closer to the influence of Kuala Lumpur. If you begin your shopping adventure in Kota Bharu, you will see the largest selection of traditional items first as you proceed south and later east toward the modern metropolis of Kuala Lumpur.

You can easily shop the East Coast in three to five days. The distances between the key shopping cities of Kota Bharu, Kuala Trengganu, and Kuantan are not great and the roads are relatively good except during the rainy season. The distance between cities usually can be driven

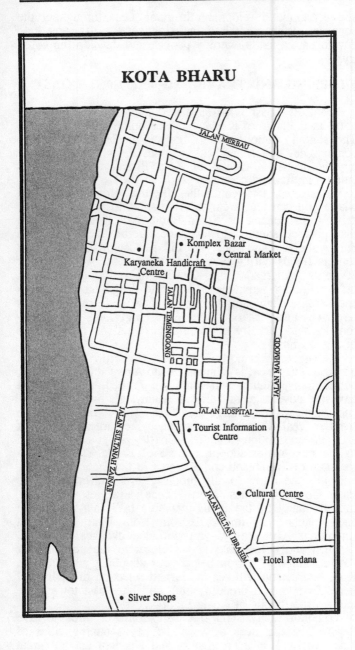

within three to five hours. If you plan your schedule well,
you can cover Kota Bharu in one or two days and Kuala
Trengganu and Kuantan in one day each. However, if you
wish to include sightseeing, festivals, the beaches, scuba
diving, and island hopping in your travel plans as well as
excursions to the Thai border and some of the popular
jungle and lake regions, plan to spend at least a week to
10 days exploring the East Coast.

KOTA BHARU

Kota Bharu is the capital of the State of Kelantan,
which means the "Land of Lighting". Located in the
northeast corner of peninsular Malaysia and bordering with
Thailand, Kelantan is one of Malaysia's most noted centers
for arts and crafts. Kelantan silver, textiles, pottery, bamboo weaving, mats, handbags, baskets, and kites are famous throughout Malaysia. Indeed, you will see many of
their products in the shops of Kuala Lumpur and Penang.

Given its close proximity to Southern Thailand, Kelantan is also a center for imported clothes and handicrafts
from Thailand. Shop the streets of Kota Bharu and you
will quickly discover a wonderful mix of Malay and Thai
products selling in the markets and shops.

The Streets of Kota Bharu

Like many upcountry and East Coast towns, Kota Bharu
is a relatively quiet and easy going commercial and government center. Bathed in the heat, humidity, and torential
rains of the tropics, it has a worn, make-shift, rustic, and
chaotic look about it. The people are friendly and inquisitive and at times helpful. Service is marginal although
well meaning.

Situated along the Kelantan River, the center of town is
lined with numerous two and three-story architecturally
unexciting commercial and government buildings. The
tallest buildings in town are hotels. You can easily walk
the downtown section within 45 minutes. Most downtown
shops and places of interest are within a 10 minute walk.

Most shopping in Kota Bharu takes place during the day
between the hours of 9am and 6pm, Saturday through
Wednesday. Like the rest of the East Coast, offices and
stores are closed a half day on Thursday and all day Friday. Unlike many other cities in Malaysia, Kota Bharu
does not have a night market. The major night-time activity centers around a few open-air food stalls.

Kota Bharu is divided into two distinct shopping areas.
The first area is the **downtown commercial section** near

the Central Market. It is bordered by Jalan Pintu Pong, Jalan Kebun Sultan, Jalan Mahmud, Jalan Hospital, and Jalan Temenggong. The best way to shop this area is to go directly to the Central Market. From there you can easily walk to the nearby shops, department stores, hotels, the handicraft center, and the state museum.

The second shopping area is found on the **northern outskirts of town** along the road to Pantai Cinta Berahi or the Beach of Passionate Love. This is the area's cottage industry center. It is lined with numerous shophouses offering a large selection of locally made textiles, arts, and crafts.

When you arrive in Kota Bharu, we strongly recommend that you first visit the **Tourist Information Centre** on Jalan Sultan Ibrahim. Here you can pick up maps and tourist literature on the area as well as ask any questions you might have regarding shopping and traveling in Kelantan and Kota Bharu. Be sure to pick up a good map of the city as well as a copy of *The Visitor's Guide to Kelantan*. The newly formed Tourist Police operate from this office, and they are very helpful in assisting travelers. With this stop you should be able to gain an excellent overview of the area from which you can better target your shopping and travel plans.

Your second visit should be to the **museum** (Istana Jahar) where you will see an excellent historical display of local arts and crafts. The two floors of this beautifully carved traditional Malay building are filled with nicely displayed wayang puppets, tops, knives (*kris*), costumes, songket, musical instruments, drums, jewelry, silverware, and porcelain.

Shopping Products and Places

Situated at the heart of Malaysia's richest cultural and ceremonial area, Kota Bharu's major shopping attractions are **textiles (batik and songket), silver, kites, tops, pottery, and woven products** such as mengkuang mats and baskets. While most of these items are made in villages outside Kota Bharu, they are available in Kota Bharu's many shops. The Central Market, handicraft center (Kratangan Kelantan), and several shops in the city as well as along the road to the Beach of Passionate Love (Cottage Industry Centre) offer good selections of these products.

If you visit the shophouses and factories in and around Kota Bharu, you will be able to see craftsmen at work making these products and you can purchase items in the factory shops. However, don't expect villages to yield many or better buying opportunities than the factories and shops around Kota Bharu. If you want to buy directly from the craftsmen in villages who are supplying the shops in Kota Bharu, you may be wasting your time. Especially in the case of textiles and woven products, shops commission these works in the villages. They provide villagers with the materials and designs and pay them by the piece work. As a result, few villagers sell their products directly to tourists. Most shopping, therefore, is concentrated in the market, handicraft center, shops, and shophouses of Kota Bharu.

Downtown Shopping

Downtown Kota Bharu has a few shopping attractions worth exploring. Its **Central Market** (Pasar Pusat Kota Bharu), located on Jalan Pintu Pong and across the street from the Shopping Bazaar (Bazaar Membeli-Belah), is one of the best organized and most interesting ones we found in Malaysia. This octagon shaped three-story structure combines a wet and dry market under one roof. Its a friendly, colorful, and relatively clean market, and a great place to take pictures, chat with the local vendors, and make a few small purchases. Assuming you are not in the market for fresh meats, vegetables, fruits, groceries, and cheap eats, go directly to the third floor where you will find numerous stalls selling batik, songket, clothes, footwear, ceramics, handbags, mats, brassware, plastic flowers, and a large assortment of housewares. The batik comes from Kelantan, Trengganu, and southern Thailand. While many of these items may appeal to tourists, most are being sold to local consumers. So don't expect to find a great deal here that you will purchase for your own use or as souvenirs and gifts for friends. The third floor also offers the best vantage point to take photos of the colorful market activity taking place on the first floor of this building.

Just across the street from the Central Market is a three-story shopping bazaar, **Komplex Bazar Buluh Kubu**, where you may find handicrafts, jewelry, and clothes more suitable to your interests. Small shops in this complex sell batik, songket, clothes, footwear, kites, jewelry, ceramics, books, luggage, baskets, silk flowers, rattan items, and tops. Look for **Noikayati Mahmud** (Lot 2, No. 49) on the second floor for some nice jewelry. **Nik Kraftangan & Karyanika** (Lot 2, No. 23) has a small but good selection of handicrafts, especially kites, ceramics, and silk flowers. On the end of the third floor look for **A. A. Krat** (Lot 3, No. 23). This is a relatively large handicraft shop offering a good selection of pottery, baskets, rattan, tops, and Thai bronzeware. Another end shop, **Gedung Seni**

(Lot 3, No. 22) also has a good selection of handicrafts, including kites, porcelain, knives and daggers (*kris*), brass, pottery, wayang puppets, tops, and fans. As you further explore the third floor -- both front and back aisles -- you will find a few other shops offering similar types of hand-crafted items.

Across the street from the shopping bazaar is a clothing bazaar operated outdoors along the first floor of a commercial building. You will find lots of cheap clothes here, especially jackets -- both imported and local.

Next door to the Central Market is Kota Bharu's largest department store -- **Pandai Timur**. The four-story building sells typical department store items. You will find a jewelry section here on the second floor that primarily sells gold jewelry. The full service supermarket and the fast photo service on the first floor are worth visiting if you have grocery and film needs. Kentucky Fried Chicken is situated at the end of this building -- a testimony to the fact that international fast-food fare has arrived in this cosmopolitan corner of Malaysia!

Just three blocks east of the Central Market and near the museum is the **Karyaneka Handicraft Centre** (Pusat Kraftangan Karyaneka). This government operated store has a good selection of pottery, silver, wood carvings, batik, songket, copper plated art, kites, decorative shell hangings, drums, wayang kulit puppets, baskets, bags, tops, and batik paintings. We especially like the unique floral paintings on embossed copper which are done by a local artist and which we did not find in any other shops.

If you are interested in local silver products, be sure to visit the shops along Jalan Sultanah Zainab in the southern section of town. **Kelantan Traditional Craft & Antiques** (3970 Jalan Sultanah Zainab) offers a large selection of silver products (serving pieces, paper weights, letter openers, jewelry, candle stick holders, ash trays, spoons) as well as wayang puppets, batik, ceramics, pottery, kites, and antiques. They also have two shops north of town (**Tuan Haji Jaccob & Sons.**), a showroom in Kuala Lumpur, and export activity with Japan and Australia. A few doors down from here is **Kelantan Silvercraft Mahd. Salleh & Sons** which also offers a wide range of silver products and handicrafts. It also operates the store next door that sells Selangor Pewter.

Other shopping areas within town include **Jalan Temenggong**, the main street which is lined with shops selling local goods, and **Jalan Tok Hakim**, which has several jewelry shops. The first-class **Hotel Perdana** on Jalan Mahmud has representatives from two local shops selling handicrafts in the hotel lobby.

Cottage Industry Centre

Kota Bharu's second major shopping area is the **Cottage Industry Centre** which is a five kilometer stretch of road north of town leading to the Beach of Passionate Love. Numerous shops line both sides of this road. Most of them are also the homes of businesspeople who maintain a showroom out front from which they sell all kinds of local handicrafts. Many shops only specialize in textiles -- batik and songket -- or kites. Others offer a large variety of handicrafts under one roof.

Beginning at the southern section of this road, you will come to several batik and songket shops. **Cik Minah Hj. Omar,** on the right side of the road, has a nice selection of silk and cotton yardage and clothes as well as batik and songket. Directly across the street is another similar shop, **Haji Idris Omar. Syarikat Sri Kijang, Che Zainab Hj. Che Noh, Hajah Cik Bidah,** and **Rashidah's** also are nearby and sell similar selections of batik, songket, and silk yardage and clothes.

About two more kilometers down this road you will come to two shops offering some of best selections of the popular Kelantan kites: **Nik Mohd. Noor Abdullah** and **Ismail Bin Josuh.** These shops also sell other handicrafts, such as batik, silver, fans, porcelain, and carved elephants from Thailand.

The next major shop is **Tuan Haji Yaacob & Sons** which consists of two shops next to each another. The shop on the right has a good selection of silver, antiques, batik, kites, paintings, pewter, knives (*kris*), wayang puppets, songket, silk scarves, tops, pots, and ceramics. The second shop is more elegant and better displays the same types of products found in the first shop.

One of the larger handicraft shops in this area is the **Local Handicraft Centre,** which has a good selection of kites, batik paintings, silver, placemats, tops, batik, songket, Thai lacquer animals, hats, fans, latterns, and tablecloths.

Other shops to look for along the remainder of this road are **Ishah Batik, Norbatik,** and **Wan Roslida Batek** -- shops frequented by many tour buses. At this point you come to the end of the road and the Cottage Industry Centre as you enter the Beach of Passionate Love, a misnomer for a rather average looking beach!

Enjoying Your Stay

Kelantan and Kota Bharu have a great deal to offer those who wish to get close to a people and their culture.

As the cultural center of the Malays, Kelantan proudly presents its people and culture through numerous performances, ceremonies, and crafts. From February through October on Mondays, Wednesdays, and Saturdays you can attend performances of top-spinning (Gasing), kite-flying, shadow puppet theater (wayang kulit), self-defence (silat) at the **Kelantan Cultural Centre** (Gelanggang Seni) located across the street from the Hotel Perdana on Jalan Mahmud. Be sure to pick up a copy of the current *Kelantan Cultural Events* brochure at the Tourist Information Centre. It gives the schedule of upcoming cultural events at the Centre. Also check on the specific dates for the annual Kelantan Top Spinning Competition (usually held in September), Kelantan Giant Drum Festival (usually held in June), as well as the International Kite Festival of Kelantan (usually held in April).

Local sightseeing attractions within Kota Bharu include the **Museum (Istana Jahar), The State Mosque,** and the **Istana Balai Besar** or "The Palace With the Large Audience Hall" -- a beautifully carved building housing the Throne Room, the Hall of Audience, and the State Legislative Assembly Hall -- located next to the Museum.

Outside Kota Bharu you can drive to the Thai border to shop at the Thai town of Sungaikalok, visit several nice beaches within 25 kilometers of the cities (Beach of Passionate Love, Beach of Whispering Breeze, Beach of Melody), the famous fishing village of Kuala Besar, Southeast Asia's largest reclining Buddha (Wat Photivihan), waterfalls, and the oldest mosque in Malaysia (Masjid Kampung Laut).

The best hotel in town is the first-class Hotel Perdana on Jalan Mahmud. Nothing fancy, but it does have the basic amenities one would expect in an upcountry first-class hotel. You also will find many inexpensive hotels and accommodations in the city as well as along the beaches.

Several tours of the area are available. The Hotel Perdana, for example, sponsors morning and afternoon tours. The morning tour takes you to the Central Market, Museum, Istanta Balai Besar (palace), Cottage Industries Centre, Silver Centre, a kite-making and batik factory, and the Beach of Passionate Love. The afternoon tour goes to Sabak Beach, the fishing village, Istana Negeri, raft houses, the Reclining Buddha, and a silvercraft and antique centre. They also sponsor river trips. Call 785000 for information on these and other tours sponsored through the Hotel Perdana. The Tourist Information Centre also sponsors half-day and full-day tours of the area as well as three-day tours into villages, up rivers, and into the jungle. Call

785534 or 783543 for information.

KUALA TRENGGANU

Kuala Trengganu, the capital of the State of Trengganu, is located 165 kilometers south of Kota Bharu, approximately half way between Kota Bharu and Kuantan. Situated on the mouth of the Sungai Trengganu River and facing the South China Sea, this is a bustling city of wide streets, tall buildings, a charming historical waterfront, and a colorful market. It is one of the wealthier cities along the East Coast, having benefited enormously from Trengganu's rich natural resources of oil, fisheries, and agriculture.

Kuala Trengganu functions as a good transitional point for travelers along the East Coast. It combines the best of traditional Malay culture with the amenities of a fine resort travel destination. If you are coming from Kota Bharu, for example, you may feel you have just entered a resort area after having experienced a few of the rigors of traveling "upcountry".

Trengganu is rich in Malay culture. Its arts and crafts are alive and well in Kuala Trengganu's many shops and factories. But Kuala Trengganu also offers some of the best beaches and water related activities on the East Coast. It boasts gorgeous white sand beaches, idyllic islands, picturesque lagoons and fishing villages, and some of the finest marine life in Southeast Asia. Its tourist infrastructure, exemplified by the deluxe Pantai Primula Hotel and the Tanjung Jara Beach Hotel, is well on its way to making Trengganu a major center for tourism. Indeed, Trengganu has a well deserved reputation for being one of the favorite destinations for many travelers and holiday-makers who want to just relax and enjoy the surf and sun. It has everything you might expect from a seaside resort, and more. Best of all, it offers some good shopping opportunities that can be enjoyed in a fine resort setting.

The Streets of Kuala Trengganu

Kuala Trengganu is an inviting city of wide streets, boulevards, impressive high-rise buildings, a charming historical Chinese section, a bustling waterfront, and colorful market. It's a relatively easy city to navigate -- once you identify the major streets and learn that many streets follow a circular pattern.

It's easiest to get around Trengganu if you have a car. However, in Trengganu it is difficult to rent a car. You are well advised to come to Trengganu with a car. You should have no problem renting a car in places such as

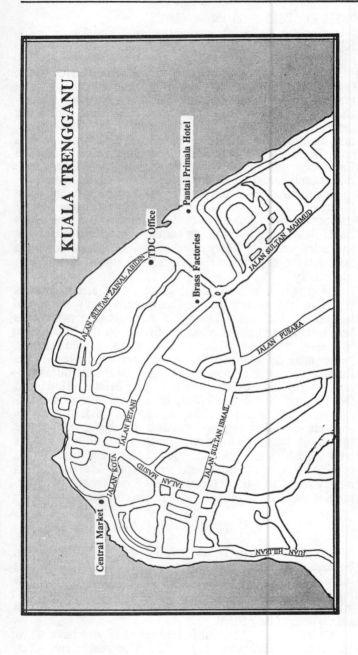

Kuantan, Kuala Lumpur, or Penang.

Like Kota Bharu, shopping in Kuala Trengganu is divided into two distinct areas. The first area is the **downtown commercial section** which is concentrated in the northwest section of this urban peninsula, at the confluence of the Sungai Trengganu River and the South China Sea. This shopping area is bordered by Jalan Sultan Ismail, Jalan Masjid, Jalan Tok Lam, Jalan Kota, Jalan Petani, Jalan Bandar, and Jalan Sultan Zainal Albidin. Here you will find the Central Market, rows of small shophouses, and the major hotels.

The second major shopping area is the **cottage industry center** located south of the city along a 15 kilometer stretch of coastal road that leads to Kuantan. Here you will find several shops as well as a handicraft center offering everything from dried fish to brassware and woven mats.

Upon arriving in Kuala Trengganu, we recommend that you first visit the **Tourist Development Corporation Office** on Jalan Sultan Zainal Abidin (Tel: 621-433) for information on the city and outlying area. This is one of the larger tourist information offices on the East Coast. Be sure to pick up a good map and tourist brochures on the area. The staff in this office are very helpful, so do ask questions to better help you plan your visit. We also highly recommend visiting the **State Museum** at Jalan Cherong Lanjut. This excellent museum is one of the finest in all of Malaysia, rivaling some of the collections at the National Museum in Kuala Lumpur. One of the highlights of the museum is its fine collection of knives (*kris*), the making of which is still an art form practiced in Trengganu today.

Shopping Products and Places

Trengganu's major shopping strengths are similar to those of Kota Bharu: batik, songket weaving, silver, woodcarving, brassware, pottery, and pandan weaving (hats, bags, food covers, floor mats, and decorative wall pieces). Trengganu is especially noted for its yellow and white brassware using the lost wax process, intricate woodcarvings, and mengkuang (pandanus) mat weaving. The attractive Trengganu mats are especially good buys. In addition, Trengganu is famous for kris making, boat making, and silk production.

However, you will see some major differences in the colors and styles of Trengganu handicrafts. Colors tend to be brighter, and designs are more appealing to tourists. Indeed, designers from Kuala Lumpur are having a definite impact on handicrafts in Trengganu. The pandan weaving is a case in point. You will find many lovely hats, bags, floor mats, and decorative wall pieces which would make attractive additions to many Western homes. A good place to see such designs is the **Handicraft Center.** The styles and colors of batik, songket, and silk also are more appealing to tourists than those found in Kota Bharu. A good place to see new designs is at the **Suterasemai** silk factory and showroom south of Kuala Trengganu.

Handicraft production in Kuala Trengganu is organized similarly to that in Kota Bharu. Villagers produce most of the handicrafts on an exclusive commission basis for shops in and around Kuala Trengganu who provide them with materials and designs. Therefore, don't expect to buy handicrafts directly from the villages since villages primarily produce for their sponsors. You can visit a few brassware factories in town, watch handicraft demonstrations at the Handicraft Center, and make purchases at the same time. For unique Malay silk, you can observe the production process at the Suterasemai factory and make purchases at their showroom.

Downtown Shopping

For the most part downtown Kuala Trengganu has limited shopping opportunities for international travelers. Most shops and department stores are stocked with goods for local consumers. As a result, we suggest you concentrate most of your downtown shopping in and around the **Central Market.**

Located adjacent to the Trengganu River at the end of Jalan Kota, the **Central Market** is a little confusing to first-time visitors. You can easily miss its best part if you don't know where to go. The market can be approached from two entrances. If you enter by way of the parking garage at the end of Jalan Kota, you will immediately come to a colorful and chaotic area of vendors sitting on the pavement selling fresh fruits and vegetables. To get to the main market building from this area, you will have wind through the maze of traffic -- keeping to your right -- until you come to an entrance to an enclosed market building. As you enter this crowded building, you will see more vendors selling fresh fruits and vegetables as well as fresh meats, cooking ingredients, and household goods. But you will want to go to the second floor, the entrance to which is found at the other end of the building. So be sure to walk all the way through this building until you come to the other entrance which has the stairway to the second floor. It would be best, however, to enter the market at this main entrance.

The second floor of the Central Market is a "must" stop in this city. This shopping arcade boasts one of the best collections of small shops on the East Coast selling batik, songket, brassware, woven items, stuffed toys, Thai bronzeware, and other handicrafts. Here, you will find well organized small shops lining both sides of a large hallway. You will find some beautiful songket in several of the shops, and a very large selection of brassware items, such as cooking utensils, vases, serving trays, candles, and ash trays.

Just outside the entrance of the Central Market you will find several shops selling woven items, such as baskets and mats. At the corner of Jalan Mesjid and Jalan Jail several vendor stalls offer inexpensive clothes. If you are on Jalan Masjid, you might want to browse through a small, congested, and somewhat touristy handicraft shop, **Nor Atikah's Songket** (A5 Jalan Masjid), for batik, songket, kites, and Thai items. At 73 Jalan Paya Bunga you will find **Usaha Desa**, a one-stop shopping center offering local handicrafts as well as contemporary hand-printed batik fashion wear.

If you are interested in observing the production of batik and brassware, consider visiting **Inche Wan Ismail**, a small house and workshop located just off of the main commercial section of town at 32 Kg. Ladang Sekolah, Jalan Sultan Zainal Abidin. You will see a sign along the road to direct you to this house-workshop. You can see men doing printed batik as well as watch the lost wax process as the molds for making brassware are fired in mounds of smoking charcoal. Expect to leave this house smelling like charcoal!

South of the City

Another major shopping area for Kuala Trengganu is the coastal road south of town on the way to Kuantan. Since the total distance you must travel to visit most of the shops and factories is 15 kilometers, you will need a car to shop this area properly. Most of the shops are located along the road. However, you will see an occasional sign that will point you into the direction of a village or town. We followed these signs and concluded they led to nowhere -- someone forget to take them down from a few years ago!

One of the most innovative silk-weaving companies in Malaysia, **Suterasemai**, is located at Kuala Ibai, just off the main southern road, approximately six kilometers from Kuala Trengganu. This place is a little hard to find since it is off the main road. As soon as you cross a small bridge look for a green and yellow sign on the left and then be prepared to immediately turn right into an industrial estate area. As you follow the road for another kilometer, look for a green fenced compound with several new red buildings. You can tour the factory as well as purchase silk fabric and clothes in the showroom. The clothing designs are limited but they may appeal to you. We found the ads for this company more attractive than their actual products. Nonetheless, the clothes here are probably the most fashionable found along the East Coast.

As you travel the remainder of the main road, you will find several small shops selling a combination of salted fish and handicrafts. The salted fish from this area are very popular, and shops package them in plastic bags from which they hang the fish in front of their shop. The most popular handicraft items in this area are the woven mats, baskets, and bags as well as batik and brassware.

The **Malaysian Handicraft Centre** (also known as the Karyaneka Handicraft Centre) is one of the "must" stops along this road. It is located approximately 15 kilometers south of the city on the lefthand side of the road. Its showroom is filled with a large variety of locally produced handicrafts: baskets, bags, placemats, hats, mats, stuffed animals, silver jewelry, batik, songket, silk, kites, pottery, woodcarvings, and model boats. Be sure to go to the back of this building where you can observe the making of handicrafts. Several girls demonstrate the making of mats and purses. We especially like their innovative designs for functional beach mats -- complete with a large compartment to carry your beachwear and related items that also can be used as a sand-filled pillow! You can also meet the designers here who are responsible for introducing new ideas and designs to the production of local handicrafts.

Enjoying Your Stay

There's much to see and do in Trengganu. Within the town you can visit the bustling waterfront, stroll through the historic Chinese section (Jalan Bandar), observe traditional boat making and village life at Pulau Duyong (an island in the river across from the downtown jetty), and visit the stately mosque on Jalan Masjid and the Maziah Palace (Istana Maziah) near Bukit Puteri. The finest hotel in town is the **Pantai Primula Hotel**, a pleasant surprise after visiting Kota Bharu. They have excellent restaurants (Cacade Grill and Rhusila Coffee Shop) and a complete program of sports and sponsor day trips to Kapus Island (Paulau Kapas).

Outside the city most activities center around the beaches and jungles. Trengganu is one of the finest places in Malaysia to swim, scuba dive, snorkel, wind surf, enjoy picturesque islands, and explore through jungles. A marine and divers paradise, it is often favorably compared by locals to Australia's Great Barrier Reef. **Four islands in particular are popular tourist destinations** -- Pulau Redang, Pulau Perhentian, Pulau Kapas, and Pulau Tenggol. These islands can be reached by boat, and they have overnight accommodations for visitors. Other popular destinations include **Marang Fishing Village** (15 kilometers from town), **Sekayu Waterfalls** (56 kilometers from town), **Kenyir Dam** (Malaysia's largest dam), and **Rantau Abang Beach** (60 kilometers south of town) with its famous giant leather back turtles -- the largest weighing 1,000 kilos! One of the finest beach resorts is **Tanjung Jara Beach Hotel** which is located 60 kilometers south of Kuala Trengganu.

You will find several travel agencies in Kuala Trengganu that offer a variety of tours and can assist you in planning your own individualized itinerary. Check at the Tourist Development Corporation office and your hotel for recommended tour groups.

KUANTAN

Kuantan, a major East Coast city in the State of Pahang, is just a few hours drive from Kuala Trengganu and Kuala Lumpur as well as the southern State of Johore and Singapore. Pahang, Malaysia's largest state, is a popular tourist destination for its hill stations, jungle adventures, lakes, beaches, and islands. Given its close proximity to Kuala Lumpur, Johore, and Singapore, Kuantan has become a popular seaside resort for weekend travelers, holiday-makers, and tourists. Of our three East Coast cities, Kuantan is the most popular destination for tourists. Resort hotels, including a Club Med just north of the city as well as the international standard Hyatt Kuantan and Merlin Inn Resort, make this an extremely pleasant location to enjoy its wonderful beaches, islands, and recreational activities or just relax to soak up the sun and surf while enjoying the amenities of deluxe resort accommodations.

Being both close to Kuala Lumpur and a seaside resort, shopping in Kuantan reflects the influence of Kuala Lumpur and the tastes of tourists. You will find, for example, more and more products made and designed in Kuala Lumpur appearing in the shops of Kuantan. You also see numerous handicrafts imported from Kota Bharu and Kuala Trengganu in these same shops. While Kuantan is not a

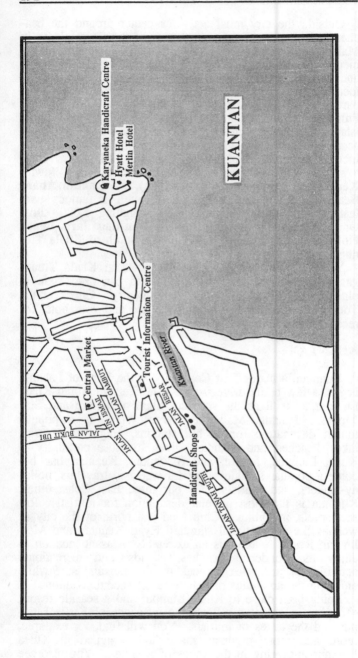

shopper's paradise, it has much to offer anyone who wants to enjoy a relaxing atmosphere as well as do some shopping at the same time.

The Streets of Kuantan

Situated in a lovely coastal setting of white sand beaches and tropic vegetation, Kuantan is one of those idyllic places you could spend lazy days doing nothing of any particular importance. It's a colorful, bustling town of rustic charm and easy going character.

Being a small town, Kuantan is relatively easy to get around in although it is somewhat spread out along the river. The major resort hotels are located within four kilometers of downtown Kuantan along the city's popular beach, Telok Chempedak. The town itself has three major streets -- Jalan Besar/Jalan Tanah Puteh, Jalan Mahkota, and Jalan Datuk Wong Ah Jang/Jalan Tun Ismail -- lined with the usual mix of commercial buildings, government offices, and food and market vendors. You can easily walk these main streets within one hour.

Shopping Products and Places

You will find a mix of locally produced and imported products in Kuantan, many items you may have seen already in Kuala Trengganu, Kota Bharu, or Kuala Lumpur. The emphasis here again is on East Coast handicrafts: batik, songket, mats, baskets, wayang puppets, kites, brassware, and windchimes. However, shops also tend to cater to their international client by stocking many imported items, such as Indonesian and Thai handicrafts, as well as such beach resort items as T-shirts and swimwear. Look for Balinese masks from Indonesia and umbrellas and woodcarved elephants and lotus figures from Thailand. You will also find a few shops carrying items from Sarawak, such as pua textiles. You will make a few discoveries such as local batik paintings and one of the best antique shops in Malaysia here in Kuantan.

Shopping in Kuantan takes place either near the resort hotels or in the downtown commercial area. If you stay at the Hyatt Kuantan resort hotel, next door you will find one of Kuantan's best shopping areas -- **Karyaneka Handicraft Centre** which consists of several small vendor shops selling local as well as imported handicrafts. In the downtown area look for the **Central Market** as well as several shops selling batik, handicrafts, and antiques. Altogether, you can easily shop this town in one day.

You will find plenty of tourist information to plan your stay in Kuantan and Pahang. Most major hotels will provide you with maps and brochures. The **Tourist Information Centre** on Jalan Makhota also may be helpful.

Downtown Shopping

Shopping in downtown Kuantan primarily centers on the Central Market as well as on a row of handicraft shops, a batik factory, and an antique store. The **Central Market**, or Pasar Lambak, is located on Jalan Tun Ismail, just behind the town bus terminal. Except for another market experience, you may not find much of interest here. The markets in Kota Bharu and Kuala Trenggenu are much more interesting and worth visiting than this one. This is a combined wet and dry market. Just outside the first floor you will find several vendors selling cheap clothes, fake leather items imported from Thailand, numerous knick knacks, and fruits. The first floor of the market is devoted to fresh fruits, vegetables, and meats. The second floor consists of several vendor stalls selling groceries, pots and pans, and silk flowers as well as a few restaurants, tailors, and seamstresses.

Along **Jalan Besar**, just southwest of the Samudra Riverview Hotel, you will find a row of four shop-houses selling a large variety of nice handicrafts: **Perniagaan Min** (45-6), **Mat Jais Bin Talik** (45-8), **Wan Enterprise** (45-5), and **Sal's Kraf** (45-4). The women running these shops are very friendly and eager to assist you. Each shop sells nearly the same items, so this is a good place to do some comparative shopping. You will find these shops crammed with baskets, mats, kites, wayang puppets, shell windchimes, stuffed animals, kris, bird cages, and fans. Directly across the street you will see several local jewelry and dry fish stores.

If you continue southwest on Jalan Besar, it changes its name to **Jalan Tanah Putih**. As you are about to leave town, you will see a sign on your right directing you to **Batik RM**. Follow the sign for approximately 200 meters until you come to a family compound that also functions as a batik factory and showroom. Here you can see the traditional batik making process. You can also purchase batik fabrics and paintings. The batik paintings are done by a local artist -- Ayam -- who paints both traditional and modern scenes. His paintings cost from M$40 to M$200. Batik RM is the company that makes the special fabrics and T-shirts for the local Club Med resort.

As you return to town, turn left onto **Jalan Dato Wong Ah Jang**. Here you will discover Kuantan's only antique shop and one of Malaysia's best antique shops -- **Golden-light Antique and Curios** (E-1486 Jalan Dato Wong Ah Jang). Indeed, we found it better than most shops in Malacca, the reputed antique center of Malaysia. This shop is packed wall to wall with a large collection of handicrafts and antiques. You will find old Chinese ceramics, Burmese tapestries, pewterware, quail traps, coconut scrapers, Khmer jars, silver figures, jewelry, knives (kris), and fishermen's tackle boxes. Be sure to look at the back room which has the latest acquisitions awaiting to be cleaned before displaying them out front.

Kuantan also has a night market with vendors selling the typical night market items -- clothes, footwear, foods, and household goods. However, the **Sunday Market** is the best market to attend.

Resort Shopping

Most of the major resort hotels, such as the Hyatt, Merlin, and Ramada, have small souvenir shops selling local handicrafts and beachwear. These shops primarily service the needs of their hotel guests rather than appeal to shoppers from outside the hotel.

The major shopping area for the resort hotels is the **Karyaneka Handicraft Centre** which is located near the wonderful beach at Telok Chempedek next to the Hyatt Kuantan Hotel. Here you will find a series of small shops under one roof selling a large variety of beachwear and handicrafts from Malaysia, Thailand, and Indonesia: T-shirts, swimsuits, batik, mats, paintings, placements, pottery, jewelry, ceramics, kites, wind chimes, bags, baskets, fans, masks, and umbrellas. We especially like **Shop #10** which has a very nice collection of traditional and abstract paintings by Noor Aishah and Mohd. Akif, prints, ceramics, Chinese embroidiery, and placemats. This is one of the more stylish shops on the East Coast. Indeed, many of the items in this shop are brought in from the Central (arts and crafts) Market in Kuala Lumpur and thus reflect the styles and talent of Kuala Lumpur. Several other shops, such as Shops #2, 4, and 9, also offer good quality and stylish handicrafts that are more appealing to tourists that what you might find further north in Kota Bharu.

Enjoying Your Stay

The State of Pahang has some of the most varied tourist attractions in all of Malaysia, from beaches to jungles to cool hill stations and lakes. You can choose several different styles of travel in Pahang -- beach resorts, swimming and scuba diving, wilderness adventures and nature trips, and cruises.

Pahang's three major hill stations are the **Cameron Highlands**, in the northwest corner of Pahang and accessible by road from Kuala Lumpur, and **Fraser's Hill** and **Genting Highlands**, both in Western Pahang and very near Kuala Lumpur. If you enjoy gambling, **Genting Highlands** is the only place in Malaysia with legalized gambling. A concrete resort entertainment center located on top of breathtaking mountains surrounding Kuala Lumpur, Genting Highlands is a one to two-hour drive from Kuala Lumpur. **Cameron Highlands** and **Fraser's Hill** are both good places to get away, relax, and enjoy the lush jungles and cool atmospheres. Cameron Highlands is the more developed of these two hill stations but both are rustic and relaxed.

The legendary **Tasek Chini**, 13 lakes located 70 kilometers southwest of Kuantan, is becoming a popular tourist destination. A mythical monster and sunken ancient Khmer city are reputed to exist in Tasek Chini. Go to see for yourself, but also enjoy the scenic trip there as well as the local flora and fauna.

The royal town of **Pekan**, 50 kilometers south of Kuantan, is an important cultural center of Pahang. Here you can observe the making of textiles as well as visit the State Museum to see its fine collection of artifacts.

If you enjoy islands, **Tioman Island** off the coast of southern Pahang may be just your place. This is the largest island off the East Coast and is the fabled Bali Hai Island appearing in the movie *South Pacific*. It offers inexpensive to expensive resort accommodations. You will find a full range of recreational activities to keep you busy, from scuba diving and snorkeling to fishing. There are a few other islands in this same area as well as off the coast of the State of Johor that are open for tourism.

Other interesting sights in Pahang include the Sungei Ular fishing village, the Gunung Tapis Park and the National Park (Taman Negara) for jungle flora and fauna, and the Charah Caves. Information on all of these and other sights is available at the Tourist Information Centre as well as through several tour groups, such as Mayflower Acme Tours (Hyatt Kuantan Hotel, Tel. 521-469), in Kuantan who sponsor a variety of tours to these and other destinations.

Chapter Ten
KUALA LUMPUR

Kuala Lumpur, the capital of Malaysia and "KL" to its residents and seasoned visitors, is one of Asia's most surprising, pleasant, friendly, and inexpensive cities. While many Asian cities are unattractive nightmares of winding streets, congested commercial centers, ugly architecture, and chaotic traffic patterns, Kuala Lumpur sets a different tone altogether.

KL is an attractive and liveable city. It boasts beautiful architecture, spacious gardens and parks, open soccer and cricket fields, wide thoroughfares, colorful markets, and modern hotels, office buildings and shopping centers -- all nestled at the foot of surrounding misty hills and mountains. At times congested with cars, nonetheless, the traffic moves well during most days except for the weekends when KL residents take to the roads to enjoy their weekend holiday.

GETTING TO KNOW YOU

Fast-paced Kuala Lumpur is a visual and cultural feast. It's a splash of many colors shaped by a stamp of orderliness. One of the most modern cities in Asia, KL is a comfortable, convenient, and enticing city to visit, one which will challenge your stereotypes of Southeast Asia and Malaysia.

Reflecting the convergence of a British colonial past, which emphasized planning and public orderliness, and a long history of ethnic diversity, Kuala Lumpur exhibits some of the most interesting architecture and lifestyles in Asia. Its Moorish municipal building, railway station, and mosques, with beautiful arabesque arches, minarets, and domes provide a serene character to KL's dynamic and boldly changing skyline and mix well with historical British colonial architecture and attractive modern hotels, office buildings, and shopping centers.

Worn Chinese shophouses, Indian vendors, and Malay food stalls meandering through Kuala Lumpur's central business district give the city a sense of traditional ethnic commerce best evidenced in Penang and other upcountry towns. Colorful Chinatown, night markets, and handicraft centers juxtaposed with KL's Golden Triangle of upscale shopping centers infuse the city with a certain energy and character, further demonstrating that this is indeed both a traditional and modern Chinese, Malay, and Indian city all rolled up into one big cultural potpourri. It's the mix of so many different elements into the whole that makes this such an interesting place to explore.

Kuala Lumpur is where the action is. During the past two decades the skyline of this city has changed dramatically, attendant with the infusion of new money, business, more money, and more business. Suffering a major recession in the mid-1980s, today Kuala Lumpur is rebounding with renewed vigor. It is one of the most modern cities in Asia. This is the seat of the federal government, where politicians and administrators determine the fate of this rapidly developing nation. This is where new ideas germinate and fashions emanate for a nation on the fast track to becoming a major player among Asia's other newly industrialized nations. It's where Malaysians look to the small but dynamic state of Singapore on its southern shores and wonder why Malaysia shouldn't, too, do as well in drawing the attention and wealth of the world to its shores. Indeed, KL's strategists are planning accordingly to challenge Singapore's reputation as the shopping paradise of Southeast Asia.

Best of all for us, Kuala Lumpur is where the shopping action is! It's not quite Singapore yet, but it has all the makings of an up-start Singapore about to come of age. The basic tourist infrastructure of good hotels, restaurants, transportation, and sights is in place along with shops galore. This is a non-stop shopping city boasting a large number of attractive shopping centers, department stores, hotel shopping arcades, shophouses, and markets. What it needs now are more tourists, greater product variety, and more appealing designs to jump-start this infrastructure into faster action. While KL today is where Singapore was 10 years ago, it may quickly close the gap in the next few years as efforts proceed to transform this city into another shopper's paradise.

Kuala Lumpur is good for two to three days of dedicated shopping. Shop its streets, shopping centers, hotel shopping arcades, department stores, and markets and you will go away with a truly unique shopping experience.

THE STREETS OF KL

Situated at the confluence of the Klang and Gombak rivers, Kuala Lumpur, the "muddy estuary", is a big sprawling city of nearly 2 million people. It's a relatively easy city to get around in given its superb street system, flowing traffic, and ample public transportation. The streets are clean, orderly, and convenient to walk and cross. Except in the midday heat, you should enjoy walking the streets, discovering new shops, purchasing unique items, marveling at the new and old architecture, watching a kaleidoscope of exotic peoples and sights, and listening to the throbbing sounds of a busy city. Most major shopping sections of the city can be reached by taxi within 15 minutes of each other.

Kuala Lumpur's major shopping areas are concentrated in three sections of the city. The older more traditional shopping area is located in and around the **city center** (Old Town) along Jalan Tuanku Abdul Rahman, Jalan Masjid India, Jalan Tun Perak, Jalan Sultan Mohammed Benteng, and Jalan Cheng Lock. Here, you will find row after row of shophouses, department stores, emporiums, demonstration centers, and vendor stalls selling everything from textiles, clothes, and handicrafts to the latest in cosmetics and electronic goods. This is the area of famous Chinatown, City Hall, High Court, Selangor Club, Central Market, National Mosque, and Railway Station. You can easily walk this area within an hour or two, but you are likely to spend at least a half-day exploring the many shops on both the main and side streets. If you include sightseeing with your shopping, this area can take two to three days to complete.

The second major shopping area is termed **"The Golden Triangle"**. This is KL's version of Singapore's Orchard Road. Located directly east of the city center, this is

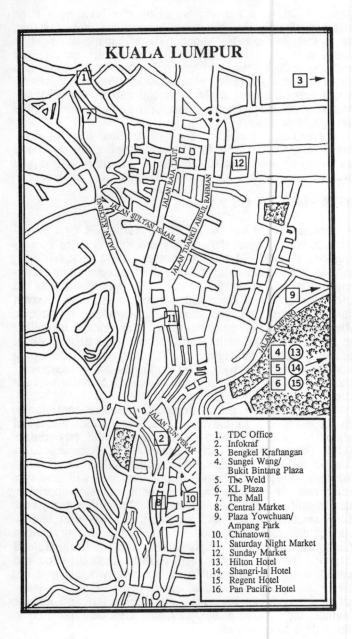

KUALA LUMPUR

1. TDC Office
2. Infokraf
3. Bengkel Kraftangan
4. Sungei Wang/
   Bukit Bintang Plaza
5. The Weld
6. KL Plaza
7. The Mall
8. Central Market
9. Plaza Yowchuan/
   Ampang Park
10. Chinatown
11. Saturday Night Market
12. Sunday Market
13. Hilton Hotel
14. Shangri-la Hotel
15. Regent Hotel
16. Pan Pacific Hotel

the most up-scale shopping area in Malaysia. It consists of major hotels (Regent, Hilton, Shangri-La, Merlin, Equatorial, and Federal) and modern shopping centers (Sungei Wang Plaza, Bukit Bintang Plaza, Kuala Lumpur Plaza, Plaza Yow Chuan, and Ambang Park). Within this area you will also find KL's best handicraft center (Karyaneka) and art galleries (10 Kiapeng and AP Gallery). Locals view this as an expensive area where wealthy people stay and shop. Accordingly, this is also where you will find the best quality shopping. Since this is a big area, you will need to spend at least two days going from one shopping center and hotel shopping arcade to another if you want to shop this area properly.

KL's third major shopping area is north of the city center along **Jalan Chow Kit Baru**, just south of the Putra World Trade Centre which houses the Tourist Development Corporation. Shopping in this area is highlighted by the Pan Pacific Hotel shopping arcade and The Mall shopping center. This is a newly developing shopping area that should continue to grow in the forseeable future. You can easily shop this area in half a day.

Nightime shopping is also a treat. Most of the major shopping centers remain open until 9pm. Chinatown at night is fascinating, with hundreds of vendor stalls selling a large variety of cheap clothes, imitation watches and leather goods, and souvenirs. The main street in Chinatown is closed as vendors set up their temporary, densely packed stalls. Next to Chinatown, the Saturday Night Market along Jalan Tuanku Abdul Rahman is the most colorful of the evening markets. This street, too, is blocked off as a colorful mixture of vendors and buyers fill the streets. The Sunday Night Market in Kampong Baru, the best in the city just a few years ago, no longer attracts the crowds as do Chinatown and Jalan Tuanku Abdul Rahman.

Given the distances both within and between shopping areas, we recommend that you use taxis. Metered taxis are inexpensive in Kuala Lumpur, with most short distance rides costing M$2-3. Since most drivers speak English, cabs are comfortable and convenient, traffic usually flows well, and maps are good, you should have no problem getting around the city to visit most of the major shopping areas.

Once you arrive in Kuala Lumpur, be sure to pick up a good map and tourist literature provided by the Tourist Development Corporation. While your hotel should have this information, you can also visit the TDC office at the Putra World Trade Centre on Jalan Tun Razak (between Jalan Kuching and Jalan Ipoh), the tall building just behind the Pan Pacific Hotel and the new The Mall shopping center. Local bookstores also carry a few maps and guide books on Kuala Lumpur. We particularly like the "Kuala Lumpur Discovery Map" which outlines many of the shopping areas and sites. Lynn Witham's *Malaysia: A Foreigner's Guide* is useful for those who want to get into the details of daily living in Kuala Lumpur. While the map is difficult to find and is somewhat dated, the book is widely distributed in the major bookstores of KL.

WHAT TO BUY

Kuala Lumpur is a cosmopolitan city of many surprises. As the capital of the country, it is also the center for trade, commerce, and tourism. Here's where you will find the latest in fashion, design, and quality products from both Malaysia and abroad. You will discover, for example, exquisitely designed Malay handicrafts at two government-sponsored shops -- Infokraf and the Karyaneka Handicraft Centre. These shops offer excellent quality and designs not found elsewhere in Malaysia. You may become an enthusiastic buyer of some wonderful Malaysian oils and watercolors depicting rural scenes on sale at 10 Kiapeng Art Gallery and A.P. Art Gallery. Or you may get caught up in buying cheap clothes and copy watches in Chinatown's night market. If you have a fondness for Asian arts and antiques as well as tribal artifacts, you will find shops offering items from China, Thailand, Burma, Borneo, Sumatra, Bali, Irian Jaya, and Papua New Guinea. As you will quickly discover, shopping in Kuala Lumpur offers something for everyone.

Kuala Lumpur's major shopping strengths are in the areas of locally produced handicrafts, textiles (batik and songket), clothes, art, and jewelry as well as imported handicrafts, arts, antiques, and duty-free items. While most shops and shopping centers primarily cater to local residents, more and more shops are orienting their product lines to KL's increasingly cosmopolitan and international population.

Handicrafts

Handicrafts, which include arts and crafts, are KL's major shopping strength for two reasons. First, they are found in abundance in the city's many handicraft and demonstration centers, export showrooms, and shops. Second, the quality and designs of handicrafts in KL are much more appealing to tourists and international buyers than those found elsewhere in Malaysia.

Take two major handicraft centers in Kuala Lumpur and

compare their handicrafts with those found in other areas of Malaysia. One of your first stops should be **Infokraf** on Jalan Tun Perak, which is attached to the Moorish looking old High Court building which, in turn, is adjacent to City Hall building and across from the Selangor Club. Infokraf is the handicraft promotional arm of the national Ministry of Rural Development (MRD), the ministry involved with promoting the development and export of Malay handicrafts. MRD helps train villagers to make export quality handicrafts as well as assists in marketing the finished products through government-run handicraft centers (Karyaneka shops) and private firms. Most important of all, MRD has a cadre of talented artists and designers who introduce new products and designs that are more appealing to tourists and the export market. The Infokraf office, therefore, is designed as a showroom to promote the export of handicrafts abroad. Infokraf consists of two parts: a showroom with very nice displays of handicrafts from various states (these change every three months) and a shop where you can purchase handicrafts. You will find many attractive handicrafts here -- baskets, mats, place-mats, batik, purses, silver jewelry, and pots -- that should integrate nicely into your home.

The second handicraft center worth visiting is the **Karyaneka Handicraft Centre** on Jalan Bukit Bintang, which is within a five minute walk east of either the Hilton Hotel or Regent Hotel. Also sponsored by the Ministry of Rural Development, the management here has changed hands three times in the past year. At present this center has one of the nicest displays of handicrafts found anywhere in Malaysia -- a tribute to the present management. This stands in sharp contrast to the rather drab and tasteless products and designs we saw here in previous years.

The Karyaneka Handicraft Centre consists of several small air-conditioned houses, each displaying handicrafts of individual states. If you tour each house, you will get an excellent overview of the full range of handicrafts produced in Malaysia. Each house summarizes the handicraft traditions of a particular state. You can see, for example, the difference between "Batik Solo" and "Batik Jawa" techniques in the Penang house; understand the production and use of pua (warp-ikat) fabrics, rattan bags, glazed pottery, and embroidered beads in the Sarawak house; appreciate songket fabrics, brassware, mengkuang weaving, woodcarving, kites, and batik in the Trengganu house; and watch the making of coconut crafts in the Johor house. You can observe handicrafts and a few craftsmen -- but not buy -- in these houses.

After completing the tour of the houses, you should visit

the showroom at the end of the compound. This shop has an extensive collection of handcrafted items for sale. And you will be tempted to buy. The quality and designs are superb, demonstrating once again the influence of new designers on Malaysian handicrafts. You will find designer batik clothes; lovely songket using innovative patterns and beautiful colors; stylish pillow covers, baskets, pottery, purses, bags, and briefcases; attractive silver jewelry, pewterware, woodcarvings, ceramics, floor and table mats, and framed batik and songket pictures. We hope the current management will stay and continue to offer such a fine product line. And while you are on the grounds of the Karyaneka Handicraft Centre, be sure to visit the National Crafts Museum located just behind the showroom. They have an excellent collection of silver, bronze, woodcarvings, baskets, mats, batik, songket, clothes, bags, umbrellas, pottery, copper and brass pictures, and kites from throughout Malaysia.

One other government handicraft center recently opened in KL, **Bengkel Kraftangan**, located on Jalan Semarak. You may have difficulty finding this place given recent changes in street names. Jalan Semarak is the new name for Jalan Gurney, although most taxi drivers still know it as Jalan Gurney. Our advice: use both street names when giving directions to a taxi driver. This handicraft center consists of several open-air building where villagers demonstrate the making of various handicrafts. Under the sponsorship of the Territorial Ministry and the Prime Minister's Department, this handicraft center duplicates much of what you can see at Infokraf and Karyaneka Handicraft Centre -- minus the more stylish designs of these other handicraft centers. The emphasis here, however, is on seeing actual handicraft demonstrations. Most of the designs and styles are very traditional and thus less appealing to many tourists. You will see, for example, artists producing oil paintings of country scenes, craftsmen working with stained glass, and weavers working with rattan in producing baskets and mats. After visiting the buildings, you can purchase items in the central showroom. Observing village traditions, you must take off your shoes before entering this showroom.

Outside these government sponsored handicraft demonstration centers and showrooms you will find one private initiative to develop a demonstration center. **10 Kiapeng Art Gallery** at 10 Kiapeng Road is opening an Art Craft and Design Centre on its premises where visitors can observe the making of fine arts and crafts at the workshop stalls in front of the main gallery building. Some of the craftsmen selling their works in the Central Market demonstrate at this gallery.

You will find numerous small shops and vendors selling handicrafts. One such place is the **Central Market** on Jalan Cheng Lock, located in the shadows of one of KL's modern Moorish architectural masterpieces, the giant Dayabumi Complex building. This is KL's old wet market which has been transformed into a popular arts and crafts center. Over 75 shops and vendor stalls occupy the two levels of this historic building. On the first floor you will see artists, craftsmen, and shopkeepers selling paintings, leather goods, woodcarvings, baskets, mats, plants, stamps, and cosmetics. It's one big bazaar filled with curios and fast food restaurants. The Kentucky Fried Chicken restaurant, for example, is one of the most interesting we have encountered for its service. It hires young deaf people as waiters and waitresses who communicate well with patrons.

On the second floor of the Central Market you will find some of the better quality arts and crafts shops. We especially like **D'Suri** for baskets, mats, and bags. The quality of D'Suri's handicrafts is similar to those found at Infokraf. All items here are made by wives of settlers under the administration of the Federal Land Development Authority. In fact, D'Suri used to supply Infokraf with these same handicrafts. We also like **Dayang Ceramica** which has one of the largest collections of Balinese woodcarvings, Buddhas, kris, wayang puppets, kites, silver, Thai lacquer elephants, baskets, ceramics, T-shirts, tops, fans, placemats, batik coasters, and Sarawak glazed pottery and pua in KL. **Aveen's**, a small colorful shop, has a unique collection of Vietnamese silk textiles, Burmese kalagas, Indian paintings, and Tibetian and Nepalese arts and crafts. If you are interested in crafts from Sarawak, visit **Longhouse Handicraft** with its unique collection of pua textiles, baskets, mats, bags, and glazed pottery as well as T-shirts.

The emphasis of the Central Market is on the trendy and touristy rather than traditional or classy. If you are in the market for inexpensive tourist trinkets and souvenirs, go here for your shopping. But don't expect to do quality shopping at the Central Market. The shops offer a wide variety of local and imported arts and crafts. You will find everything from local etchings, T-shirts, butterflies, and jewelry to Balinese carvings, Thai lacquerware, and Chinese furniture.

You will also find handicraft shops in the various shopping centers and in the art and antique shops of hotel shopping arcades (see our next discussion on arts and antiques in KL). **The Mall** shopping center, located on Jalan Chow Kit Baru, has several handicraft stalls located on the fourth floor in the charming Medan Hang Tuah market bazaar area. They sell Chinese porcelain, pua, batik, Burmese kalagas, Balinese carvings, pottery, baskets, and paintings. **Bukit Bintang Plaza**, at the corner of Jalan Bintang and Jalan Sultan Ismail, has three such shops on its lower level: Syarikat Fortune Arts & Crafts, AA Batek & Craft, and Ardi. **Plaza Yowchuan**, an upscale shopping center at the corner of Jalan Ampang and Jalan Tun Razak, has a few good quality handicraft shops: Sharon's Amazing Grace, Thai Shop, Peking Handicrafts, and Silkroad. Directly across the street is **Ampang Park** shopping center. Here you will find Kembali (#123) and Khalid Batik (#148) for unique batik designs and hand-crafted items as well as Star Gems & Gifts for a wide range of handicrafts.

Jalan Tuanku Abdul Rahman and **Jalan Masjid India** in the central city are also centers for Malay, Chinese, and Indian handicrafts. On Jalan Tuanku Abdul Rahman look for Mee Sing Co., Peiping Lace Co., and Sohan Singh & Sons. On Jalan Masjid India, Kwality Arts (#70-A) has a small but good selection of Indian bronzeware and woodcarvings.

And don't forget that the local **prison** also produces handicrafts for sale. The prison is located on Jalan Hang Tuah. It has a handicraft shop from which you can purchase rattan furniture, mats, and small woven items made by the prisoners. You will find good prices here, but don't expect great quality since the workers do not do this work as part of a long-term career in arts and crafts!

Arts, Antiques, and Home Decorative Items

Kuala Lumpur has several shops offering a wide range of fine arts, collectibles, antiques, and home decorative items. These range from unique watercolors and oil paintings to Chinese antiques and primitive arts. To shop KL's arts and antiques, you will need to visit galleries, exhibits, markets, hotel shopping arcades, and small street-front shops throughout the city.

The art scene in Kuala Lumpur is not well known both inside and outside Malaysia. Nonetheless, we have un-covered some basic facts of art life in KL that can make for some wonderful shopping if you have fine art on your mind. We find, for example, the works of several Malaysian artists, especially those working in watercolor, to be superb. And shopping for this art is one of the more interesting adventures, one that puts you in touch with a very interesting community of artists. Since the marketing of art in Malaysia is not confined to art galleries, you may wish to visit the National Art Gallery to make contact with individual artists as well as explore private art galleries and hotel exhibitions where you can purchase art directly through dealers.

Historically Malaysian artists have expressed themselves in craft mediums, such as textiles, silver, brass, and wood. What was serious traditional art for them is often considered handicrafts for Westerners. Western fine arts are relatively new to Malaysia. Such media as oil, watercolor, and sculpture were introduced by the British during the colonial period. A few Malaysians were influenced by the Western traditions as well as studied fine art abroad. The single most important Western influence on Malaysian artists has been abstract expressionism. This influence is clearly evident in the paintings and sculptures displayed at the **National Art Gallery**, which is located directly across from the railway station on Jalan Hishamuddin. Stroll through the four floors of this building and you will quickly see the bias toward abstract expressionism. Other Malay artists use the media of watercolors and oils but express the more traditional rural landscapes and urban scenes. These paintings can be seen in a few galleries, such as 10 Kiapeng Art Gallery and A.P. Art Gallery. Some of Malaysia's famous artists include Eng Tay, Ibrahim Hussein, Sharifah Fatimah Syed Zubir, Chong Fee Ming, Amron Omar, Choony Kam Kow, as well as the director of the National Art Gallery, Tuan Syed Ahmad Jamal.

Few Malaysian artists can support themselves on the basis of their art alone since there is little market for their art in Malaysia. Their major buyers are Westerners who appreciate such art. Within Malaysia the big buyers are hotels and corporations that decorate their Western buildings with local watercolors and oils. As a result many artists work as instructors at local schools and universities and pursue their art on a part-time basis.

Many visitors to Malaysia may find this Western-style art very attractive. We, for example, have purchased some stunning watercolors by two very talented artists: Keng Seng Choo and Lye Yau Fatt. If you are interested in purchasing art, you can do so by contacting four different sources: the artists, the National Art Gallery, private galleries, and hotel exhibitions. We recommend that you first visit the **National Art Gallery**. Should you identify a particular artist whose work you would like to purchase, go to the fourth floor administrative offices and ask the director -- who also is an accomplished artist -- how to contact the artist. He should be able to put you in touch with the artist who may then invite you to his studio or home to see and purchase his works.

This is the best way to make direct contact with individual artists who exhibit at the gallery and who are part of a loose network of artists centered around the National Art Gallery. Since most of these artists have full-time jobs as educators rather than as practicing artists, you will have to plug into these networks to locate your favorite artist. Keep in mind that much of the art in this gallery is abstract and thus many of the artists you will contact through this source will be abstract painters.

Kuala Lumpur has two good galleries you can visit to see exhibits and purchase fine art. **10 Kiapeng Art Gallery**, behind the Hilton Hotel on Jalan Kiapeng, is an excellent gallery. Opened in 1987, it has quickly become a center for many of Malaysia's best artists. It exhibits the works of artists from all over Malaysia. Prices range from M$800 to M$1250 for good quality framed and matted watercolors and oils. Another good gallery is **A.P. Art Gallery** which has shops at The Weld shopping plaza on Jalan Raja Chulan near the Shangri-la Hotel, Wisma Damansara on Jalan Semantan, the Central Market, and at 905 Persiaran Tun Ismail (Galeri Kumpulan Anak Alam). A.P. Art Gallery also operates the small shop at the National Art Gallery.

You can also purchase art at various exhibitions and shows held in KL's hotels. Each year Esso sponsors the Young Contemporaries Exhibition and Shell sponsors the National Open Art Exhibition at the National Art Gallery. You can purchase art at these popular exhibits. Check with the National Art Gallery for the exact dates and times of the exhibits. The National Open Art Exhibition is always held in January. Also consult the local newspaper, check with the major hotels, or contact 10 Kiapeng Art Gallery and A.P. Art Gallery to learn when and where these and other art exhibitions will be held.

Paintings can also be found at the new **Bengkel Kraftangan** handicraft center on Jalan Semarak (Jalan Gurney). One craft house is devoted to painting traditional rural scenes. This is amateur art which may appeal to many tourists. Also, you will find several young artists, many of whom are art school dropouts, selling their works on the pavement along **Jalan Masjid India**. They are usually there during the day.

Several shops also offer a wide range of Chinese arts and antiques. Many of these shops are located along **Jalan Tuanku Abdul Rahman**. Look for **Peiping Lace Co.**, for example, which has two shops (217 and 223 Jalan Tuanku Abdul Rahman) offering a good selection of Chinese arts and antiques. The first shop specializes in cloisonne, lace, linen, and ceramics. Should you be interested in hand woven carpets, be sure to visit the second floor where you will find one of the best selections of Persian, Afgan, Pakistani, and Indian carpets in KL. The second shop primarily offers furniture, jade, ivory, and screens. **China Arts Co.** at 219 Jalan Tuanku Abdul Rahman sells screens, lacquer, ceramics, furniture, and cloissone. **T.K. NG. Antiques** at 166 Jalan Tuanku Abdul Rahman is a small shop offering porcelain from the Han, Tang, Sung, Yuan, Ming, and Ching dynasties along with a variety of gemstones. **Mee Sing Co.** at 158 Jalan Tuanku Abdul Rahman offers a good selection of cloisonne, ceramics, furniture, silver, woodcarvings, brass and pewter.

Some of the best art and antique shops are found in KL's major hotel shopping arcades. One of our favorites is **King's Art** which has two shops -- one at the Regent Hotel and the other at the UBN Tower (adjacent to the Shangri-La Hotel). While these are ostensibly small shops, their service goes far beyond the confines of the existing floor space. These two shops are filled with an excellent collection of good quality Chinese ivory, jade, semi-precious stones, fine porcelain and pottery, Buddhas, snuff bottles, paintings, jewelry, and other works of art as well as souvenirs for tourists interested in buying gifts. Spend some time poking around the shelves, surveying walls, and exploring every nook and cranny of this shop. For some reason we always discover some exquisite items tucked behind the door or behind a chair or display case! The shops also have a few tribal artifacts from Sumatra and Sarawak. In fact, the husband and wife team that owns these two shops -- Sunny and Jenny Tee -- have a good eye for acquiring quality pieces from China, Hong Kong, Thailand, Indonesia, and Sarawak. Should you have special needs, they will special-order items as well as commission woodcarvings to your specifications. Ask to see their photo albums to survey other buying options as well as for placing special orders. They are known to commission the construction of big boats, carved poles, and decorative doors! The quality of products, service, and pricing here are excellent -- one of our very favorite shops in Malaysia.

A few shops in the **Hilton Hotel Shopping Arcade** also offer a good selection of arts and antiques. In fact, this arcade has the largest number of quality art and antique shops in KL. One of our favorite shops here is **Lim Arts & Crafts**. This shop is filled with a mixture of arts, antiques, and handicrafts, such as jewelry, ivory, jade, Burmese tapestries, kris, wayang puppets, Balinese masks, Chinese porcelain, Khmer silver, bronze, opium weights, cloisonne, and Buddhas. The service here is extremely friendly, prices are good after discounting, and buying is fun. Next door you will find the **Garuda Antique Shop**, a unique shop specializing in arts and antiques from Indonesia. We find this shop excessively expensive and unwilling to bargain much. Nonetheless, it does have a very nice collection of Batak staffs, Javanese kris, ceramics, Buddhas, batik, Sumba ikat textiles, Indonesian lacquer, and Asmat tribal artifacts. If you are planning to visit Indonesia next, go here to see the types of items you are likely to buy in Indonesia -- at one-fourth the price charged here! **Dynasty Art & Crafts** also has a good collection of porcelain, jade, cloisonne, furniture, jewelry, Buddhas, kris, and pua.

At the **Shangri-la Hotel Shopping Arcade** look for **King's Art** and **The Gems Shop**. This is the main shop for King's Art and where the owner, Sunny Tee, is likely to be found. Like its counterpart shop in the Regent Hotel, this shop is filled with good quality arts and antiques along with tourist quality handicrafts and souvenirs. The Gems Shop is also a mixture of arts, antiques, and handicrafts. They have a good selection of ivory, jewelry, Balinese masks, wayang puppets, kites, pewter, silver, Thai lacquerware, and primitive woodcarvings. Another branch of this shop is found in the Pan Pacific Hotel Shopping Arcade.

The **Pan Pacific Hotel**, across from The Mall on Jalan Chow Kit Baru, has one good art and antique shop which also stocks the usual range of Asian handicrafts. Look for **The Gemsque Shop** on the second floor shopping arcade. This shop sells ivory, jade, Balinese masks, Chinese carvings, celadon, jewelry, and a few primitive Batak woodcarved pieces.

If you are looking for an old-fashioned dusty, delapidated, musty, and rather disorienting antique shop crammed floor to ceiling with treasures galore, go to **Ahmed Toko Antik** located in the Sunday Market at Kampong Bharu. This is the type of antique shop you would encounter in many parts of Indonesia -- one requiring you to dig through what some might think is junk. This shop is actually open every day as well as during the Sunday Market which is actually held Saturday night. This is one of KL's best antique shops, especially if you are looking for a collection of primitive artifacts from Malaysia, Indonesia, and Papua New Guinea. Here, you will find ivory, porcelain, Khmer silver, Balinese masks, batik, ikat textiles, Buddhas, knives, drums, kites, clocks, quail traps, canes, tops, batik presses, brassware, boxes, coconut scrapers, lamps, musical instruments, wayang puppets, and primitive woodcarvings. Just around the corner is a smaller antique shop called **Ahmad-Curios**. It offers wayang puppets, knives, masks, bronzes, silver, pottery, and woodcarvings. Be sure to check your purchases for water damage -- both shops periodically flood when the nearby river overflows its banks and inundates the Sunday Market area. Bargaining is in order for both of these shops as well as for the other nearby shops and vendor stalls.

You will also find several home decorative shops in KL. Many of these shops primarily import items from abroad. For example, on the fourth level of **The Mall** shopping center, you will find several home decorative and designer shops. These include **Kamal's** for carpets and crafts, the **Design Centre** for imported fabrics, **Konimal** for Korean chests, and **Decor** for rattan furniture and accessories. **Plaza Yowchuan** also has a few shops specializing in home decorative items: the **Thai Shop** and **Silkroad** for Thai decorative items, **Decor** for rattan furniture and accessories, and **Hamid Carpets & Handicrafts** and **Oriental Carpet Gallery** for nice quality Oriental carpets. We especially like **Unique Decorators** on the first floor of Ampang Park shopping city with its large collection of porcelain vases, brass pieces, Korean chests, and abacus lamps -- the first we have seen outside Hong Kong.

Pewterware

Several shops throughout KL sell pewterware. However, the premier shop is **Selangor Pewter** at 231 Jalan Tuanku Abdul Rahman. This is the main showroom for all of the Selangor Pewter shops in Malaysia. It displays very fine quality pewterware as well as Austrian crystal and English China. You will find some very innovative pewter designs, lines, and collections, such as the Royal Collection, Garfield Pewter Collection, Gerald Benny Collection. You may discover a picture frame, box, tea set, or pin that might make a perfect gift or an addition to your collection of handcrafted items.

We are especially impressed with Selangor Pewter's new pewter designs and product lines which make such pewterware more appealing to international travelers -- something we have not seen on previous visits to Malaysia. Faced with increased competition from other pewter companies, as well as expectations for a growing export market, Selangor Pewter now has an innovative team of English, Scandinavian, and Malay designers who are creating some fabulous new designs to appeal to a larger international audience. While you are in this shop be sure to pick up a copy of their catalog which outlines product lines as well as explains the making of and caring for pewterware.

You also may want to visit the **Selangor Pewter Fac-**

tory at 4 Jalan Usahawan Enam (Tel. 4221000). Here, you can observe the making of pewterware. Most of the pewterware found in other shops in KL is Selangor Pewter. In fact, you will quickly discover that this company has one of the most extensive market networks in Malaysia. Shops everywhere seem to carry some form of Selangor Pewter!

Batik and Other Textiles

If you love textiles, several KL shops have much to offer in the way of fabrics, clothes, and art forms. Malaysia's largest batik shop -- KL's equivalent to Bangkok's Jim Thompson Silk House or Jakarta's Iwan Tirta -- and most popular with tourists is **Batek Malaysia** in the Wisma Kraftangan Building at 9 Jalan Tun Perak which is near the famous Masjid Jame (Jame Mosque) at the confluence of the Klang and Gombak river in downtown KL. Two floors of this shop offer a wide range of batik fabrics as well as ready-made clothes for both men and women. The second floor also sells some Malaysian handicrafts. While this is a big and popular shop, we have yet to get excited about the colors, designs, and styling of these fabrics and clothes. Like many of the batik factories and shops in Malaysia, they are in need of some creative designers who are familiar with the wider world of fashion and design. Batek Malaysia has branch shops in the International Departure Lounge of the Kuala Lumpur International Airport as well as at 114 Jalan Bukit Bintang.

If you are interested in observing the batik making process, visit the **Kutang Kraf Batik Factory** which is located 15 kilometers west of the city along Jalan Damansara in Kampong Sungai Pencala. You can also purchase hand-drawn and block-printed batik at the factory shop. The factory and shop are open Monday through Friday, 9:30am to 5pm, and on Saturday from 9:30am to 4pm.

Some of the best batik shops in Malaysia are small boutiques that have commissioned their own designs and fashioned clothes for international audiences. We feel the best such shop is **Batik Permai** which is located on the first floor of the Hilton Hotel Shopping Arcade. This shop offers some truly unique batik designs and products, from quilted reversible bedspreads to caftans and hand-painted batik silk. **Modern Batik**, a small shop on the second floor of the KL Plaza, offers nice hand-painted silk batik and does tailoring. **Sri Zayu Boutique** on the second floor of the Ampang Park shopping center also offers some nice ready-made batik clothes.

The **Karyaneka Handicraft Centre** on Jalan Bukit

Bintang has an excellent selection of designer
songket fabrics, ready-made clothes, and handcra
You will also find some handcrafted items using
lar Sarawak pua or ikat fabrics.

If your interests include ikat textiles from Sarawak
(pua), go to **Longhouse Handicraft** on the second floor of
the Central Market. This is one of the first shops in KL
that specializes in handicrafts and textiles from Borneo.
Several other shops in the Central Market also sell batik
fabric and ready-made clothes.

Thai silk is also found in a few KL shops. **Bogies Thai
Silk**, a Bangkok-based Thai company, is located on the
third level of The Mall shopping center. It sells good
quality and very fashionable silk fabric and ready-made
clothes.

If you are interested in Indian fabrics and sarees, one of
the most innovative fabric and dress-making shops is **Adek**
on the third floor of Plaza Yaochuan. Operated by the
noted designer Datin Ibrahim, this shop makes very fashionable Indian sarees.

A nice shop specializing in Malay women's dresses
(saree) but using Italian silks and Malay batik patterns
printed on Chinese silk is **Baju Kurong** in the Pan Pacific
Hotel shopping arcade.

Along Jalan Tuanku Abdul Rahman and Jalan Masjid
India you will find several shops selling batik, songket,
silk, and cotton fabrics. Look for the **Globe Silk Store**
and **Mun Loong** department stores on Jalan Tuanku Abdul
Rahman and several street stalls at the corner of Jalan
Bunus Enam and Jalan Tuanku Abdul Rahman. Along
Jalan Masjid India look for **Alankar Textiles** (#74), **Saradhas** (#86), and **Haniffa Textiles** (#149) for Indian
textiles. If you are in the market for Indonesian batik, stop
at **Toko Batek Indonesia** at 2004 Jalan Masjid India.

Ampang Park shopping center houses two shops producing unique batik designs: **Kembali** (#123) has some
nice batik among its Balinese handicrafts. **Khalid Batik**
(#148) produces exclusive hand-painted batik designs for
women's and men's clothes, screens, wall hangings, and T-
shirts. We especially like their unique batik paintings.

Clothes and Accessories

Malaysia is quickly becoming one of the world's leading
manufacturers and exporters of inexpensive clothes. At the
same time, you will find several fashionable shops selling
the latest in designer clothes from Malaysia, Singapore,
Hong Kong, Taiwan, Italy, and France as well as tailors
and dressmakers who produce good quality garments to

your specifications.

Inexpensive clothes produced in Malaysia, Thailand, Hong Kong, and Taiwan are found throughout the shopping centers and street shops of KL. However, the favorite place for locals to shop is the **Night Market in Chinatown.** Every evening vendors set up stalls from which they sell tons of inexpensive clothes -- T-shirts, jackets, jeans, dresses, blouses, and under garments. Many locals claim the prices here are as much as one-third of what one might pay for the same items in department stores. Be forewarned of four considerations before buying clothes in Chinatown: the quality of garments is also cheap; the sizes may not fit because most are for locals who may be much smaller than you; many of the items are poor quality fakes, such as the Benetton jackets imported from Thailand; and the Night Market is extremely crowded and congested to the point where you may quickly feel claustrophobic in the midst of all the hanging clothes, noisy hawkers, and clinging people! Nonetheless, shopping for inexpensive clothing in Chinatown may well become one of the highlights of your visit to KL!

More fashionable, expensive, and quality clothing is found where you would expect -- at the more fashionable shopping centers, department stores, and hotel shopping arcades. If you are interested in seeing the work of young struggling Malaysian clothes designers, visit **Focus** on the third level of The Mall shopping center. This is the only shop in Malaysia that brings together the works of leading Malaysian designers such as Richard Ong, Alistair Tan, Dominic Sio, Phin, Sherry, Yen, and Koji Ronnie. We are particularly impressed with the innovative batik designs, in both classic and executive-type wear, created by Richard Ong. Several other clothing shops and boutiques in The Mall as well as its adjacent Yaohan Department Store carry local and imported clothes. **Designers' Row,** for example, on the third level carries fashionable European imported women's clothes. **Bogies Thai Silk,** also on the third level, offers excellent quality Thai silk garments.

The five most fashionable centers for imported name brand clothes as well as for excellent tailors are the Hilton Hotel Shopping Arcade, the Shangri-la Hotel Shopping Arcade, Regent Hotel Shopping Arcade, The Weld shopping center, and KL Plaza. The first floor of the **Hilton Hotel Shopping Arcade** houses such European name-brand shops as **Gucci, Loewe, Lanvin,** and **Ermenegildo Zegna.** You will also find three local boutiques worth visiting: **Batik Permai, Cottage,** and **La Donna.** On the second floor (fourth level) look for **Couture** and **Spark Manshop,** a men's tailor shop.

The **Shangri-la Hotel Shopping Arcade** has four very nice boutiques and tailoring shops: **La Fenme, Spark Manshop, The Monument,** and **Seijun.** Seijun is one of KL's finest boutiques and dressmakers, a haute couture shop using Italian and French fabrics. Seijun has another shop in Plaza Yowchuan.

The **Regent Hotel Shopping Arcade** only has two shops: **Flair Boutique** for fashionable women's batik clothes, and **Calan** for very fine men's ready-made suits, shirts, and accessories.

The **Weld** shopping center also has several European name brand shops for upscale clothes shoppers: **Benetton, Bruno Magli, Lacoste,** and **Etienne Aigner.** Le Salon is a nice boutique. You will find two good men's shops: **Antenna by Isetan** for ready-made clothes and **Jim's Shop** for custom tailoring.

KL Plaza is home to such name brand clothing shops as **Polo, Ralph Lauren, Givenchy,** and **Christian Dior,** all located on the first level. Also, look for **Top Man, My Place Fashion,** and **Sugar Boutique** on the second level. And **Jim's Shop,** also found in The Weld shopping center, is a nice men's tailor located on the third level.

Jewelry

Kuala Lumpur has a few jewelry stores worth visiting should jewelry be on your shopping itinerary. However, jewelry is not one of KL's major shopping strengths. Similar to the pattern found in shopping for brand-name imported clothes, the nicest jewelry stores are found in KL's major shopping centers, hotels, and department stores.

At **Plaza Yowchuan** you will find four very good jewelry stores. **K.M. Oli Mohamed** has an excellent selection of pearls and loose stones. **Storch Jewellry** specializes in good quality jewelry, watches, and silver tableware. **Selberan** has a good selection of jewelry. We especially like **Juita** which produces unique neck pieces using semi-precious stones and beads.

KL Plaza has four excellent jewelry stores: **De Silva,** a long established family jeweler with branch shops in other cities, **Kedai Emas Kelvin Gems, Kevin Gems,** and **Selberan Jewelry.**

The **Weld** shopping center on Jalan Raja Chulan has one shop worth visiting, **The Jewel Mine.** Owned by the Globe Silk Store on Jalan Tuanku Abdul Rahman, this shop offers some lovely jewelry pieces.

If you are primarily in the market for gold jewelry and jade, you will find four jewelry shops next to each other on the first floor of **Bukit Bintang Plaza.** This is a good place to compare prices on such jewelry.

Each of the major hotel shopping arcades will have one or two shops selling jewelry. The **Hilton Hotel Shopping Arcade**, for example, houses **Chopard**, a shop offering excellent quality Swiss watches. The **Regent Hotel Shopping Arcade** has one small shop, **The Joailliers**.

Duty-Free

Kuala Lumpur is aggressively promoting itself as a major duty-free shopping center in comparison to Singapore. The international departure lounge of **Subang International Airport** has been transformed into a shopper's haven for a large variety of duty-free items. Several shops offer sporting goods, cameras, jewelry, electronic goods, liquor, cigarettes, luggage, and chocolates. While you are here be sure to pick up a copy of *Malaysian Duty-Free Shopping Guide* which includes a floor plan of the airport as well as an extensive listing of prices for liquors, cigarettes, tobacco, perfume, cosmetics, chocolates, batik, handicrafts, pewterware, cameras, audio video equipment, watches, pens, fashion and leather goods, and sporting goods. You will find major brand names, and the prices appear to be good. They are excellent if you come from a country which places high duties on such items. If you plan to do some duty-free shopping, make sure you arrive at the airport early so you can spend some time exploring these shops.

You will also find a duty-free shop, **Wealthouse Duty Free**, at The Mall shopping center in Kuala Lumpur. Located on the ground floor next to the Yaohan Department Store, this shop primarily sells duty-free liquor and cigarettes. If you buy here, you must show the salesperson your passport and departure ticket. You pick up your purchases at the airport when you depart. Since the prices here are the same as at the airport, we are not sure what the advantage is in purchasing your liquor and cigarettes here rather than at the airport shops.

The More You Look

Kuala Lumpur is a surprising city in transition. While it may not yet be a shopping paradise or a threat to Singapore's shopping dominance, it is by no means a shopping slouch. Shopping here is continuously improving with the development of new shops, shopping centers, and product lines. One of the most important changes taking place with KL shopping is the general improvement in the quality and designs of both local and imported products. The changes are especially evident in the cases of Malaysian handicrafts, pewterware, clothing, and art. Expect to discover more such changes with these and other product lines when you shop the streets of KL.

Malaysian handcrafted items are found in abundance, and many make wonderful gifts, souvenirs, and home decorative items. At the same time, we are surprised to find so many handcrafted items from abroad appearing in several KL shops. Many of these products, such as primitive artifacts from Sumatra, Borneo, Sulawesi, and Papua New Guinea, are unique items not readily available elsewhere, including Singapore as well as the countries of origin. Compared to what you might pay in Singapore for comparable artifacts found in Kuala Lumpur, the prices in KL are generally better.

If you are like us, you will discover the unexpected when shopping in Kuala Lumpur. We normally don't expect to do much shopping here, but we manage to come away with many unexpected purchases -- almost as many as we make in Singapore.

You, too, may get lucky when shopping in KL. Explore the streets, shops, and markets of KL and you may discover some lovely handmade furniture, unique textiles, beautiful woodcarvings, striking jewelry, trendy clothes, unusual antiques, gorgeous Oriental carpets, fabulous watercolors and oil paintings, or fashionable home decorative items you had not planned to buy.

There is only one way to make such discoveries in KL: go shopping in as many shopping areas as possible as you expose yourself to a new shopping world of shopping centers, hotel shopping arcades, department stores, street shops, and markets.

The more you look, the more you will discover. We expect to be surprised with even more discoveries when we again shop in KL. If present trends continue, next year will be an even better year for shopping in KL. Given the rapid changes taking place in Kuala Lumpur's shopping scene, each year will bring new and exciting shopping discoveries.

WHERE TO SHOP

Shopping in Kuala Lumpur is relatively easy once you orient yourself to KL's major streets, landmarks, and shopping areas. The major shopping areas are concentrated in and around the old central city which begins at the confluence of the Klang and Gambok rivers. Each area is within 10 to 15 minutes of the other areas. While you can easily walk within each area, it is best to take taxis be-

between areas. Taxis are inexpensive and relatively easy to find at hotels and shopping centers. Buses are even cheaper, but they are not as convenient if you must carry several packages. If you decide to walk, be sure to take it easy since the high heat and humidity of this city can quickly debilitate walkers.

Shopping is found throughout Kuala Lumpur and its nearby suburbs. However, for most visitors interested in buying unique Malay items, it is best to approach the city as being divided into three distinct shopping areas.

Shopping Areas

Kuala Lumpur is divided into three major shopping areas. The **central city** is KL's high density commercial and governmental center as well as the older section of the city. Here you will find some of KL's major shopping streets, such as Jalan Tuanku Abdul Rahman, Jalan Masjid India, and Jalan Tun Razak. It's where you will find the Central Market, Chinatown, and Infokraf, where shopping takes place in department stores, small shops, vendor stalls, and colorful night markets. It's one of Asia's most interesting and attractive central cities noted for such beautiful landmarks as City Hall, High Court, Selangor Club, Masjid Jame, and Dayabumi Complex -- an area of traditional mosques and minarets and modern Moorish architecture. It's a pleasant walking area that tends to yield many surprises as you walk its colorful streets. Immediately to the south of this area is KL's famous Railway Station which is also across the street from the National Art Gallery and the KL Visitor's Centre.

The second major shopping area is known as **The Golden Triangle**. This is KL's upscale shopping area just a few minutes east of the central city. Bordered by Jalan Ampang on the north and Jalan Imbi on the south and linked together by Jalan Sultan Ismail (The Golden Mile), Jalan Raja Chulan, and Jalan Bukit Bintang, this area is defined by several major hotels and shopping centers within walking distance of each other that form a triangle when plotted on a map. This is where you will find quality imported goods, major department stores, fashionable boutiques, and fine restaurants. This is KL's answer to Singapore's Orchard Road. The primary hotels consist of The Regent, Kuala Lumpur Hilton, and Shangri-La Hotel, hotels which also have nice shopping arcades. Other hotels, such as The Merlin, Hotel Equatorial, Holiday Inn, and the Federal Hotel are nearby. The major shopping centers include the huge Sungei Wang Plaza/Bintang Plaza shopping complex and KL's two most exclusive shopping centers, The Weld and KL Plaza.

KL's third major shopping area is what we call, for the lack of a better term, **peripheral shopping centers**. This is a collection of shopping centers lying outside, yet near, the other two shopping areas. These consist of The Mall shopping center and the Pan Pacific Hotel to the north of the central city at the Putra World Trade Centre on Jalan Chow Kit Chuan; the Plaza Yowchuan-Ampang Park shopping complex on Jalan Ampang and the Bengkel Kraftangan handicraft center on Jalan Semarak (Gurney) northeast of the Golden Triangle; and the Karyaneka Handicraft Centre immediately to the east of the Golden Triangle. This is a mixed area of handicraft centers, fashionable boutiques, department stores, and fast-food restaurants catering to tourists and middle to upper-class shoppers.

Shopping Centers

Kuala Lumpur has several shopping centers that are popular with locals and tourists alike. They range from the chic to the ordinary. All are air-conditioned, multistory shopping malls filled with hundreds of small shops, department stores, and eateries. They tend to be brightly lit, crowded, and noisy. For many locals, and especially for young people, this is where the action is for shopping, eating, and socializing. If you are looking for good department stores, fashionable clothes and accessories, fine jewelry, and attractive home decorative items, these centers have it all.

The major shopping centers, in order of class and quality, are as follows:

MAJOR SHOPPING CENTERS

- **The Weld:** Just down the street from the Shangri-La Hotel on the corner of Jalan P. Ramlee and Jalan Raja Chulan, this is KL's newest and classiest shopping center. Compared to many other shopping centers, this one is small. But it's packed with some exquisite shops selling the latest in imported brand name clothes and accessories: **Benetton, Bruno Magli, Lacoste, Etienne Aigner, Le Salon,** and **Antenna by Isetan.** You will find two art galleries here -- **A.P. Art Gallery** and **Worldwide Art and Frame** --and a nice jewelry shop -- **The Jewel Mine.** If you are the market for good quality men's tailoring, **Jim's Shop** is the place to go. The

Weld also has a **Times Bookshop**, department store (Guardian), grocery, and a McDonalds and Pizza Hut.

- **KL Plaza:** This was KL's best shopping center until The Weld opened in 1988. Nonetheless, it still retains its class with several shops offering some of the best quality products in KL which tend to be both imported and expensive. Located along Jalan Bukit Bintang east of the intersection with Jalan Sultan Ismail near the Regent Hotel and Bukit Bintang Plaza, KL Plaza consists of four floors of shops. Most of the shops are concentrated on the first two levels--ground and first floor. Anchored by one of the classiest **Mun Loong Department Store** branches in KL, here you will find some top menswear shops: **Polo Ralph Lauren, Givenchy,** and **Christian Dior.** A branch shop of the excellent men's tailor, **Jim's Shop,** is found on the third level. If you are in the market for jewelry, you've come to the right place: **Selberan Jewelry, De Silva, Kedai Emas Kelvin Gems,** and **Kevin Gems.** You'll also find some unique silk batik clothes and designs in a small boutique on the second level -- **Modern Batik.** A&W Root Beer is the major fast-food restaurant here.

- **The Mall:** This is one of KL's newest and more innovative shopping centers. It's also the second largest shopping center in KL. Located two kilometers north of the central city, across from the Pan Pacific Hotel and the Putra World Trade Centre on Jalan Chow Kit Baru, The Mall is a five-story shopping center fronted with a large glassed-in atrium. This attractive building is anchored by the excellent **Yaohan Department Store** and a McDonald's and topped with a street bazaar and food center -- **Medah Hang Tuah** -- you will find boutiques, home decorative, gift and souvenir, florist, optical, shoe, tailor, jewelry, electronic, carpet, and home furnishing shops along with restaurants throughout this center. **Selberan Jewelry** has a branch shop here. **Bogies Thai Silk** offers nicely tailored and colorful Thai silk.

- **Designer's Row** is a trendy boutique with very nice imported European clothes and accessories. **Focus** is one of KL's most unique boutiques specializing only in Malaysian designer clothes by such designers as Richard Ong, Alistair Tan, Dominic Sio, Phin, Sherry, Yen, and Koji Ronnie. On the fourth level you will find several home decorative and furnishing shops offering fabrics (**Design Centre**), wicker furniture and baskets (**Decor**), and Korean chests (**Konimal**). One of the highlights of The Mall is the historical theme shopping and eating center on the fifth level -- **Medan Hang Tuah.** Built in a pre-war colonial style, complete with replicas of pre-war building facades commonly found along the famous Batu Road and Malacca and Penang streets, this center consists of several small vendor stalls selling Malaysian handicrafts, gifts, and souvenirs, an art exhibition hall, and hawker food stalls selling tempting Malay dishes. The Mall also has one duty-free shop -- Wealthouse Duty Free - which is located on the ground floor next to Yaohan Department Store. It primarily sells liquor and tobacco which can be purchased here to be picked up at the airport as one departs.

- **Plaza Yowchuan/Ampang Park:** **Plaza Yowchuan** and **Ampang Park** are two shopping centers across the street from each other on the corner of Jalan Ampang and Jalan Tun Razak. Plaza Yowchuan is an exclusive shopping center catering to KL's upper middle and upper classes with many imported and stylish products. Ampang Park, while not as classy as Plaza Yowchuan, is more middle class. It, too, has much to offer shoppers. **Plaza Yowchuan** is filled with smart boutiques, tailors, jewelry, shoe, accessory, handicraft, carpet, and home decorative shops. For nice jewelry, visit **K.M. Oli Mohamed, Storch Jewellry,** and **Selberan. Juita** offers some very unique and attractive neck pieces using semi-precious stones and beads. **Seijun Boutique** has some gorgeous fabrics and designs and does haute couture work. **Etienne Aigner** also has a shop here,

and Adek makes fashionable one-of-a-kind sarees. If you are in the market for Oriental carpets, two shops offer good selections: **Hamid Carpets & Handicrafts** and **Oriental Carpet Gallery**. **Decor**, a home decorative shop specializing in wicker furniture, also has a branch shop here. Both **Silkroad** and the **Thai Shop** offer excellent handcrafted and home decorative items from Thailand. For handicrafts, visit **Sharon's Amazing Grace** and **Peking Handicrafts**. You will also find an excellent branch of the **Times Bookshop** as well as a supermarket, McDonalds, Pizza Hut, and Dunkin' Donuts on the ground floor. **Ampang Park** is a popular shopping center for locals in search of clothes, accessories, and household goods. We especially like **Kembali** and **Khalid Batik** for unique batik designs and handcrafted items from Indonesia. **Star Gems & Gifts** has a good collection of local and imported handicrafts, including ceramics, baskets, jewelry, batik, woodcarvings, and Balinese masks. For home decorative items, **Unique Decorators** offers a large selection of porcelain, lamps, brass, and Korean chests. **May Jones** and **Sri Zayn Boutique** on the second level have nice stylish clothes.

- **Sungei Wang Plaza/Bukit Bintang Plaza:** This is KL's largest shopping complex. Consisting of two shopping centers joined together at Jalan Bukit Bintang and Jalan Sultan Ismail, it's very popular with local shoppers. It's big, bright, crowded, and loud. Sungei Wang Plaza has 550 shops offering a wide variety of goods and services. It has everything from department stores and a hawker food center to cinemas and a roller skating rink. As a full service shopping center, you will find tailor shops, jewelry stores, trendy boutiques, home furnishing shops, hairstylists, bookstores, handicraft shops, and much more. The **Parkson Grand** is a nice department store, and it has an excellent grocery store on its lower level. We don't know if these shops will appeal to you given their local product orientations. Local PR literature boasts that this center is the ultimate one stop shopping experience and that there is no place like it for shopping except perhaps Harrods of London. Such hyperbole seems unwarranted after having visited this shopping center several times. But go see for yourself. We're not that impressed. The place is big, bright, crowded, and loud, but we feel the products lack the quality and class we prefer when shopping in exotic places. Oriented toward young people and trendy styles, and with prices appealing to the local middle-class, the shops here do not scream *"take me home"*. **Bukit Bintang Plaza** is smaller than Sungei Wang Plaza, but it has similar types of shops and products. Its **Metro Jaya Department Store** is very nice, with quality products throughout its four levels. If you are interested in gold jewelry, visit the four jewelry shops adjacent to each other on the first floor. This shopping center appeals to us in the same manner as Sungei Wang Plaza.

- **Other shopping centers:** You will find a few other shopping centers in KL. However, most of these are small shopping centers frequented primarily by local residents who shop for clothes and household goods. Examples of such places in the central city include **Campbell Shopping Complex, Pertama Complex,** and **Wilayah Complex,** all on Jalan Dang Wangi, and **Kota Raya Shopping Complex** on Jalan Cheng Lock.

Major Department Stores

KL has several very good quality department stores offering a large variety of locally produced and imported goods. Most of these department stores are located in the shopping centers and have bookstore and local handicraft sections. KL's major department stores include:

DEPARTMENT STORES

- **Yaohan:** Anchors The Mall shopping complex. A popular Japanese department store occupying five levels of The Mall.

- **Guardian:** A small department store in The Weld shopping center.

- **Mun Loong:** Classy department store anchoring KL Plaza. Another branch found on Jalan Tuanku Abdul Rahman.

- **Metro Jaya:** A major department store occupying four levels of the Bukit Bintang Plaza. Also located in the basement of the Pertama Complex at the corner of Jalan Tuanku Abdul Rahman and Jalan Dang Wangi.

- **Parkson Grand:** Found in Sungei Wang Plaza. Has a good grocery store on the lower level.

Hotel Shopping Arcades

While most hotels have one or two sundry shops selling souvenirs, books, and travel supplies for hotel guests, KL's four major hotels also have shopping arcades which appeal to shoppers from outside the hotel. KL's premier hotel shopping arcade is found at the **Hilton Hotel.** Three other hotels, the **Shangri-La, Regent,** and the **Pan Pacific,** have small shopping arcades by comparison.

HOTEL SHOPPING ARCADES

- **Hilton Hotel Shopping Arcade:** Located at the Kuala Lumpur Hilton Hotel on Jalan Sultan Ismail. Recently renovated, upgraded, and enlarged, this still remains the top hotel shopping arcade in KL -- and in Malaysia. Two floors of shops offer outstanding quality products and services. The first floor primarily has classy shops selling famous imported name-brand clothes and accessories such as **Gucci, Loewe, Ermenegildo Zegna,** and **Lanvin.** You will also find a **Selangor Pewter** shop here as well as three fine boutiques -- **Cottage, La Donna,** and **Batik Permai.** We especially like the unique silk batik clothes and quilts produced by **Batik Permai.** This, in fact, is our favorite batik shop in KL. The second floor (indicated as fourth level on the elevator) is devoted to art, antique, and tailor shops. **Lim Arts & Crafts** is one of our favorite shops. It offers a wide range of good quality products (jewelry, ivory, jade, tapestries, wayang puppets, Balinese masks, porcelain, silver, bronze figures, opium weights, cloissone, and Buddha statues) along with excellent service and reasonable prices. **Dynasty Arts & Crafts** also has nice selections of porcelain, jade, jewelry, cloissone, and furniture. **Garuda Antiques Shop** specializes in quality Indonesian arts, such as Batak staffs, Asmat carvings, Sumba textiles, and lacquerware. We find this shop to have good quality but somewhat overpriced. If you are interested in men's tailoring, **Spark Manshop** is a good quality tailor.

- **Shangri-La Hotel Shopping Arcade:** Located in the UBN Tower adjacent to the Shangri-La Hotel at the corner of Jalan Sultan Ismail and Jalan P. Ramlee, this is a small shopping arcade compared to the one found in the Kuala Lumpur Hilton Hotel. Nonetheless, it has some excellent quality shops. One of our favorite shops is **King's Art**, which offers a good selection of Chinese, Malaysian, Thai, and primitive arts and crafts (ivory, jade, cloissone, textiles, Balinese masks, wayang puppets, Malay kris, jewelry, snuff bottles, paintings, and primitive woodcarvings). The owner, Sunny Tee, offers good service and will do special orders upon request. We also like **The Gems Shop** which has an extensive collection of arts and antiques, including ivory, jewelry, cloisonne, pewter, silver, Thai lacquerware, wayang puppets, kites, and primitive woodcarvings. One of the finest boutiques and dressmakers in KL is also found in this shopping arcade: **Seijun.** This shop offers exquisite Italian and French fabrics and does haute couture work. **The Monument** is another good boutique in this arcade.

- **The Regent Hotel Shopping Arcade:** Located in the Regent Hotel at the corner of Jalan Sultan Ismail and Jalan Imbi, this two-floor arcade has a few nice shops selling clothes, jewelry, arts, antiques, gifts, and souvenirs. **The Joailliers** is a small jewelry shop offering good quality items. **Flair Boutique** specializes in fashionable batik clothes. **Calan** is an exclusive menswear shop selling only imported ready-made suits and shirts. **King's Art**, a branch of the same shop at the Shangri-La Hotel, is an excellent arts, antique, and souvenir shop. You will also find a **Selangor Pewter** and a gift and souvenir shop here.

- **Pan Pacific Hotel Shopping Arcade:** Located in the Putra World Trade Centre directly across the street from The Mall shopping center on Jalan Chow Kit Baru, this is a very small shopping arcade. **Pia Lisash Fashion House & Interior Design** is a small boutique with nice women's clothes and accessories. **Baju Kurong** specializes in making beautiful Malay women's dresses from Italian and Chinese silks with Malay batik patterns. **The Gemsque Shop** is an arts, antique, and souvenir shop offering similar items as its sister shop (The Gems Shop) in the Shangri-La Hotel Shopping Arcade.

Street Shops

KL's major concentration of street shops is along Jalan Tuanku Abdul Rahman and Jalan Mesjid India and a few adjacent streets in the central city. Starting at the intersection of Jalan Tuanku Abdul Rahman and Jalan Dang Wang (Campbell Road) and walking south along Jalan Tuanku Abdul Rahman until you reach Jalan Melayu, you will find several interesting art, antique, fabric, and clothing shops lining both sides of this major shopping street. This is a colorful street of small shops, street vendors, and talented blind musicians playing swinging music on the latest electronic instruments. **Selangor Pewter** has its major showroom at 231 Jalan Tuanku Abdul Rahman. Just a few doors south are the two shops of **Peiping Lace Co.** with its extensive collection of Chinese furniture, ivory, jade, ceramics, cloisonne, and lace. Be sure to visit the second floor of the shop at 217 Jalan Tuanku Abdul Rahman if you are interested in Oriental rugs. Other shops along this street worth browsing through are **China Arts Co.** (#219), **Ming** (#166), **T.K. NG. Antique** (#162), **Mee Sing Co.** (#158), and **Sohan Singh & Sons** (#156). You will also find two department stores along this street -- **Globe Silk**

Store and **Mun Loong** -- and street stalls selling clothes and fabrics at the corner of Lorong Bunus Enam. **Aked Ibu Kota** is a shopping arcade offering numerous products of interest to visitors, such as batik, songket, woodcarvings, and copper-tooling.

Along **Jalan Masjid India** look for **Kwality Arts** (#70A) for Indian brass and woodcarved items; **Toko Batik Indonesia** (#2004) for Indonesian batik shirts, sarongs, and fabrics; and **Alankar Textiles** (#74), **Haniffa Textiles** (#149), and **Saradhas** (#86) for Indian textiles.

On nearby **Jalan Tun Perak** you will find **Batek Malaysia Berhad** (#9), KL's largest batik shop. Its two floors have a combination of batik fabrics, ready-made clothes, and Malaysian handicrafts.

Handicraft Centers

Reflecting Malaysia's major strength in the arts and crafts, four centers have developed in KL to promote the production and marketing of handicrafts:

HANDICRAFT CENTERS

- **Infokraf:** Located on Jalan Tun Perak next to the High Court Building, Infokraf is the most international center promoting Malaysian handicrafts. It is designed to promote the export of Malaysian handicrafts by displaying changing exhibits of attractive local products. Infokraf consists of a showroom and a shop where you can purchase very nice quality handicrafts designed to be appropriate for Western homes.

- **Karyaneka Handicraft Center:** Located on Jalan Bukit Bintang. Consists of several handicraft display houses and a large shop selling excellent quality and beautifully designed handicrafts.

- **Bengkel Kraftangan:** KL's newest handicraft center located on Jalan Semarak (also named Jalan Gurney). Consists of several handicraft demonstration buildings as well as a shop selling handcrafted products. Products tend to follow more traditional designs than found at Infokraf or Karyaneka Handicraft Center.

> • **Central Market:** Located in the heart of the
> central city on Jalan Cheng Lock, this is a
> center for over 75 vendor stalls and small
> shops selling a wide range of locally prod-
> uced and imported handcrafted items.   A
> good place to spend a few hours browsing
> from shop to shop.

Markets

KL has both day and night markets. The day markets
are the traditional wet and dry markets which sell a combination of fresh fruits, vegetables, meats, clothes, and
housewares. The night markets primarily sell hawker food
and inexpensive clothes.

At one time KL had one central market which has now
been converted to an arts and crafts center on Jalan Cheng
Lock and appropriately called the Central Market.   With
the closing of this as a traditional market, several daytime
markets have developed throughout KL to service neighborhood populations. If you are interested in seeing such
markets, ask for information on the location of these markets at your hotel or at the Tourist Information Centre.

Kuala Lumpur's most interesting markets are the night
markets. KL has three such markets worth visiting: Chinatown, Saturday Night Market, and Sunday Night Market.
We list these markets in the order of quality, interest, and
adventure:

> ──────── **MAJOR NIGHT MARKETS** ────────
>
> • **Chinatown:**   Bounded by Jalan Petaling,
> Jalan Sultan, and Jalan Bandar, this is by far
> the most colorful and interesting night market
> (*pasar malam*) in KL. Held every night in
> the heart of Chinatown, two blocks of this
> street are closed off to traffic as more than
> 100 vendors set up stalls to sell an incredible
> variety of goods. Navigating through crow-
> ded, congested, brightly lit, and noisy narrow
> pathways, you will discover stall after stall
> selling cheap Malaysian, Thai, Taiwanese,
> and Hong Kong clothes, copy watches, foot-
> wear, cassettes, leather, sunglasses, belts,
> bags, jewelry, radios, alarm clocks, luggage,
> and food.   Very popular market for local
> residents who come here to get good bargains
> on inexpensive clothes. You can really have

a fun evening exploring this night market, if you don't mind the crowds! Warning: most of the clothes are sized for small Asian bodies. If you don't have such a body, chances are many of these clothes will not fit you. During the day Chinatown is well and alive with numerous shop-houses selling a vast array of textiles, household goods, herbs and medicinal remedies, and food.

- **Saturday Night Market:** Held every Saturday night along Jalan Tuanku Abdul Rahman, this is the best of the weekend markets. Beginning at the intersection with Jalan Selat 4, the remainder of Jalan Tuanku Abdul Rahman in closed to auto traffic on Saturday night. If you walk this street, you will see a kaleidoscope of activities and products for sale. This is essentially a Malay, rather than Indian or Chinese, market. It's much better than the much praised Sunday, or Kampong Bharu, Market. You will see many vendors along this street selling footwear, baskets, bags, toys, silk flowers, watches, books, cassettes, clothes, wallets, belts, jewelry, and pottery. Blind musicians, who also occupy this stretch of the street during the day, play loud music which give the street activities a mood. You will also see several "snake oil" salesmen demonstrating their products and praising their incredible curative powers! Their loud, colorful, and dramatic presentations are well worth a photo.

- **Sunday Market:** This is a real misnomer. The so-called Sunday Night Market is held on Saturday night in Kampong Bharu. Once considered the most interesting night market in KL, today it is quickly fading into obscurity as fewer people visit this market. They have all gone to Chinatown or Jalan Tuanku Abdul Rahman. Nonetheless, this is still an active market. It may be worth a visit should you be interested in hawker food and making a few sociological observations. In addition to the numerous food stalls, vendors sell clothes, fabrics, toys, cassettes, pillows, fruits, and vegetables. You will find one of KL's best antique shops here -- **Ahmed Toko**

> **Antik** -- which is also open during the day. This shop alone is worth a visit to this market.

ENJOYING YOUR STAY

As the center of Malaysia, Kuala Lumpur has much to offer international travelers both within and outside KL. In addition to some surprising shopping opportunities, KL offers some excellent sightseeing opportunities. Much of the sightseeing includes observing many of KL's unique architectural landmarks. Within Kuala Lumpur you will find:

ADDED ATTRACTIONS

- **National Museum:** A fine example of modern Malay architecture. Located on Jalan Damansara just off Jalan Sultan Hismamuddin near the railway station and the Kuala Lumpur Visitor's Centre, this is a fine museum with a good collection of traditional Malay jewelry and artifacts. The Cultural Gallery on the first floor has nice displays of ceremonies, costumes, and etiquette of the Malays, Chinese, and Indians in Malaysia. The Social History Gallery, also on the first floor, has excellent displays of Malaysian architecture, traditional Malay houses, and artifacts.

- **Old City Hall/High Court/Selangor Club:** Located in the heart of the central city along Jalan Tun Razak, these are three of Asia's most interesting and attractive architectural landmarks. The Moorish style Old City Hall and High Court buildings are topped with copper domed minarets. The Selangor Club's colonial-style architecture and expansive cricket field reminds one of the British imprint of orderliness on this city. This is a great location to take pictures showing the juxtaposition of historical architecture in the shadows of KL's modern, high-rise skyline.

- **Railway Station:** Another of KL's Moorish architectural marvels. Located along Jalan Sultan Hishamuddin just south of the city center and across the street from the National Art Gallery and Kuala Lumpur Visitors' Centre.

- **Dayabumi Complex:** One of Asia's most attractive contemporary Moorish buildings located just behind the Central Market. You can visit the top floor (helipad above the 35th floor) of this building to get a panoramic view of the city.

- **National Mosque:** An example of Malaysian contemporary architecture and one of the largest mosques in Asia. Located at the intersection of Jalan Lembah Perdana and Jalan Sultan Hismamuddin near the railway station.

- **Masjid Jame:** A beautiful old mosque located in the city center at the confluence of the Klang and Gombak rivers, where Kuala Lumpur was first founded.

Other interesting sights in Kuala Lumpur include the **Parliament House, Lake Gardens, National Monument, Chan See Shu Yuen Temple, Sri Mahamariamman Temple,** and the **Sultan Abdul Samad Building** (Clock Tower).

Further from the central city and within a half-day driving distance of KL are several worthwhile attractions:

- **National Zoo and Aquarium:** Located 12 kilometers from the city center, this attractive area has over 1000 species of Malaysian flora and fauna.

- **Mimaland:** A popular recreational center located 18 kilometers from Kuala Lumpur on the road to Genting Highlands. Includes swimming, boating, fishing, and jungle trekking. Complete with accommodations.

- **Genting Highlands:** Located one and a half hours from Kuala Lumpur, this mountain top resort is Malaysia's only gambling center. Complete with a casino (off limits to Malaysian citizens), game rooms, a recreational park, hotels, and restaurants, this is a very popular center for tourists. Shopping opportunities are limited to one hotel shop. Go only if interested in gambling and avoid driving the winding road at night, especially if you have become a big casino winner (such winners have been known to be ambushed on their way home!).

- **Batu Caves:** Located 13 kilometers from the city center, this large limestone formation is the site of a popular Hindu shrine and the annual Thaipusam pilgrimage ceremonies.

- **Templer Park:** A beautiful and relaxing park located 22 kilometers from Kuala Lumpur and 10 kilometers from Batu Caves. Includes bubbling streams, waterfalls, and pools and a large variety of flora and fauna.

Several tour groups cover these sights in their half and full-day tours. Contact the **KL Tourist Information Centre** (Jalan Sultan Hishamuddin) or the **Tourist Development Commission** (in the Putra World Trade Centre) for information on these sights as well as various tour companies. Examples of reputable tour companies include **Tour East, Masmara Travel & Tours, Mayflower Acme Tours, Richfield Tours, Tour Fifty-One, Amshield World Travel**, and **Reliance SMAS Tours**.

KL's four top hotels are the **Shangri-la Hotel, Kuala Lumpur Hilton Hotel**, and **Regent Hotel**, all located along Jalan Sultan Ismail, and the **Pan Pacific Hotel** in the Putra World Trade Centre on Jalan Chow Kit Baru. The **Shangri-La Hotel** is Malaysia's, and one of Asia's, very best hotels. However, the recently renovated **Kuala Lumpur Hilton Hotel** gets rave reviews for its service, ambiance, and location. The **Plaza Hotel** is considered to be KL's best economy class hotel.

You will find many excellent restaurants in KL. The best continental restaurant is the award winning **Suasa Brasserie** in the Regent Hotel -- a "must" dining spot for those who want to experience the very best of ambiance, service, and food in KL. Other excellent restaurants include the **Shang Palace** (Chinese) in the Shangri-La Hotel, **Melaka Grill** (Continental and local) in the Hilton Hotel, the **Keyaki** (Oriental) in the Pan Pacific Hotel, the **Marco Polo** (Chinese and Continental), **Happy Valley Seafood and Sharkfin Restaurant** (very expensive!), **Yasmine Restaurant** (Malay), **Shiraz Restaurant** (Indian), **The**

Lion (Malay, Chinese, Thai), and **Moghul Mahel** (Northern Indian and Pakistani). Delicious and inexpensive hawker food (satay, curry, noodle, and rice dishes) is widely available in the night markets and shopping centers.

Chapter Eleven

MALACCA

Malacca, also known as Melaka, is one of Malaysia's oldest, most colorful, and unique cities. This is where modern Malaysian history began in 1511 with the arrival of the Portugese and the subsequent influx of Chinese, Indians, and other Europeans. A very traditional city with a melting pot of cultures, this city is a historical and cultural experience well worth the visit. It's a quaint city of contrasts, where the blend of the old and new is clearly evident in Malacca's many colorful temples, aging homes, cluttered shops, and narrow, congested streets. Best of all, Malacca offers some unique shopping not found elsewhere in Malaysia.

GETTING TO KNOW YOU

Malacca is a port city located on Malaysia's busy West Coast approximately two hours drive from Kuala Lumpur. Known as the Venice of Malaysia, it was settled nearly 500 years ago by the Portugese, Chinese, Indians, and Dutch as one of Southeast Asia's major trading centers and strategic cities controlling the lucrative trade passing through the Straits of Malacca. Today it remains a quaint and pleasant city of merchants, fishermen, and tourists.

You can easily reach Malacca from Kuala Lumpur by road. In fact, the main road from Kuala Lumpur to Malacca is one of the best in Malaysia. The drive takes less than two hours. If your only purpose in going to Malacca is to shop and do a little sightseeing, consider commuting from KL to spend the day in Malacca rather than staying overnight. You can easily cover most of the major shopping areas and do basic sightseeing -- including a visit to Taman Mini Malaysia -- in a day. However, if you wish to do extensive sightseeing as well as sample Malacca's wonderful local cuisine, spend at least one night here.

Malacca's major shopping strengths are twofold: antiques and handicrafts. Indeed, Malacca is considered Malaysia's "mecca" for antiques. Here you can explore shop after shop filled with a combination of Portugese, Dutch, and Chinese antiques and imported handicrafts. Malaysian handicrafts are found in abundance both within the city and at the nearby cultural center, Taman Mini Malaysia.

The streets of Malacca are relatively easy to navigate. City maps and tourist literature are some of the best you will find for any city in Malaysia. In addition, shopping within the city is concentrated along two streets which are within easy walking distance of each other.

You will want to start your visit at the **Malacca Tourist Information Centre** which is located next to the Malacca River on the square occupied by the famous Christ Church and The Stadthuys where Jalan Gereja meets Jalans Kota, Guayside, Hang Jebat and Laksamana. Be sure to pick up some of their excellent maps (*Melaka Map and Guide* and *Melaka Town and Road Map*) and TDC's award-winning guide book, *A Visitor's Guide to Melaka*. The personnel here are very helpful. From here you can easily walk to the three major shopping streets near the square: Jalan Hang Jebat, Jalan Taman, and Jalan Bunga Raya. **Jalan Hang Jebat** is Malacca's famous antique mecca. Here you can explore more than 25 antique shops that line both sides of this street for three blocks. **Jalan Taman** is a street of small tourist-type vendor stalls selling similar types of handicrafts and souvenirs -- mainly baskets, mats, and other items made of rattan and pandanus.

Other shopping areas in and around Malacca include shopping centers along **Jalan Hang Tuah, Jalan Bunga Raya**, and **Jalan Kilang** (renamed Jalan Tun Ali) as well as **Taman Mini Malaysia**, an outdoor Malaysia-in-miniature theme park located 15 kilometers from Malacca which also includes handicraft and souvenir stalls and a Karyaneka (Infokraf) showroom displaying top quality Malay handicrafts. You will see a road sign directing you to

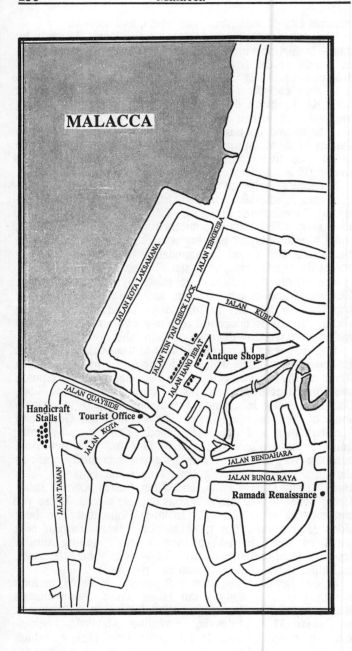

MALACCA

JALAN KOTA LAKSAMANA

JALAN TENGKERA

JALAN TUN TAN CHENG LOCK

JALAN HANG JEBAT

JALAN KUBU

Antique Shops

JALAN QUAYSIDE

Handicraft Stalls

Tourist Office ●

JALAN KOTA

JALAN TAMAN

JALAN BENDAHARA

JALAN BUNGA RAYA

Ramada Renaissance ●

hats, bags, baskets, bronze items, woodcarvings, jewelry, shell items, tacky paintings, and food. Unless you happen to find something worthwhile here, you can quickly shop this area of redundant shops and products in less than 10 minutes. This is not our idea of a good time nor good shopping.

Taman Mini Malaysia's Handicrafts

Located 15 kilometers from Malacca at Ayer Keroh, Taman Mini Malaysia is Malaysia's attempt to provide an outdoor theme park representing Malaysia's cultural heritage. It primarily consists of 13 houses -- each representing the traditional architecture and lifestyles found in each of Malaysia's 13 states -- a handicraft showroom, and handicraft and food stalls. If ever you wanted to see the changing designs and quality of Malaysian handicrafts, this is the place to come to visit two different shopping areas. As soon as you pass through the ticket turnstile, turn left and enter the first building. Here you will find a display showroom operated by Karyaneka (Malaysian Handicraft Development Corporation) which also runs Infokraf in Kuala Lumpur. You will see several small displays designed to promote the export of Malaysian handicrafts. Most of the displays feature home furnishings and clothes, all expertly designed to appeal to a quality export market. Like Infokraf in KL, these are very attractive handicrafts. But unlike Infokraf, this is strictly a showroom where you can look and touch; you cannot purchase any of the items. This place merely whets your appetite to visit the Infokraf showroom and shop in KL.

Next door to this showroom are the more traditional handicraft and souvenir stalls primarily appealing to tourists rather than serious shoppers looking for quality home decorative and collector items. The selections and quality here are better than you will find at the stalls on Jalan Taman in downtown Malacca, but nothing of special note. Here you will find a full range of handcrafted items and knickknacks: baskets, pottery, paintings, batik, mats, bronze, jewelry, and shells.

ENJOYING YOUR STAY

Being an historical port town with a potpourri of multiracial cultures, Malacca is rich in history and culture. There is much to see and do here from sightseeing to sampling its local cuisine. You can visit several old churches, museums, the oldest functioning Chinese temple in Malaysia (Cheng Hoon Teng Temple), take a river cruise, or visit the colorful Portugese Square on Friday night to see dances of the various ethnic groups. Malacca's major attractions include **The Stadthuys (Historical and Literature Museum), Christ Church, A Famosa, St. Paul's Church, Malacca Sultanate Palace (Cultural Museum), St. Francis Xavier's Church, Baba Nyonya Heritage, Kompong Ling Mosque, Portuguese Square, Portuguese Settlement, St. John's Fort,** and the **Malacca Zoo.** Information on these and other local attractions is available at the Malacca Tourist Information Centre (adjacent to The Stadthuys and Christ Church) as well as through hotels and tour groups in Malacca.

If you are planning to stay overnight in Malacca, the best hotel is the **Ramada Renaissance** on Jalan Munshi Abdullah. This deluxe hotel also has an excellent coffee shop serving a local Nonya noon buffet as well as a fine continental restaurant -- **Taming Sari Grill Room.** Other major hotels in downtown Malacca include the **Merlin Melaka** and **City Bayview.**

Chapter Twelve

SARAWAK AND KUCHING

Shopping and traveling in Malaysia takes on a whole new dimension as you leave Peninsular Malaysia for East Malaysia on the island of Borneo. Here you encounter some of the most exotic and adventuresome shopping in Malaysia. This is the Malaysia that conjures up images of plantations, steaming jungles, wild rivers, ferocious tribespeople, headhunters, missionaries, and the colonial Southeast Asia of the British adventurer and rajah James Brooke and novelist W. Somerset Maugham. It's where you can move back into a fascinating colonial history and emerge with some wonderful purchases that will forever remind you of this intriguing country and its exotic peoples, marvelous places, and unique products.

East Malaysia is divided into two relatively autonomous states -- Sarawak and Sabah -- which occupy the northern third of the island of Borneo. The tiny Sultanate of Brunei lies between these two states, and Indonesia occupies the remaining two-thirds of the island it calls Kalimantan. For purposes of shopping, Sarawak has the most to offer visitors and thus this state, its capital city of Kuching, and river and jungle hinterland are the primary destinations for shoppers to East Malaysia.

GETTING TO KNOW YOU

Shopping in Sarawak and Kuching is unlike shopping anywhere else in Malaysia. If you visited Penang, the East Coast, Kuala Lumpur, and Malacca, you primarily shopped in urban centers for Malay handicrafts. Only in Kuantan and Kuala Lumpur did you come across shops selling artifacts and textiles from Sarawak. On the other hand, you will find some Malay handicrafts in East Malaysia, but the primary emphasis in Sarawak is on tribal artifacts, textiles, and collectibles.

Sarawak, the "Land of the Hornbills", is Malaysia's largest state covering an area of 124,000 square kilometers. Occupying the northwest tip of Borneo, Sarawak's 700 kilometers of coastline faces the South China Sea and is dotted with plantations and river towns. The mountainous interior has a few river trading towns and a great deal of impenetrable jungle occupied by numerous tribes which formerly took heads but are now pacified, Christianized, and increasingly commercialized. Known for their animistic beliefs, ceremonies, primitive lifestyles, longhouses, and unique arts and crafts, much of shopping in East Malaysia centers on the products produced by these colorful tribes.

Sarawak's population of 1.7 million is divided into indigenous and non-indigenous groups. The indigenous population consists of Iban (30%), Malays (20%), Bidayuh (8%), Melanau (5%), and several small tribal groups such as the Kenyah, Kayan, Kelabit, and Penan (5%). Non-indigenous groups are the Chinese (30%) and others (2%).

Kuching, the capital of Sarawak, is a city of nearly 70,000 people. Primarily a Chinese city (60 percent), its ethnic mix also includes Malays (25 percent), Dayak (10 percent), and Indians, Europeans, and other groups (5 percent). Lazily spread out along the meandering Sungai River, Kuching is the major shopping destination for all of East Malaysia. The town has several shops and shopping arcades offering excellent quality handcrafted items produced by Sarawak's major tribesmen -- Iban (Dayak), Kayan, and Kenyan -- who primarily live further up the river in small villages and jungle communities. Kuching is also a center for contemporary fine arts, clothes, handicrafts, and souvenirs. For the more adventuresome, one can take a boat into tribal villages to visit longhouses and buy artifacts and handicrafts directly from the tribespeople. However, as we will see shortly, Kuching should be your major shopping destination.

You will find several other smaller towns in Sarawak:

Sibu, Mukah, Kapit Bintulu, Belaga, Miri, Marudi, Bario, Limbang, and Lawas. Connected to Kuching by regularly scheduled flights, most of these towns function as river trading towns. While few of these towns have much to offer shoppers, they are important stations from which to explore the surrounding hinterland.

Given the frontier, jungle, tribal, and Chinese nature of Sarawak, shopping here takes on a totally different character from that of shopping in the more urban, middle-class, and resort areas of peninsular Malaysia. In Sarawak you know you are in a different place and time. This is a mysterious, exotic, and intriguing country of extremely interesting peoples and cultures. What they produce makes shopping in Sarawak some of the best and most interesting we found anywhere in Malaysia.

Indeed, if you are interested in the traditional cultures of tribal peoples, you've come to the right place. But get here soon, because much of the quality shopping for tribal artifacts is quickly disappearing and being replaced by handicrafts of questionable quality. The cities are largely run by Chinese (commerce) and Malays (government), but the dense jungle areas are dominated by numerous tribal peoples who still practice many of their traditional ways. The combined impact of Christianity and trade, as well as disinterest on the part of Malaysians in collecting old items, has resulted in the presence of exquisite tribal artifacts -- many of museum quality -- in the shops of Kuching. Buy now, if you can, since there will be no tomorrow for these products.

THE STREETS OF KUCHING AND ITS ENVIRONS

Kuching has the feel of a small but vibrant frontier town. Straddling both sides of the Sungai River, the older part of the city is located along the southern bank of the river. Here you will find the major hotels -- Holiday Inn and Kuching Hilton -- markets, and commercial and residential areas. The city is also developing a new town on the north side of the river which at present primarily has government buildings and residential areas. It is joined to the southside by a single bridge.

Given the relatively small and compact size of Kuching, you can easily walk the downtown commercial area -- including the major hotels, shopping arcades, markets, and street shops -- and view the most historical sights within a few hours. Narrow one-way streets tend to meander in numerous directions, but they are easily understood once you locate yourself in relationship to the hotels, museum, and shopping centers. The major commercial street is

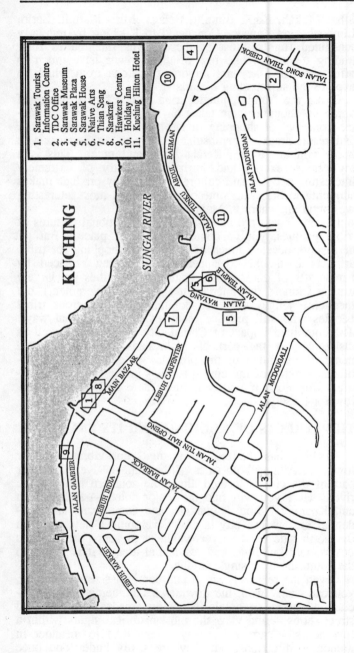

KUCHING

SUNGAI RIVER

1. Sarawak Tourist
   Information Centre
2. TDC Office
3. Sarawak Museum
4. Sarawak Plaza
5. Sarawak House
6. Native Arts
7. Thian Seng
8. Sarakraf
9. Hawkers Centre
10. Holiday Inn
11. Kuching Hilton Hotel

JALAN SONG THIAN CHEOK

JALAN PADUNGAN

JALAN ABDUL RAHMAN

JALAN TUNKU

JALAN TEMPLE

JALAN WAYANG

JALAN MCDOUGALL

LEBUH CARPENTER

MAIN BAZAAR

JALAN TUN HAJI OPENG

JALAN BARRACK

JALAN GAMBIER

LEBUH INDIA

LEBUH MARKET

Jalan Tunku Abul Rahman, which passes in front of the Holiday Inn and the Kuching Hilton Hotel, and then continues west where it changes its name to **Main Bazaar** and **Jalan Gambier**. Along this street you will find the city markets, the tourist information office, and several shops selling everything from food and household goods to tribal artifacts. Several streets adjacent to Main Bazaar also house Kuching's major shops: Jalan Temple, Lebun Wayang, Lebun Carpenter, and Lebun India.

The best way to orient yourself to Kuching and Sarawak is to visit the **Sarawak Tourist Information Centre** which faces the river on Jalan Main Bazaar. This centre, open from 8am to 12:45pm and from 2pm to 4:15pm, has numerous maps and brochures on the city and state as well as a nice historical display and two shops--an arts and crafts shop, Sarakraf, and a souvenir shop. Ask for the *Welcome to Sarawak* packet which is filled with useful information, including maps and brochures on handicrafts, for planning your visit to Sarawak. This office also operates an airport information desk from 8am to 1:30pm and from 7pm to 9pm Monday through Saturday.

The national **Tourist Development Corporation** (TDC) also has an office on Jalan Padungan (AIA Building) where you can pick up similar information found at the Sarawak Tourist Information Centre. However, we recommend that you visit the Sarawak Tourist Information Centre instead because it is best organized to assist visitors.

Another first stop should be the **Sarawak Museum** at Jalan MacDougall and Jalan Tun Haji Openg. This is one of the best museums in all of Southeast Asia. However, it has its limitations for individuals interested in learning more about the tribal artifacts. Consisting of two buildings, the museum is filled with social, cultural, and historical exhibits. The older building has natural history exhibits (animals) on the first floor and social and cultural exhibits (model longhouse, instruments, games, baskets, weaving, handicrafts, weapons, beads, knives, woodcarvings) on the second floor. The newer building, located on Jalan Tun Haji Openg, and reached by an overhead bridge, is the museum's ethnographic gallery. Here you will find several nice displays of Sarawak's various ethnic groups, Chinese ceramics and furniture, intricately carved Javanese chests, brassware, and special exhibits. This section also has a museum shop -- the **Sarawak Arts Shops** -- selling books, baskets, and woodcarvings.

Overall, this is an interesting museum with a decided bias toward Chinese ceramics. It largely neglects what one would expect from such a museum -- an extensive collection of tribal artifacts depicted as legitimate works of art.

The museum, instead, tends to treat the most important groups in Sarawak somewhat superficially -- as curious cultural entities. Consequently, if you are interested in learning more about specific tribal artifacts, the museum's cultural displays only emphasize the ethnic, cultural, and social differences between tribes. One would hope such a distinguished museum would begin recognizing tribal artifacts as being as significant to collect and classify as Chinese ceramics, brassware, and Javanese chests. In the meantime, most tribal artifacts of museum quality are quickly disappearing into the collections of museums and individuals outside Malaysia who have a greater appreciation for the value of such items.

Navigating the streets of Kuching can be difficult if you do not have your own transportation. Unlike many other cities in Malaysia, Kuching does not have the ubiquitous trishaws to get around town. Your major alternative is to take taxis which are located at the major hotels. However, don't expect great service from the local taxi drivers. The taxis in Kuching can be difficult to find and use at times. Taxis do not use meters, so you will have to get some idea of the charge before you get in the cab, and taxi drivers are not adverse to overcharging you. In general, most short distance rides -- from the Holiday Inn, for example, to the Sarawak Museum -- cost $M2 or $M3. But for some reason taxi drivers have the maddening habit of getting lost. Be sure to take a map with you, do not assume the taxi driver knows where he is going, and help direct him as much as possible. You may find it more convenient to rent your own car or hire a car with driver through one of the local tour companies.

Kuching has several **tour companies** that provide daily scheduled tours of the city as well as the surrounding countryside, including one to five-day river safaris to visit the Iban longhouses. These companies can also custom-design itineraries to meet your travel and shopping needs. While no tours are specially organized on shopping, most tours do allow you to stop along the way to do some shopping. It's best to go to the Sarawak Tourist Information Centre on Jalan Main Bazaar to get information on the various tours. This office has brochures, can answer any of your questions, and assist you with booking reservations with the various tour companies.

If you are interested in background reading on Sarawak, visit the H. N. Mohad. Yahia & Son bookstore in the Holiday Inn as well as the Sarawak Arts Shop in the Sarawak Museum. While the bookstores tend to inflate their prices greatly -- 100% or more -- they do have unique collections of books on Sarawak that are difficult to find elsewhere. If you are interested in Iban textiles, especially the beautiful "pua" warp-ikat weavings, we highly recommend purchasing a copy of Edric Ong's *Pua: Iban Weavings of Sarawak* which is available at the museum and in a few arts, crafts, and book shops in Kuching.

WHAT TO BUY

Sarawak and Kuching are rich areas for purchasing locally produced items which primarily consist of antiques, artifacts, fine arts, textiles, handicrafts, and pottery. Here you can purchase some lovely items not available elsewhere in Malaysia. Better still, you shop in the midst of a living museum of craftspeople who still produce excellent quality products for collectors, home decorators, and tourists.

Much of Sarawak's most interesting shopping is of little interest to locals. Tribal artifacts and textiles, for example, are important symbols of Sarawak's tribal heritage, but local Chinese and Malays have little interest in these items. Like many other Asians, they tend to prefer new items and have difficulty understanding why anyone would want to buy old -- and expensive -- items which also might have some bad spirits associated with their past owners. At the same time, much of the national heritage is being sold off to museums, dealers, collectors, and tourists who have developed an appreciation for the techniques, craftsmanship, and social and cultural significance of such artifacts. Unfortunately, when Malaysians finally do develop an appreciation for such artifacts -- probably in another 20 years -- most of the good quality artifacts will be found abroad. This is good news for you but bad news for those intent on preserving Malaysia's cultural heritage.

However, one of the problems in Malaysia is political -- whose cultural heritage should be preserved? So far the government and museums have been preoccupied with preserving some aspects of the cultural heritage of Malaysia's three major competing ethnic groups -- Malays, Chinese, and Indians. The Aboriginals (*orang asli*) on Peninsular Malaysia and the tribal peoples on Borneo are not politically significant groups and thus they have not been viewed as important for cultural preservation. If anything, they are often viewed as primitive and backward, as exotic yet embarrassing cultural oddities that need to be quickly brought into the modern 20th century. As a result, the tribal peoples receive rather cursory treatment as cultural entities and oddities to be understood in an anthropological sense rather than as treated as skilled artists and craftsmen whose traditions should be preserved and further promoted for purposes other than production of tourist handicrafts. In the meantime, it's open shopping season for whatever tribal artifacts still remain in Sarawak.

As you shop in Sarawak, we hope you would develop a full appreciation for the heritage of the many tribal groups and share your knowledge with others. In this sense shopping becomes a cultural tour de force as you learn about the unique lifestyles, talents, and beliefs of tribal peoples who are so near, yet so far, from your own world of fast planes and cars that brought you here in the first place.

Antiques and Artifacts

Kuching is the major city in Borneo for purchasing antiques and artifacts. Antiques consist of Chinese ceramics, canons, knives (kris), musical instruments, and furniture previously found amongst the Chinese, Malay, and European communities. If you collect Ming and Chin Dynasty ceramics, you will find a few shops offering old ceramics which testify to the lengthy Chinese presence in Sarawak. A good starting point is a small tailor shop which also sells Chinese ceramics from a few shelves in its back room -- **Chop Seng Ann** (68 Main Bazaar). Shops selling tribal artifacts also offer canons, knives, brassware, musical instruments, and furniture.

Some of the most interesting shopping in Sarawak centers on tribal artifacts. These consist of masks, woodcarvings, beads, war shields, parang (headhunting knives), blow guns, baskets, colorful hornbill carvings, beaded baby carriers, doors, drums, spears, pig sticks, mats, fish traps, tobacco containers, betel nut sets, head dresses, boxes, ceremonial containers, and textiles. Many of these items have religious significance whereas others are more utilitarian in function. All are handcrafted by tribespeople living along the rivers and in the jungles.

Be forewarned, however, that prices for tribal artifacts are extremely high. A good quality headhunting knife, for example, can cost M$1000 or more. Expect to pay at least M$2000 for a decent quality baby carrier. And masks tend to start at M$500. Such prices are primarily due to the present state of the buying trade, and what may well be a buying crisis in the near future. Many artifacts have already been purchased by collectors and museums outside Malaysia and fewer artifacts are being made today. But more important, most tribal artifacts are considered family heirlooms. Decisions to sell these heirlooms are not made lightly, and they often bring great embarrassment to individuals and families. The only times they are sold to traders is when families need money or when missionaries persuade tribes to get rid of such items because of the pagan beliefs and practices associated with them. Today, fewer and fewer tribal artifacts are finding their way into the shops. In some instances wealthy Ibans are actually buying back these heirlooms and thus competing with traders who increasingly are having difficulty finding good quality artifacts. Artifacts that do find their way into the shops are very expensive and increasingly rare to find. Within the next five years few good quality tribal artifacts will be available. They will most likely be replaced by copies and contemporary handicrafts. If interested in these artifacts, buy now and be prepared to pay high prices.

You will find six good tribal artifact shops in Kuching. Four of the shops are owned by two families who each operate two shops on or adjacent to Jalan Main Bazaar. **Thian Seng** (48 Main Bazaar, Tel. 242918) is the largest and oldest shop in town. This shop is filled with antiques, tribal artifacts, and textiles. As you enter the shop you will notice this family also operates a gold jewelry business at the front of the shop. Most of the tribal artifacts are found toward the back of the shop and in a rear room. You will need to focus your eyes for a few minutes since few things are displayed for ease of examination. Examine the floor, walls, and ceiling for collectibles. You will find ceramics, canons, woodcarvings, wood hornbills, brass, war shields, knives, musical instruments, baskets, doors, baby carriers, drums, textiles, clothes, spears, silver coins, mats, fish traps, and bronze betel nut sets, and beaded head dresses here. The quality is good and this shop has a reputation for reliability. Thian Seng also has a second shop -- **Native Arts** (Tel. 424886) -- located one block away at 94 Main Bazaar. While this shop has a smaller selection of antiques and artifacts than Thian Seng, you may find items here that are not available at the other shop. You will find carved poles, shields, hats, pig sticks, baskets, baby carriers, knives, spears, gongs, textiles, silver, canons, and brass items here. Products are much better displayed in this shop.

Two other nearby shops also offer excellent quality antiques and tribal artifacts. **Sarawak House** (Tel. 424035) at 80 Main Bazaar nicely displays excellent quality baskets, drums, masks, textiles, carved poles, silver, mats, and woodcarvings. This is actually the second Sarawak House shop. The main shop, with a larger collection of tribal artifacts, is located just around the corner at 39 Jalan Wayang (Tel. 252531). Here you can meet the owner, Richard Yong, who is an enthusiastic collector of tribal artifacts. He has an eye for good quality pieces and is very knowledgeable about each piece. Expect to do some of the best quality shopping in all of Malaysia for tribal artifacts in this shop.

The **Borneo Art Gallery** in the Sarawak Plaza, adjacent to the Holiday Inn, also has a nice collection of tribal artifacts and textiles. A relatively small shop, nonetheless you will find good quality items here, especially woodcarvings, masks, pig sticks, textiles, gongs, pottery, jewelry, and textiles. This shop also stocks some contemporary woodcarvings as well as clothes and books.

Tan & Sons Souvenirs & Handicraft Shop at 54 Jalan Padungan (Tel. 412998), near the Holiday Inn and Kuching Hilton Hotel, also carries some tribal artifacts and antiques along with many tourist quality handicrafts. Look for large colorful hornbill carvings here along with ceramics, spears, baskets, shields, textiles, and beaded jewelry.

A few other shops in Kuching also carry some tribal artifacts. **The Curio Shoppe**, a small and hard-to-find shop on the lobby floor of the Kuching Hilton Hotel, has some nice woodcarvings, baskets, and pig sticks at relatively good prices. The shop at the Sarawak Museum -- **Sarawak Arts Shop** -- also has a few tribal artifacts, such as carvings and baskets. **Eonco**, located at 5 Jalan Pearses near the new Civic Center, also carries a few good quality artifacts, particularly old woodcarvings and pig sticks.

Outside Kuching you can find some shopping for tribal artifacts. However, do not expect to find a great deal on your own. The shops in Kuching have their own group of buyers, many of whom are members of the local tribes that now reside in the urban areas, who regularly go into the villages to buy from fellow tribespeople. At best you are likely to find recently completed handicrafts rather than good quality artifacts. However, if you go up river to the trading town of Kapit, stop at **Lai Lai** on Main Bazaar. This shop functions as a pawnbroker, regularly buying and selling to tribespeople who need cash. Depending on your timing, you may find some quality artifacts at this shop.

Textiles

The Ibans produce some lovely ikat, or warp-tie dyed, textiles that are highly prized by collectors and home decorators. Known as "*pua kumbu*", these colorful textiles are produced by Iban women. They are used for a variety of purposes, from body coverings to ceremonial cloths. Each textile is a handwoven work of art with intricate designs created from a warp-ikat weaving and tie dyeing process. The designs reflect many symbols of Iban society, culture, and religious beliefs. The most common figures appearing in these textiles are animal figures such as crocodiles, deer tiger, snakes, frogs, birds, and lizards. Most of these animals either have some spiritual significance or represent important Iban food sources. Other designs depict trees, plants, fruits, weapons, canoes, fish-traps, paddles, and river crossings -- all significant produce, products, and processes in the daily lives of Ibans. The colors are derived from natural dyes and tend to be muted ochre and tans as well as some blues, although ochre tends to predominate. The newer textiles, many of which use commercial dyes, tend to have greater contrast and brighter colors and are less tightly woven.

If you want to learn more about these fascinating textiles, we highly recommend purchasing a copy of Edric Ong's *Pua: Iban Weavings of Sarawak* which is available at the Sarawak Museum and a few arts and crafts shops in Kuching. This book explains the techniques and significance of these Iban weavings. The *Welcome to Sarawak* packet you receive from the Sarawak Tourist Information Centre includes a brochure explaining these textiles. Many visitors to Sarawak fall in love with these textiles and become avid collectors. You may want to buy one or two for your home. They make lovely home decorative pieces.

You will find many new Iban textiles as well as some old pieces in Kuching. The newer pieces, of course, are much less expensive than the older ones. Overall, however, the prices on these textiles are very reasonable considering the amount of work involved and the artistic accomplishments of the weavers. An old but good quality 18" x 48" pua can still be purchased for around M$250. We recommend buying the older pieces because the colors and workmanship in these textiles tend to be much nicer than the newer ones and they have greater value. The best places to buy these textiles are in the artifact shops in Kuching. **Native Arts** and **Thian Seng** on Main Bazaar each have nice collections of old and new pua. **Borneo Art Gallery** in the Sarawak Plaza also sells the textiles, many of which are newer pieces. The **Sarakraf** shop at the Sarawak Tourist Information Centre and the **Sarawak Arts Shop** at the Sarawak Museum also offer a good selection of these textiles.

Serious collectors and buyers of Iban textiles may want to contact Edric Ong directly at Atelier Sarawak, 33 Jalan P. Ramlee, Kuching (Tel. 420042). Edric is very active in promoting local textiles as well as textiles throughout Southeast Asia.

Contemporary Art

Sarawak has several talented artists working in contemporary mediums and idioms, but shoppers will have difficulty finding their works given the present structure of the contemporary art market in Sarawak. The artists primarily work in oils, watercolors, and batik. You can see much of their work at the **Art Gallery** (open from 9:15am to 5pm Monday through Friday) in the new Civic Center building. In many respects this is a much nicer gallery than the National Art Gallery in Kuala Lumpur. Most paintings depict local themes, such as jungles, rivers, boats, longhouses, tribespeople, and street scenes of Kuching. We especially like Ramsey Ong's portraits, Melton Kais' cubist treatment of village scenes, Foo Syn Choon's Chinese style watercolors, and the batik paintings of Lee Hock Kia, Stephen Teo, and Saga Ak Jenang.

Purchasing fine art in Kuching is another matter altogether. No shops or galleries specialize in this type of art. Most of the artists work full-time as teachers or in other occupations. They occasionally have art exhibits and shows where you can purchase their works. Assuming you will not be in Kuching during one of the shows, our best advice for shopping for contemporary art is to contact the artists directly. Start at the Art Gallery to review the art work on display. If you see paintings by an artist you like, take down the name and contact the artist through one of two sources: Edric Ong, Atelier Sarawak, 33 Jalan P. Ramlee, Tel. 420042 or Rhaphael Scot Ah Beng, Tel. 248422 (ext. 260) or 457622. Edric is very active in promoting the local artist community and thus he can put you in direct contact with the local artists. However, we only recommend that you contact these individuals if you are a serious shopper for fine art rather than just a curious window shopper. These are busy people who volunteer their time to assist struggling artists and promote modern art in Sarawak.

You will find one batik artist with his own gallery in town. **Sarawak Batik Art Shop**, located on Temple Street, just around the corner from Main Bazaar and across the street from the Tua Pek Kong Temple, has the batik paintings of the noted artist Pang Ling. While this shop often looks closed because the windows are covered and it has a closed front door, it usually is open; just open the front door and walk in. The artist is usually in this shop. He proudly shows his works and may even share his scrap book which includes photos of his many exhibits over the past 40 years. He does some very lovely batik paintings depicting native and kampong scenes. He also sells some beautiful all-occasion cards which include photos of his most famous paintings. This shop is worth the visit if you want to see some good quality batik paintings as well as meet the artist. Prices of his paintings range from M$170 to M$2500.

Handicrafts and Souvenirs

Like other areas in Malaysia, Sarawak has become a handicraft and souvenir center offering locally produced products as well as items from other parts of Malaysia. The typical mix of handicrafts and souvenirs found in Sarawak includes pottery, carvings, baskets, jewelry, brief cases, pillow covers, batik shirts, fans, hats, T-shirts, serving trays, blow pipes, cards, purses, beads, and cassettes of traditional Iban, Keyah, and Punan music. They are marketed primarily to visiting tourists who wish to purchase momentos of their trip to Sarawak.

Kuching has a few good handicraft and souvenir shops worth visiting. Some of these shops also sell tribal artifacts and textiles. However, the tribal artifacts in such shops tend to be newly carved war shields, masks, and figures stained brown and made specially for the tourist market. You may or may not find this work attractive and its artistic value is questionable. One enterprising businessman in the town of Sibu has 10 craftsmen turning out these "new artifacts" for tourists which sometimes borders on tourist kitsch. Several styles of brief cases and purses integrate pua textiles into their leather designs. One of first stops should be **Sarakraf**, the arts and crafts shop adjacent to the Sarawak Tourist Information Centre on Main Bazaar. This shop has an excellent collection of good quality handcrafted items you may or may not find in other Kuching shops: pottery, pua, woodcarvings, art prints, brief cases, hats, blow pipes, baskets, spears, batik paintings, purses, songket, cassettes, and T-shirts. You will also find some unique necklaces here but they are imported from Singapore and Japan rather than made locally or in Malaysia. At the other end of this building is a small souvenir shop selling pewter, food (birdnests, pepper, tea, shrimp paste, honey), postcards, and mounted butterflies.

Appoximately four kilometers west of the city center at 324/325 Satok Road is a local branch of **Karyaneka** (Tel. 415761), the government-sponsored handicraft shop. This shop is hard to find since it is outside the central business district and tucked behind numerous commercial buildings. Call if you need directions. This shop has a good selection of woven purses, hats, and baskets as well as woodcarvings, fans, drums, silk batik, briefcases, food covers, hats, batik shirts, pua, and unique handcrafted silver figures in the form of longhouses and war shields.

You will find a few other good handicraft shops in Kuching. The **Sarawak Arts Shop** at the Sarawak Museum has good quality baskets, pua, shields, pottery, woven articles, and T-shirts. This shop also posts a sign stating that their prices may be expensive, but the curator of the museum guarantees the items. **Tan & Sons Souvenirs & Handicraft Shop** at 54 Jalan Padungan has a nice selection of handcrafted baskets, jewelry, brassware, porcelain, vases, purses, and woodcarvings. **The Curio Shoppe** in the Kuching Hilton Hotel offers a small but good selection of woodcarvings, pottery, baskets, masks, pua, brass, spears, knives, pig sticks, bags, jewelry, and T-shirts. Both the **Borneo Art Gallery** and the **Sarawak Souvenir Centre** in the Sarawak Plaza offer a good range of handicrafts and souvenirs, although the Borneo Art Gallery tends to sell more high quality artifacts and handicrafts than the other shop which is more oriented to selling tourist souvenirs. **Eeze Trading**, located just east of the Holiday Inn and Sarawak Plaza on Jalan Tuanku Abdul Rahman (Lot 250, Section 49), is a small handicraft and souvenir shop offering pewter, woven purses, postcards, woodcarvings, pottery, food, and liquor. It also operates the handicraft and souvenir shop on the second floor of the airport. The **Sarawak Batik Art Shop** on Jalan Temple carries a few handcrafted items, such as baskets, pua, pottery, and hats, in addition to its batik paintings. **Borneo Handicraft** on Jalan Tun Hju Openg and **Seng Chiang Jewellers and Goldsmith** at 13 Jalan Gartak both have small collections of handicrafts and souvenirs.

The **Malaysian Handicraft Centre**, across the river and on the road to Damai Beach, is a training, production, and exhibition center for locally produced handicrafts. Young men and women produce a large variety of handicrafts which are sold during the center's yearly exhibition as well as to Sarakraf and other shops in Malaysia. If you are in Kuching during August, you can see the yearly exhibit which takes place in several small demonstration buildings. In the meantime, you can visit this center, observe the craftsmen at work, and have commissioned works done to your specifications.

Further outside Kuching is the new **Sarawak Cultural Village and Heritage Centre** adjacent to the Holiday Inn Damai Beach. This "Mini Sarawak" provides visitors an opportunity to view traditional dances and the arts and crafts of Sarawak.

Pottery

Sarawak is famous for a distinctively designed and

colored pottery. Using both traditional Dayak and Chinese designs, craftspeople draw a variety of multi-colored decorative motifs on what become figurines, flower vases, plant and flower pots, ash trays, bowls, and decorative items. While we have yet to acquire a taste for this type of pottery, many tourists find it attractive and buy pieces for gifts and souvenirs.

Kuching's major pottery center is located 9 kilometers from town along the road to the airport, **Penrissen Road.** One of the best pottery factories and shops is **Yong Huat Heng Earthenware** at 5th Mile Penrissen Road (Tel. 451540). This shop has some of the best designs and colors. You can tour the factory and observe the women painting the pottery and the men working with their hands in preparing the clay and throwing the pots. Other factory-shops in the area to look for include **Wong Siap Hup Pottery Factory, Joo Yee Ceramic Factory, Ng Lee Seng, T. E. Pottery Centre.** If you purchase large pieces, be sure they are packed well. This pottery tends to be more fragile than many other types of pottery.

Clothes and Accessories

Kuching may not be a fashion center in Malaysia, but it does have a few shops selling uniquely designed clothes and accessories as well as many shops selling inexpensive clothes and textiles. **Eonco,** for example, located at 5 Jalan Pearses (near the new Civic Center on Jalan Golf Links, Tel. 414686), produces interesting ready-made clothes that are designed in Kuching but finished in The Philippines. Eonco also has some unique accessories -- handbags, jewelry, shoes. **Diane de Boutique,** located next to the Fata Hotel at the circle on Jalan Tabuan, makes lovely dresses and evening gowns; we especially like their use of Indonesian batik in many of their clothes. The **Thai Silk Centre and Gifts** in the Sarawak Plaza has good quality Thai silk which can be made into clothes. **Kuching Plaza** has several men's tailor shops on its third and fourth floor.

If you are in the market for inexpensive clothes, head for the **Hawkers Centre** along the river on Jalan Gambier (Main Bazaar). Consisting of two large enclosed buildings and similar to the vendor stalls in Kuala Lumpur's Chinatown, numerous small stalls are crammed together offering inexpensive clothes, footwear, cosmetics, and bags. Be sure to bargain hard here, perhaps getting as much as a 50 percent discount on items.

If you are interested in purchasing textiles, especially batik, head for the many cloth shops that line Jalan India.

You will also find a few fabric and clothing stores along Main Bazaar, such as **Sin Ching Loong** (#57) and **Fang Kee** (#61) for batik.

Several of the handicraft shops will have a rack or two of ready-made shirts, blouses, or skirts using batik or local designs. You may find some unique garments in these shops that are not available elsewhere in Sarawak or Malaysia.

Jewelry

Kuching has a few jewelry shops which may be of interest to visitors. Most of these shops sell traditional gold jewelry, silver pieces, beaded jewelry, and necklaces. **Khadjijah & DeSilva Jewellers**, located next to the Sarawak Batik Art Shop at 5 Temploye Street, offers a good selection of jewelry, gems, loose stones, pearls, and unique silver crafted longhouses and hornbills in display cases. These latter items make lovely souvenirs of Sarawak. This shop's owner is related to the noted DeSilva family of jewelers located in Penang, Kuala Lumpur, and Singapore.

Two of the major artifact and handicraft shops also sell traditional gold jewelry: **Thian Seng** (48 Main Bazaar) and **Seng Chiang Jewellers and Goldsmith** (13 Jalan Gartak).

Fashionable jewelry and accessories are sold at several of the handicraft shops. **Sarakraf** at the Sarawak Tourist Information Centre on Main Bazaar, for example, offers some attractive neckpieces which are imported from Singapore and Japan. **Tan & Sons Souvenirs & Handicraft Shop** at 54 Jalan Padungan also has some nice handcrafted jewelry including beaded items.

WHERE TO SHOP

Shopping in Sarawak is primarily centered on the capital of Kuching. While you will find some shopping in other towns as well as in a few villages, we recommend that you plan to do most of your shopping in Kuching. Travel to the other areas in Sarawak primarily to learn about the people, visit sights, and experience adventure travel.

Shopping in Kuching centers on a few major streets, shops, shopping plazas, and markets. While you can walk to most of the major shops in the downtown area, you will need transportation if you decide to travel to shops outside this area. We recommend taking a taxi when necessary, although Kuching's taxi service leaves much to be desired.

Downtown Kuching

Downtown Kuching is where the shopping action takes place. Bordered by the Sungai River to the north, Jalan Chan Chin Ann to the east, and Jalan Gambier on the northwest, the main commercial streets run east and west as well as south of the main street -- Jalan Tuanku Abdul Rahman/Main Bazaar/Jalan Gambier. Major shopping starts with the Holiday Inn and Sarawak Plaza in the east and runs for more than one kilometer along Jalan Tunku Abdul Rahman until it reaches Jalan Gambier in the west. The major shopping streets in this area include Jalan Tuanku Abdul Rahman, Main Bazaar, Jalan Gambier, Lebuh India, Lebuh Wayang, Lebuh Temple, and Jalan Padungan.

Most of the shops along these streets are found in shopping plazas or in rows of two-story shophouses. Starting in the east along Jalan Tuanku Abdul Rahman with a row of new shophouses across the street from the Sarawak Plaza, you will find **Eeze Trading** (Lot 250, Section 49, Jalan Tuanku Abdul Rahman), a small but popular handicraft shop. The **Sarawak Plaza**, which is adjacent to the Holiday Inn, is a small but modern air-conditioned shopping center offering a department store and several specialty shops selling clothes, handicrafts, and books. The **Holiday Inn** has perhaps the best bookstore in town, **H. N. Modh. Yahia & Son**, a small shop with a good collection of hard-to-find literature on Borneo. It also has another shop on the bottom level of the Sarawak Plaza. The new **Kuching Hilton Hotel** is just a few minutes walk from the Holiday Inn along Jalan Tuanku Abdul Rahman. The hotel has one small but excellent handicraft and artifact shop -- **The Curio Shop** -- which also sells books. Somewhat hard to find because the hotel has yet to put up signs to direct visitors to this shop, The Curio Shop has good prices on several tribal artifacts, and prices on their books are the best in town.

Proceeding further west along Jalan Tuanku Abdul Rahman, you will come to the intersection of Jalan Temple, Jalan Padungan, and Jalan Main Bazaar. You will see the Tua Pek Kong Temple on your left. At this point Jalan Tuanku Abdul Rahman ends and continues west as Jalan Main Bazaar. If you turn left and walk along Jalan Temple for a few meters, you will come to the **Sarawak Batik Art Shop** which sells the batik paintings of noted local artist Pang Ling. Although this shop may look closed, just open the front door and walk in. The shop also has a few handicrafts and some attractive cards. Next door to this shop is **Khadjijah & DeSilva Jewellers** which has a small but good selection of jewelry, gems, loose stones, and pearls. Their handcrafted silver pieces in the form of long houses and hornbills are especially attractive.

Returning to the intersection, turn left onto Jalan Main Bazaar. This is Kuching's major shopping street. The left side of this street is lined with numerous shophouses selling household goods, clothes, food, artifacts, and handicrafts. In this area you will discover three of Kuching's best tribal artifact shops: **Native Arts** (94 Main Bazaar), **Sarawak House** (80 Main Bazaar), and **Thian Seng** (48 Main Bazaar). Thian Seng is the largest dealer in Sarawak and regularly supplies the Sarawak Museum with tribal artifacts; it also owns Native Arts. Sarawak House is a smaller operation, but it has some of the best quality tribal artifacts we found in Malaysia. The main shop of Sarawak House, the one with the largest collection, is located just around the corner at 39 Jalan Wayang. If you are interested in tribal artifacts, you should visit all four of these shops. They offer different types of good quality artifacts at competitive, although not inexpensive, prices. Other shops along this side of Jalan Main Bazaar include **Chop Seng Ann** (68 Main Bazaar) for Chinese ceramics and **Sin Ching Loong** (57 Main Bazaar) and **Fang Kee** (61 Main Bazaar) for batik.

The right or north side of Jalan Main Bazaar faces the river with godowns, Customs and Marine Departments, and markets. Along this side of the street you will also find the **Sarawak Tourist Information Centre** which provides a great deal of useful information on the city and area. **Sarakraf**, one of Kuching's major handicraft shops, is attached to the Centre. If you visit only one handicraft shop in Kuching, you should visit Sarakraf. You will also find a small souvenir shop attached to the left side of the Centre's building. Further west along Jalan Main Bazaar you will come to the city markets. At this point Jalan Main Bazaar changes its name to Jalan Gambier. Here you will find two buildings -- the **Hawkers Centre** -- that are filled with small vendor stalls selling inexpensive clothes, footwear, cosmetics, and accessories. This is a good place to practice your bargaining skills.

One street south of Jalan Gambier is Kuching's major textile street -- **Jalan India**. You will find several shophouses selling fabric by the meter length.

Other shops are found on several adjacent streets. **Diane de Boutique**, for example, is located next to the Fata Hotel at the circle on Jalan Tabuan. The **Sarawak Arts Shop**, the Sarawak Museum shop located on Jalan Tun Haji Openg, has a good selection of artifacts, handicrafts, and books. **Eonco**, found at 5 Jalan Pearses near the new Civic Center, has an interesting mix of locally designed clothes, accessories, and tribal artifacts. **Tan & Sons Souvenirs & Handicraft Shop**, located at 54 Jalan Padungan, has an interesting mix of tribal artifacts and handicrafts. Further outside the city center is a local branch of the **Karyaneka** handicraft shop located at 324-325 Satok Road (Tel. 415761 if you need directions). Similar to Sarakraf, it has a good selection of locally produced handicrafts.

Centers and Factories

Kuching and the surrounding area have two handicraft demonstration centers and numerous pottery factories. The handicraft demonstration centers are located across the river via the road to Damai Beach. The **Malaysian Handicraft Centre** is relatively close to Kuching. It's best to visit this training and exhibition center during the month of August. However, you can visit it any time to observe the craftspeople at work and commission any work you might want done, especially woodcarvings. The **Sarawak Cultural Village and Heritage Centre**, a "Mini Sarawak", is located next to the Holiday Inn Damai Beach.

Most of Kuching's pottery factories are located on the road to the airport -- **Penrissen Road** -- approximately nine kilometers from the center of town. Factories and shops along this road produce the colorful and distinctive Sarawak pots and Chinese dragon jars. While you will find several pottery factories and shops along this road, **Yong Huat Heng Earthenware** (5th Mile Penrissen Road, Tel. 451540) has some of the best designs and selections.

Shopping Centers and Plazas

Kuching has four major shopping centers and plazas. Most of these centers cater to local residents, and they often tend to be crowded and noisy. These consist of the following centers and plazas:

KUCHING'S SHOPPING CENTERS

- **Sarawak Plaza:** Adjacent to the Holiday Inn on Jalan Tuanku Abdul Rahman, this is a small but nice modern air-conditioned shopping center with a department store (Ngiukee) and several specialty shops offering clothes, cassettes, books, and artifacts. One of Kuching's better artifact and handicraft shops is found in this plaza -- **Borneo Art Gallery**. Also look for the **Sarawak Souvenir Centre** for local souvenirs; **Thai Silk Centre and Gifts** for good quality Thai silk and handicraft items; and **Mohamed Yahia & Sons** for books, magazines, and money changing. You will also find a Christian bookstore, clothing stores, a Kentucky Fried Chicken, and small restaurants in this shopping plaza.

• **Wisma Saberkus:** Located off Rock Road, this is Kuching's newest and largest shopping and office complex consisting of 22 stories. The first five floors have shops offering clothes, shoes, photo equipment, electronics, furniture, video, sporting goods, handicrafts, and food. A very noisy center crowded with young people, it primarily caters to local residents.

• **Kuching Plaza:** Located next to the Aurora Hotel and near the Sarawak Museum on Jalan McDougall, this is one of Kuching's most popular shopping plazas. It's four levels are filled with all types of shops servicing the needs of local residents: clothes, shoes, electronic, jewelry, accessories, luggage, cassettes, appliances, books, music, sporting goods, cards, and food. The third and fourth levels have six tailor shops some tourists patronize for their tailoring needs. You will find a camera repair shop on the first level should you need such services.

• **Electra House:** This is Kuching's first shopping arcade which opened in 1965. It is no longer as popular with local residents as it was more than a decade ago. Located on Jalan Electra directly across the street from a hawker food stall center, Electra house is a small shopping center with a few shops catering to local residents who visit the market area. It does have one small handicraft shop.

Markets

Kuching has a few markets you may wish to visit. The most colorful and interesting one is the open air produce market on Market Street. Here you can see tribespeople selling their produce to local residents in the morning.

The nearby **Open Air Market** -- directly across the street from Electra House on Jalan Electra -- is a popular hawker food center. This is a very clean food center famous for its delicious Chinese food and Malaysian desserts.

Shoppers enjoy the **Hawkers Centre**, two large buildings along the river on Jalan Gambier. Each building is crammed with small vendor stalls selling inexpensive clothes, footwear, bags, and accessories. This place is inexpensive as long as you bargain.

The **Night Market** is held every evening from 6:30pm to 10pm on Jalan Khoo Hun Yeng. Here vendors set up stalls from which they sell inexpensive clothes, batik, T-shirts, and shoes. Many of these items are imported from peninsula Malaysia, Thailand, Hong Kong, Taiwan, and Japan.

The **Sunday Morning Market**, located on Jalan Satok, is a colorful produce and livestock market. While you may not want to buy anything here, it is an interesting cultural experience. Dayaks arrive in town on Saturday evening to set up the market. It gets started about 5am on Sunday morning.

Beyond Kuching

While most of the good shopping in Sarawak is found in Kuching, you will find shops in other towns. However, as we noted earlier, do not travel to other towns or Dayak villages for the primary purpose of shopping. Most of these other areas sell local produce and imported consumer goods for local residents, and they can be expensive and inconvenient areas to reach. You may find a few locally-produced handicrafts, but nothing that would justify the expense and time involved in getting to these places. Go outside Kuching primarily to learn about the countryside and its fascinating peoples.

If you visit the town of Kapit, a bustling little trading town along the Rejang River, you will find one shop that trades in tribal artifacts and handicrafts. **Lai Lai** on Main Bazaar functions as the local pawnbroker in lending money to tribespeople in exchange for family heirlooms. Depending on when you visit this shop, you may be able to pick up some nice quality artifacts at comparatively reasonable prices.

ENJOYING YOUR STAY

Kuching is by no means the backwaters of Malaysia. It may not have the sophisticated shops of KL or the fine dining of Penang, but it has some excellent hotels and travel opportunities unparalleled for Asia. The best overall hotel is the **Holiday Inn** located on the banks of the Sungai River on Jalan Tuanku Abdul Rahman. This is a gem of a hotel, one of the best in Malaysia, with excellent views of the river from each room, excellent service, and a fine ambiance. Its restaurants and coffee shop are some of the best in Kuching. It is nicely located in relation to the major shops in Kuching. The Holiday Inn also operates a deluxe resort hotel and recreational complex -- **Holiday Inn Damai Beach** -- located approximately 25 kilometers from Kuching. This area is rapidly developing, especially with the completion of the new "Mini Sarawak" -- the Sarawak Cultural Village and Heritage Centre.

The new **Kuching Hilton Hotel** is located just a few minutes walk from the Holiday Inn along Jalan Tuanku Abdul Rahman. While not on the river, it does have a good view of the river and city. Like other Hilton Hotels, this one is well appointed, provides excellent service, and offers good restaurants. The coffee shop here is excellent and has a good view of the river and town.

After these two deluxe hotels, the character of local hotels -- as well as the price ranges -- change markedly. The **Aurora Hotel** (Jalan McDougall, Tel. 20281), **Country View Hotel** (Jalan Tan Sri Datuk Ong Kee Hiu, Tel. 24711), and **Liwah Hotel** (Jalan Siong Thien Cheok, Tel. 249222) are considered first-class hotels. You will also find inexpensive accommodations in Kuching. Contact the Sarawak Tourist Information Centre for information on these and other hotels in Kuching.

Kuching also has several good restaurants. Two of the best Chinese restaurants in Kuching are **Tsui Hua Lau** on Jalan Banhock and the **Meisan Szechuan Restaurant** in the Holiday Inn. The **Serapi Restaurant** in the Holiday Inn has excellent international cuisine, especially Indian food. You will find many small restaurants and food stalls offering excellent Chinese, Malay, and Indian dishes. The food stalls in the **Open Air Market** on Jalan Electra, across from Electra House shopping center, serves excellent Chinese dishes and Malay desserts. You will also find numerous food stalls along Jalan Main Bazaar, Jalan Gambier, and around the Night Market and other market areas.

You will find plenty to do in and around Kuching as well as in other areas of the state. One of the first activities you may wish to engage in is a survey of Kuching's major sights. Kuching is rich in history and its many buildings testify to the fact that this was more than just another colonial outpost. When you visit the Sarawak Tourist Information Centre, pick up a copy of a brochure entitled *Kuching Sarawak Buildings and Historial Sites* as well as the colorful map *Sarawak*. These items should be included in your orientation packet, "Welcome to Sarawak". With these two items you can easily take your own walking tour of Kuching. In fact, the city has put up signs throughout the downtown area directing visitors on a self-guided walking tour of the major sights.

Kuching's major sights include **Bishop's House, Astana (palace), Court House, Tua Pek Kong Temple, Indian Mosque, Fort Margherita, Square Tower, Round Tower, Sarawak Museum, Pavilion, Satok Suspension Bridge, Darul Kurnia** (residence), **Post Office,** and **Maderasah** (college). Don't forget to visit the new **Civic Center** on Jalan Golf Lines. This is one of the most attractive modern structures in all of Malaysia. The tower and restaurant offers an excellent panoramic view of Kuching and the Art Gallery houses some of Sarawak's finest oil, watercolor, and batik paintings.

Several inbound tour operators, such as **Interworld Travel Service** (110 Green Road, Tel. 252344) and **Sarawak Travel Agencies** (70 Padungan Road, Tel. 243708 and the Borneo Art Gallery in the Sarawak Plaza, Tel. 418290), offer a variety of tours that encompass both the city and the outlying areas. The typical range of tours includes:

- **Kuching City Tour** - 3 hours
- **Orang Utan Sanctuary Tour** - 3 hours
- **Sarawak River Cruise and Kampong Visit** - 2-3 hours
- **Land Dayak Longhouse Tour** - 4 hours
- **Santubong Fishing Village** - 3 hours
- **Jungle Walk** - 3-4 hours
- **Iban Longhouse Tour** - full day
- **Bako National Park Tour** - full day
- **Skrang River Safari Tour** - 2-4 days/1-3 nights

These tour operators will also custom-tailor tours to individual needs. For example, if you want a car, driver, and guide to explore the Kuching area or you want to spend 7 days exploring Dayak villages in areas largely untouched by other tourists, most tour operators can put together a travel itinerary to meet your individual needs.

Many visitors to Sarawak primarily come to visit the tribespeople in the longhouses. They tend to use Kuching as the gateway city to the more adventuresome hinterland. Indeed, one of the great highlights of many visits to Sarawak is to have a chance to go up river to meet the Dayaks

and visit their longhouses. You will find many tour groups offer one to five day river safaries that will take you
into their areas. The one-day safari will give you a glimpse of what more you might expect on an extended trip to
longhouses further up river. Expect to visit villages that
are most heavily touristed and commercialized. If you
want to see the "real Sarawak", you must be more adventuresome. You will need government permits to visit the
interior. True adventurers should read Eric Hansen's *Stranger in the Forest: On Foot Across Borneo* and Redmond
O'Hanlon's *Into the Heart of Borneo* -- both available in
major bookstores in the U.S. -- for starters to learn more
about what the interior is all about and perhaps take a little
romance out of one's proposed journey into the steaming
jungles of Borneo!

If you do visit the longhouses, the Sarawak Tourist Association recommends the following "do's and don'ts":

LONGHOUSE PREPARATION AND ETIQUETTE

- Do make prior arrangements with your tour
  operator especially if you intend to stay overnight. A longhouse is usually 'open' to everyone but don't take things for granted. Wear clothes and shoes for jungle trekking: flat
  heel comfortable shoes, slacks or jeans, light
  weight jacket and cap, and socks.

- For overnight stays, bring a flashlight, mos-
  quito repellent, earplugs, and some of your
  own supply of food and drinks. A pair of
  rubber sandals will come in handy.

- Do bring some small gifts like sweets and
  biscuits (cookies) for the children, and cigarettes for the men.

- Do realise the local people are every bit as
  proud of their way of life as you are of yo-
  urs. They are warm, hospitable, charming,
  and witty people. You can relax and feel at
  home with them but don't take any liberties.

- Don't be offended or disappointed if sometimes someone asks you to pay for a pose for
  your camera or even tries to sell you some
  handicrafts (should shoppers be so lucky!).

- Don't just enter a longhouse or walk in the *bilek* (room) inside without first asking and being given permission.

- Don't refuse the traditional welcoming drink of *tuak* (rice-wine). If you don't drink, just take a sip and say *Terima Kasih* (thank you)!

- Don't accept food and drinks with just one hand. Use both.

- Don't just push away any food offered. Touch the food and put your fingers to your lips and say *Terima Kasih*.

- Take off your footwear. Don't step onto the mat with your shoes or sandals on where you sit to chat or have your meal with your hosts.

- Don't take pictures of anyone without first asking permission.

- Don't go near a longhouse during *pantang* (taboo), a period when death or misfortune has occurred there. Someone will tell you or you may see a white flag placed near the entrance of the longhouse.

- Don't take a bath in the nude when there are people around.

- Don't show the Western way of greeting one another by kissing in front of the public.

Whatever you do, enjoy Kuching and Sarawak. This is a different world of traveling and shopping from the more urban and Malay character of Peninsula Malaysia. If you enjoy primitive artifacts, unique ikat textiles, and tribal handicrafts, Sarawak offers a wonderful world of shopping. Indeed, Kuching and Sarawak may well become your favorite travel and shopping destination in all of Malaysia!

INDEX

SINGAPORE

MALAYSIA

ORDER FORM

The following *Shopping in Exotic Places* titles can be ordered directly from the publisher. Complete the following form (or list the titles), include your name and mailing address, enclose payment, and send your order to:

> IMPACT PUBLICATIONS
> 10655 Big Oak Circle
> Manassas, VA 22111 (USA)
> Tel. 703/361-7300

All prices are in US dollars. Orders from individuals should be prepaid by check, moneyorder, or Visa or MasterCard number. If your order must be shipped outside the U.S., please include an additional US$1.50 per title for surface mail or the appropriate air mail rate for books weighting 24 ounces each. We accept telephone orders (credit cards), and orders are shipped within 48 hours.

Qty.	TITLES	Price	TOTAL
___	*Shopping in Exciting Australia and Papua New Guinea*	$13.95	___
___	*Shopping in Exotic Hong Kong*	$10.95	___
___	*Shopping in Exotic India and Nepal*	$13.95	___
___	*Shopping in Exotic Indonesia and the Philippines*	$13.95	___
___	*Shopping in Exotic Places: Your Passport to Exciting Hong Kong, Korea, Thailand, Indonesia, and Singapore*	$14.95	___
___	*Shopping in Exotic Singapore and Malaysia*	$12.95	___
___	*Shopping in Exotic Thailand*	$10.95	___
___	*Shopping the Exotic Caribbean*	$12.95	___
___	*Shopping the Exotic South Pacific: Your Passport to Exciting Australia, New Zealand, Papua New Guinea, Fiji, and Tahiti*	$15.95	___

SUBTOTAL $ ___

Virginia residents add 4.5% sales tax $ ___

Shipping/handling ($2.00 for the first title and $.50 for each additional book) $ ___